"Muy buenas noches"

THE MEXICAN EXPERIENCE · *William H. Beezley*, series editor

"Muy buenas noches"
MEXICO, TELEVISION, AND THE COLD WAR

Celeste González de Bustamante

FOREWORD BY RICHARD COLE

UNIVERSITY OF NEBRASKA PRESS · LINCOLN AND LONDON

© 2012 by the Board of Regents of
the University of Nebraska

Chapter 6 was previously published as
"Olympic Dreams and Tlatelolco Nightmares:
Imagining and Imaging Mexican Television
News," *Mexican Studies/Estudios Mexicanos* 26,
no. 1 (2010): 1–30. © 2010 by the University
of California Institute for Mexico and the
United States and the Universidad Nacional
Autónoma de México. Reprinted by per-
mission of University of California Press.

All rights reserved
Manufactured in the United
States of America

Library of Congress
Cataloging-in-Publication Data
González de Bustamante, Celeste, 1965–
"Muy buenas noches": Mexico, television,
and the Cold War / Celeste González de
Bustamante; foreword by Richard Cole.
p. cm. — (The Mexican experience)
Includes bibliographical references and index.
ISBN 978-0-8032-4010-0 (pbk.: alk. paper)
1. Television broadcasting of news—
Mexico—History—20th century.
2. Mexico—History—20th century.
3. Partido Revolucionario Institucional—
History—20th century. 4. Cold
War—Influence. I. Title.
PN4969.G66 2012
070.4'30972—dc23   2012024919

Set in Chaparral by Ashley Muehlbauer.
Designed by Nathan Putens.

To Héctor and Claire

Contents

List of Illustrations   ix

List of Tables   xi

Foreword by Richard Cole   xiii

Acknowledgments   xvii

Introduction   xxi

1   The Rise of Television in Mexico   1

2   The Invention of Tele-Traditions   31

3   Rebels and Revolutionaries   53

4   The First Television Diplomats   79

5   Hot Rockets and Cold War   107

6   Olympic Dreams and Tlatelolco Nightmares   145

7   Victory for the Brazilians and Echeverría   177

Conclusion   205

Notes   217

Bibliography   243

Index   259

Illustrations

1. XHTV, Channel 4, television studios   14
2. Television antennae on Mexico City rooftops   18
3. Fidel Castro speaking in Havana, Cuba   65
4. President López Mateos arriving with his family in Chicago   93
5. Miguel Alemán Velasco in front of a rocket at Cape Canaveral   137
6. Mission Control after *Apollo 11* splashdown on Earth   140
7. Buzz Aldrin's boot on the surface of the moon   141
8. Norma Enriqueta Basilio carrying the Olympic torch   165
9. Granadero depicted as a gorilla   168
10. "Corrupt Press" student flyers   169
11. Granadero driving a tank with the Olympic symbol   170
12. Miguel Alemán Velasco with Emilio Azcárraga Vidaurreta   185
13. Lolita Ayala, Televisa news anchor   202

Tables

1. Television newscasts produced in 1959   85
2. Telesistema Mexicano newscasts and airtimes in 1970   181
3. Estimated nationwide viewership from 1950 to 1970   181
4. Breakdown of election and World Cup coverage in 1970   190

Foreword

RICHARD COLE

ANYONE WHO knows the slightest bit about television in Latin America knows that Televisa is a cultural, political, and economic force that wields tremendous power in Mexico and the hemisphere. Over the second half of the twentieth century, Grupo Televisa became the most profitable and influential media conglomerate in the Spanish-speaking world. For decades its *telenovelas* (homegrown soap operas) have been exported to more than one hundred countries. People from as far away from Mexico as the former Yugoslavia claim to have learned to speak Spanish by watching the famed 1980s dramatic series starring Veronica Castro, *Los ricos también lloran* (The rich also cry). Yet there is still much to be learned about how this company and those who created it were able to emerge as an authority that now rivals the state and other institutions as one of the nation's most influential cultural and political entities.

The casual Spanish-language media consumer might have heard of Televisa, but he or she surely would not know how the company rose to rival Mexico's most powerful political institutions. That's because little has been published from a historical perspective about the media conglomerate, especially in English. What did viewers watch during the earliest years of television? What subjects did television news executives and reporters think viewers should watch? What topics remained offscreen and why? How did North American companies influence the medium and programming? These are just a few of the lines of inquiry Celeste González de Bustamante untangles and answers in "*Muy buenas noches*."

These questions became of paramount importance in the fall of 1968, when foreign reporters and photographers converged on Mexico for the nineteenth Olympiad, the first, and to date, only Olympics held in Latin America. As politicians and media executives attempted to put the country's brightest and most modern face forward, authoritarian whims led to mass murder in a Mexico City plaza, resulting in the deaths of hundreds of students and bystanders. Etched into the collective memory of its citizens, the massacre of the Plaza de las Tres Culturas (Plaza of Three Cultures) at Tlatelolco stands as one of the nation's greatest tragedies as well as a watershed moment when civil society began to sprout and help move the nation slowly away from the strong hand of one-party rule. At that critical juncture the visions of state officials and television executives diverged, leading to a call for nationalization of the industry. Back in the 1960s when I worked for a while on *The News*, the English-language newspaper in Mexico City, Telesistema Mexicano was the octopus of Mexican mass communication. González de Bustamante's observations on Telesistema Mexicano and the political climate during that turbulent period are right on.

"*Muy buenas noches*" focuses on the history of television news from 1950 to 1970, which tells the story of Mexico and its citizens during a crucial time in the nation's development and in the midst of Cold War international turmoil, marked by events such as Fidel Castro's takeover of Havana in 1959 and humankind's first walk on the moon in 1969. It's an epic that would be difficult—if not impossible—to tell without the help of Televisa's primary sources. Few scholars have been able to gain access to the company's rich script archive, and González de Bustamante was one of the first U.S. scholars to consult it, which allowed her to examine questions that others have written about only in broad and theoretical terms. The strength of *"Muy buenas noches"* lies in the author's ability to show how television executives presented the nation and the world to viewers and how news coverage often blurred the lines between big business interests, the goals of the Mexican state, and the lives of everyday viewers.

The benefits of a study like this are obvious for students and scholars of Mexico, but the topic of television and Mexico should also benefit Americanists in general. Why? For one, Mexico is the United States' third largest trading partner—topped only by Canada and China.[1] Moreover, Americans enjoy Mexico. It is the most popular place for U.S. tourists to vacation abroad. Additionally, in learning about what happened south of the U.S.-Mexico border, North Americans learn more about themselves. Based on the latest U.S. Census, Latinos are the fastest-growing and largest ethnic minority in the United States, and most Latinos in the United States are from Mexico. Finally, we should not forget that much of the United States was once part of Mexico, that is, until the Treaty of Guadalupe Hidalgo in 1848. Let's face it: historically, culturally, politically, and economically, the United States and Mexico are joined at the hip. The tensions and ties between both countries come into clear focus in *"Muy buenas noches."*

Acknowledgments

THIS PROJECT began at the University of Arizona, in a research seminar on the history of modern Mexico. More than ten years later it is a book. Funding for the research that forms the basis of this book came from various sources, including the Tinker Foundation, American Philosophical Society, and the University of Arizona Center for Latin American Studies.

Over the course of the past decade scores of individuals from near and far have helped me along the way, in varied and sometimes unexpected ways. Looking back, I am overwhelmed and humbled by all of the assistance and inspiration I have received, and I recognize fully that I couldn't have finished this book without the support from all of you.

In Mexico, I acknowledge and appreciate the assistance of the archivists, especially those who offered their expertise at the Biblioteca Miguel Alemán, Archivo General de la Nación, Biblioteca

Nacional, and the Archivo Histórico de la UNAM. I appreciate deeply the opportunity to have been granted access to conduct research in Televisa's news archives at Chapultepec and Estadio Azteca. In particular, I thank Licenciado Jorge Vidaurreta, Mario Arrieta Gutierrez, and Antonio Ruíz Maquedan. I am also extremely grateful to those individuals who allowed me to interview them, including Miguel Alemán Velasco, Raúl Alvarez Garín, Lolita Ayala, Pablo García Sáinz, Patricia Fournier, Adriana Labardini (who invited me into her beautiful home), Jorge Perezvega, Ana Ignacia Rodriguez, Miguel Sabido, and Jorge Saldaña.

I thank my colleagues in academic institutions in Mexico — Manuel Guerrero at the Universidad Iberoamericana and Jorge Martinez at the UNAM — who lent me their support and invaluable insights. I owe my gratitude to Guillermo Palacios, at El Colegio de Mexico, for his support and for introducing my husband Héctor and me to some of the best margaritas in the world at the San Angel Inn restaurant. My thanks and appreciation go out to the Gudiño family, our Mexico City neighbors who adore Claire and helped us feel at home while I was completing my dissertation research, and beyond.

Closer to home, I am eternally grateful for the unwavering support and gifted guidance from my adviser and now colleague at the University of Arizona, Bill Beezley. It's good to have my former mentor just a football field away, and, as they say, "once an adviser, always an adviser." I would be remiss if I didn't mention the other two of the "Three Wise Men" at the UA who've been tremendous pillars of support: Bert Barickman and Kevin Gosner. I also am deeply indebted to my mentor, dear friend, and colleague Jacqueline Sharkey, who encouraged me to go back to graduate school and who later as my director provided much-needed guidance to navigate the academic world. My friend and former supervisor, and should-be academic, Héctor González, I thank for his continual interest and encouragement.

At the UA School of Journalism, I feel blessed to be able to work with some of the best colleagues in the country, and I thank the faculty, especially Jeannine Relly, for their encouraging words and interest in my work. I thank my dear colleague and editor-supreme Bruce Itule, who read and critiqued an earlier version of the manuscript. Kevin Gosner did the same and offered a historian's take on the book. Kudos for John De Dios, who helped me prepare the images for the book, and for graduate student Kevin Andrade, who helped me in the manuscript's final stages. Thanks also go to Tom Gelsinon at the UA Mexican American Studies Department.

Over the years, the UA Center for Latin American Studies has become "*mi segunda casa*," and I would like to thank in particular Raúl Saba, Scott Whiteford, Colin Deeds, Julieta Gómez González, and professor emeritus Ed Williams, who have been wonderful colleagues and friends.

Beyond the UA mall, Roderic Camp provided encouragement and valuable insights about the politics of Mexico. At various stages of this project, I have come to know and receive support from numerous scholars, who've been a wonderful source of guidance and inspiration. These esteemed scholars include Robert Alegre, Ann Blum, Elaine Carey, Manuel Chavez, Richard Cole, Leonardo Ferreira, Bill French, James Garza, Sallie Hughes, Andrew Paxman, Otto Santa Ana, Lucila Vargas, and Eric Zolov. A special note of gratitude goes to Liza Bakewell, who not only encouraged me to finish this project but opened doors for me in Mexico City. *Gracias comadre*!

From my dissertation days and beyond I would like to thank my study group for their intellectual inspiration, including Elena Albarrán Jackson, Maritza De la Trinidad, Tracy Goode, Dina Berger, Amie Kiddle, Amanda López, Monica Rankin, Ageeth Sluis, Rachel Kram Villarreal, Gretchen Raup, Laura Shelton, and Aurea Toxqui.

I am indebted to the editors at the University of Nebraska Press: first, Heather Lundine and then Bridget Barry, as well as Susan Silver and Joeth Zucco who worked to strengthen this project.

I am eternally grateful for my close friends in Tucson, including Lili Bell, Erma Ciancimino, Hilda Greenwald, Milani Hunt, Jessica Judd, and Lynette Leija, who've put up with my crazy ways over the past several years as I've worked to finish this and other projects, and who've forgiven my absences at our gatherings.

Very close to home, I am indebted to Antonia (Toña) Rodriguez, who cared for my greatest joy, Claire, while I was conducting the research for the book. I thank my sister Shelley London, who has always been supportive of my intellectual and athletic pursuits. I thank my parents, Sam and Nina Gonzalez, who have always been there for me in California, Mexico, and Tucson, and especially during these last few years as I worked to finish the manuscript. I thank my mom for her love, child-rearing skills that she employed from Oaxaca, Mexico, to Tucson, Arizona, and her valuable taxi services. Finally, to the two people closest to me and who next to me have seen this project more than anyone else (though from a distance, looking over my shoulder as I sat at the computer), my husband, Héctor, and daughter, Claire: I will happily be offering you thanks and praise for the rest of my life!

> Those homes may lack good water services, a heater, a good gas range or a washing machine but those matter less than a TV set.
>
> Luis Becerra Celis

Introduction

PERSPIRATION FORMED on his forehead and soaked his shirt, as Emilio Azcárraga Milmo, the son of one of the country's most influential media moguls, greeted members of the news media. It had been six years in the making, and now Azcárraga Milmo was ready to unveil Estadio Azteca (Aztec Stadium). He wiped his brow, grabbed a microphone, and welcomed reporters and photographers to a press luncheon. Up until this point, Azcárraga Junior, as he was sometimes affectionately called, had walked in the shadows of his father, El León (The Lion), Emilio Azcárraga Vidaurreta, who in 1950 bellowed that he was the "czar of Mexican radio and that he would soon be the country's television czar."[1] Yet on this sweltering spring day of May 29, 1966, the day the stadium was inaugurated, Azcárraga Milmo moved beyond his father's shadow and strolled alongside the president of the republic, Gustavo Díaz Ordaz. The two men walked across a well-manicured soccer field, through a dimly lit concrete tunnel, and into a black late-model sedan. A driver paraded the president and the emerging media magnate around the hundred thousand–ton concrete structure. Azcárraga Milmo owned the stadium, as well as its home team, Club América. He had acquired the team in 1959 in anticipation of building the stadium and his company's empire.[2]

At the same time, 105,000 soccer fans gathered, as television camera operators recorded the inaugural ceremony and activities.[3] On Telesistema Mexicano's XHTV, Channel 4, announcers reported that four years after the then president Adolfo López Mateos laid the first stone of the stadium, another president helped to inaugurate it.[4] One of the two television announcers remarked that "Azcárraga Milmo and the president were about to enter the car and that the president was always with Emilio Azcárraga."[5] As the evening news began, Jacobo Zabludovsky, the best-known news anchor in Mexico City, and Pedro Ferríz Santa Cruz delivered details about the inaugural ceremonies to capital residents. Ferríz commented, "We, as Mexicans, also feel proud to have a stadium of this magnitude, and in every way it is the best out of any place in the world. I have been to Maracanã Stadium in Brazil and Wembley in England, the National in Santiago and the one in Tokyo, and, in my judgment, ours is more functional in every way."[6]

News film of Díaz Ordaz and Azcárraga Milmo walking together provide a metaphor for the close connections between the government and the media during the second half of the twentieth century. By and large scholars have concluded that Televisa, what Telesistema Mexicano would become in 1973, walked in lockstep with the government and the Partido Revolucionario Institucional (PRI, Institutional Revolutionary Party), the party that ruled for seventy-one years (1929–2000).[7] No legitimate scholar would dispute the fact that close political ties between television executives and the party help to explain the long-standing rule of the PRI, but this is only part of the picture. Just how did this occur on a daily basis and over time?

Government decisions that regulated communications and telecommunications infrastructures undoubtedly aided in the development of the television industry and enabled Televisa's success, which by the end of the twentieth century stood as one of the most powerful media companies in the world. Grupo Televisa dominated in both production and profits in the Spanish-speaking world. By 1977 the company transmitted 21,423 hours of television programming to an estimated 28 million viewers, with 60 percent of the company's programming produced domestically. The company's television advertising revenue reached US$144 million, while revenue from all advertising sales totaled US$184 million.[8]

Long before the first twenty years of television (1950–70), media barons and government officials had begun to develop political, economic, and social ties.[9] The close relationship between media magnate Rómulo O'Farrill and President Miguel Alemán Valdés opened the door for O'Farrill to act as a *prestanombre* (front name) for the sitting president in the creation of the country's first television station, XHTV.[10] On several occasions Emilio Azcárraga Milmo called himself, "a soldier of the PRI".[11] Yet despite the cozy relationship between media moguls such as Azcárraga Milmo and the PRI, the connections should not be viewed as static and without tension. Relationships were forged over time, and on occasion they were strained. In the 1950s Azcárraga Vidaurreta had to go through the president's secretary to set up meetings with Alemán, an indication that they certainly were not the best of friends.[12] In 1968 President Gustavo Díaz Ordaz criticized Telesistema Mexicano's television news coverage of the student movement and massacre at the Plaza de las Tres Culturas on October 2, despite evidence that coverage was severely limited. In the early 1970s President Luis Echeverría threatened to take over the television industry in a wave of nationalization efforts.[13]

By the end of the 1990s Azcárraga Milmo began to criticize the PRI, and his defenders said that Azcárraga Milmo never required Televisa employees to call themselves soldiers of the PRI.[14] Miguel

Alemán Velasco, son of the former president, who directed the company's first news division and who in the late 1960s and 1970s acted as a liaison between the company and the government, maintained that he never stated that he was a solider of the PRI.[15] Furthermore, longtime news anchor Jacobo Zabludovsky admitted that he had to follow the directives of Azcárraga Milmo, but *El Tigre* (The Tiger), as he was known by his friends and enemies, never told Zabludovsky to back the PRI.[16]

To continue the metaphor, when the moving image slows down the viewer notices that Díaz Ordaz and Azcárraga Milmo walked together, but not exactly in lockstep. They moved in the same direction but at a slightly different pace, and they each occupied a different space on the screen. The same can be said about the relationship between television executives and government officials from 1950 to 1970. Díaz Ordaz had a less amicable relationship with Azcárraga Milmo than his predecessors Adolfo López Mateos and Miguel Alemán Valdés had with media magnates, especially after 1968.[17]

STUDY PURPOSE AND DESIGN

From 1950 to 1970, that is, during the apexes of the PRI and the Cold War, television emerged as the newest and most valuable tool for those interested in winning the hearts and minds of citizens. This book aims to describe and explain the role that television executives, producers, and reporters played in that struggle. Directed by executives, television producers functioned as cultural authorities that would by and large reinforce the messages that political authorities wanted to be disseminated—but not always.[18]

Through five case studies that have both national and international dimensions, this book focuses on the nexus between power and culture. The case studies include (1) Mexican and Cuban revolutionaries during 1959, (2) presidential and heads of state visits at home and abroad, (3) the Space Race and the country's participation in this Cold War technopolitical competition, (4) the 1968 student movement and the Olympics, and (5) the 1970 presidential election and the World Cup. The case studies enable an investigation of power on two fundamental levels. On the international level the book explores foreign (mainly U.S.) hegemony over the nation-state and national media. From a national perspective the study hones in on the state's influence on national media, and the national media's influence on the country's citizens.

The national and international dimensions of the selected cases make them ideal subjects to examine the central theme of the book—the limits of cultural hegemony at the height of the PRI and the Cold War. Cultural hegemony is the process through which groups consent to and assimilate the ideas and beliefs of dominant classes, in this case, those who control the airwaves.[19] In a region fraught with domestic authoritarianism and strong foreign influence, it is a useful concept for understanding the complexity of how nations and ordinary citizens facing dominant powers such as the nation-state and the United States at times consented to and at other times resisted such power. T. J. Jackson Lears summed up the value of cultural hegemony for both: "intellectual historians trying to understand how ideas reinforce or undermine existing social structures and social historians seeking to reconcile the apparent contradiction between the power wielded by dominant groups and the relative cultural autonomy of subordinate groups whom they victimize.[20]

The recognition that both news producers and viewers have "relative cultural autonomy" informed the central questions for this book: How, and to what extent, did television news from 1950 to 1970 reflect or differ from the government's positions and U.S. interests? Or, put another way, what were the limits of cultural hegemony on television news? To what extent did viewers buy the messages being disseminated?

Honing in on the limits of cultural hegemony opens the door for other critical questions to be asked: How did producers of the media and television news contribute to the long-standing power of the PRI? If members of the news media played a role in legitimizing the PRI among citizens, what prompted thousands of railway workers, students, and popular groups to stand up to the ruling party in 1958, 1959, and 1968? What sorts of counter-hegemonic messages did popular groups disseminate? Questions regarding U.S. hegemony in the region can also be asked: How far did the influence of foreign news agencies reach? Did television news executives act as simple conduits of information for the Associated Press and United Press International, or did domestic producers retool stories about issues such as nuclear arms and the Space Race in their own nationalistic terms? Answering these questions moves research about early television beyond the two camps of scholarship that have emerged: those that focus on state-media relations and the so-called business hero studies that overemphasize the power of media magnates such as members of the Azcárraga family.[21] The "symbiotic relation" studies, such as Fátima Fernández Christlieb's, concentrate on the relationship between the government and media, and the government as the "instrument" of a dominant class.[22] Works based on the business-hero model stress the individual qualities of the entrepreneur as the necessary ingredient for the success of electronic media.[23] This study advances research by exploring hegemony from above and below, and from within and without, in an effort to integrate social and political history and transform both.[24]

In answering these central questions, the book posits a three-fold argument. First, during the height of the PRI and Cold War, news coverage from 1950 to 1970 overwhelmingly favored PRI and North American interests, yet tensions did arise when news reports did not conform to the preferences of government officials and foreign investors. In other words, news producers often towed the official line, but Telesistema Mexicano and later Televisa were not simple mouthpieces of the government and foreign interests. Second, when looked at on the whole, the case studies of news coverage point to a specific form of national identity, a *mexicanidad* that promoted modernity and consumer values broadcast from above. Third, viewers-cum-citizens did not always buy into what they saw on the small screen, and by the late 1960s a critical mass of citizens attempted to get their own hybrid messages heard.

The tensions examined in this book include those between government officials and media owners; modernity and efforts to maintain traditions or invent new ones; elite male media producers and popular viewers; political dissent and authoritarian rule; and the country's Janus-like image during the Cold War (an international face that portrayed the country as modern and peaceful, and a domestic face imbued with violence and repression).[25] The word "tension" is used intentionally, as it accurately reflects the relationships among television actors, both on- and offscreen.[26]

Early television news programs functioned as microcosmic windows through which viewers could see a country in turmoil. As historical artifacts, early television news reports and images provide audiovisual expressions of political and social struggle. By the second half of the twentieth century, it became evident on the streets and on television that more than one vision for the nation's future existed, and at times these *tele-visiones* (tele-visions) competed and conflicted.[27]

The book's focus on key domestic and international events and issues during the first two decades of television journalism allows for the discussion and examination of key debates that inform Mexican and Latin American history in the twentieth century, such as the role of the mass media and the formation of national identity; the limits of authoritarian regimes, including the PRI; and foreign influence in the region during the Cold War. Certainly, scholars have only begun to scratch the surface regarding the significance of non–super powers during the Cold War.[28] In this way, the book aims not to furnish an institutional history of television but instead seeks to describe and explain how television—through news programming—played an integral role in creating a sense of *lo mexicano* (that which is Mexican) at a time of tremendous political, social, and cultural change. Lo mexicano should be understood as a fluid concept, constructed by various societal actors. Stated another way, national identity as part of cultural history is far from static or monolithic and is, in reality, contingent and "provisional."[29] The mexicanidad that this book seeks to explain was forged from above by media producers influenced by high-ranking government officials. At the same time, the book embraces a negotiation between elite producers and popular viewers, who were also capable of creating images evoking their sense of mexicanidad.[30]

Examining the intersections between culture and power, this book also requires a foray into discussions about cultural imperialism from both within the country and abroad.[31] That foreign companies such as General Motors and Standard Oil sponsored and advertised on Latin American news programs was no accident. The practice emerged from a then new economic development model that privileged multinational corporations over a previous model that emphasized state control over industry.[32] Yet domestic entrepreneurs and news producers made editorial decisions on a daily basis regarding what should be included or excluded from news coverage. The success of Televisa, the most profitable and powerful media conglomerate in Latin America, enables renewed debates over dependency and world systems theories that relegate "peripheral nations," such as Mexico, to an eternal secondary position on a global economic and cultural stage. That the U.S. justice system ruled against Azcárraga Milmo's effort to establish a Spanish-language monopoly in 1987, as he had done in his country, requires a rethinking of dependency and world systems conceptual and theoretical frameworks. Pablo Arredondo Ramírez's and María de Lourdes Zermeno Torres's suggestion that Televisa's broadcasting of 24 horas (Mexico's longest-running news program) represents a case of "reverse cultural imperialism" may go a bit too far, but just how viewers interpret cultural products such as television news within and across national boundaries is part of a highly complicated and contested process.[33] As a theoretical construct, cultural imperialism ties scholars' hands and inhibits them from exploring the myriad of factors involved in the development of cultural industries.[34]

Moving beyond cultural imperialism and keeping in mind the concept of cultural hegemony, this study employs a theoretical framework called "hybridity of framing." The framework is useful for understanding the negotiation of meanings between international news agencies and domestic producers of journalism as well as the competing discourses between producers and viewers. Hybridity of framing draws on *cultural hybridity* and *framing*. Cultural hybridity holds that when two or more cultures converge, the social practices and beliefs of each group influence one another to the extent that a new distinct culture merges.[35] Framing, as a methodology and a theoretical construct, has gained currency among sociological and communications researchers and reflects the manner in which a news producer or writer emphasizes some elements of an event or issue over others, with the goal of making a news report meaningful.[36]

As this book's case studies demonstrate, television news producers framed events in particular ways, sometimes in a manner distinct from the perspective of state officials or foreign interests. Additionally, news producers' portrayals of events could be in conflict with how viewers interpreted events, and those viewers may have reframed the same events in ways they deemed just and meaningful. As one example, hybrid framing helps explain how news producers may have attempted to downplay student movements, but young people often interpreted the same issues or events in different ways—a conflict of visions that in some cases may have helped foster domestic and international solidarity.[37] Hybrid framing allows us to view interpretations of media messages as a negotiation and process between the individual and the media that occurs over time, rather than reduce viewers to inert media consumers. The framework also is useful in understanding the power relationship between news producers and international news agencies. The U.S. wire services Associated Press and United Press International may have described major Space Race events such as the lunar landing in way that exalted U.S. technological prowess, but Mexican television news staffs often couched reports regarding the Space Race in their own very nationalistic terms.

Former Televisa media executive Miguel Sabido's declaration that *"presidencialismo* is the key to understanding television in Mexico" is telling, but the analysis of what viewers saw on the air remains equally significant.[38] Yet studies about media content, especially for the early years of television, are hard to come by.[39] With all the theoretical works on television, there has been a certain lack of hard data, which if available would help ground existing theoretical works.[40] Part of the problem lies in the availability and accessibility of sources. Generally, private interests control scripts, television programs, images (film and video), company documents, and all the data necessary to produce systematic empirical works. The interests of private companies may or may not always coincide with those of the researcher and vice versa, so the researcher often is denied access.

Having been granted unprecedented access to Televisa's news scripts and images produced between 1950 and 1970, I have been able to analyze some hard data. Nevertheless, two factors limited my access to Televisa's archives: the *jurídico* and natural disasters. The governing body within the company known as the jurídico decides who gets access to what materials and how much material (in my case, scripts and images) an individual obtains. I was able to examine scripts produced between the years 1954 and 1970. The scripts for earlier newscasts had been lost as a result of three earthquakes, several floods, the transfer of documents from one archive location to another, and perhaps simple neglect. Many images that correspond to the scripts could not be located for the same reasons. With respect to images of the student movements and violence of 1968 and 1971, the governing body allowed me to view about twenty minutes of images. None of those images included *balaceras* (shootings) involving young dissidents.

The scripts and images that I did analyze at Televisa's news archives at Chapultepec and Estadio Azteca in Mexico City are more than faded words on onion-skin paper and dust-covered film reels and videotapes. They provide clues to answering questions about cultural and social history, including the history of the television industry. By keeping in mind the three levels of media flow—content, production and, interpretation—this study puts these artifacts into their proper historical place.[41] Scrutinizing the scripts and images in terms of content, production, and interpretation enabled an empirically based picture of the early television news industry to emerge and, as a result, helped to contribute to a deeper understanding of Mexican society during this crucial period.

Analyses of news programming can shed light on discussions regarding the rise of youth counterculture, popular social unrest, and the media's influence on society during the height of the Cold War.[42] This study demonstrates how the media served to reinforce the country's strategy of dual containment—that of containing domestic dissidents to maintain control for the national government and containing communism to maintain good relations with the United States. Through televised reports, news media helped the government implement this strategy. Additionally, understanding media during this period is essential because of the increasingly significant role that mass communications played in disseminating information to citizens in countries such as Mexico, where the majority of citizens began to receive news through television. Moreover, it was through television news programs about protests and the Olympic Games that citizens began to understand the country's relationship to the world during the Cold War.

Although diplomatic historians have tended to focus on nation-states, the analysis of television programming offers an opportunity to understand the everyday experiences and the shared national experiences of the Cold War, both of which are lacking in the existing literature.[43] Furthermore, as scholars have noted, Mexico's role in the Cold War has been neglected. This book helps resituate what currently constitutes a bipolar body of scholarship on a global conflict in a way that includes more than the United States and the Soviet Union. Finally, the analysis of the media and its role during this pivotal period remain useful because of the United States' involvement and financial interests in media production, including news content through foreign news agencies and transnational advertising agencies.[44]

Chapter 1 details how U.S. and other foreign interests influenced the development of the medium, as well as how Mexican entrepreneurs looked beyond the country's border to establish the first television networks. Transnational interests in Latin American media began long before the official inauguration of Mexican television on September 1, 1950, with the broadcast of President Miguel Alemán Valdés's fourth national address. By the early part of the twentieth century, U.S. radio networks and wire services had formed ties with Mexican domestic entrepreneurs to sell both news programming and radio receivers. By some estimates, in the 1920s Mexico was second only to Canada in terms of the importation of radio sets.[45] Yet there were limits to U.S. efforts to influence the country's cultural industries as well as its people, just as there were limits to the government's and media entrepreneurs' efforts to influence the hearts and minds of Mexican viewers. This chapter also discusses the important first steps in establishing the industry, such as the decision to implement a commercial television system, and what that meant for television programming—including television news.

Chapter 2 analyzes the origins of television news, demonstrating that, contrary to the assumption that the first decades of TV news were insignificant, these early years determined the path the medium would take and helped to explain the unique power the industry gained by the late twentieth century.[46] Indeed, by the end of the first five years of television's development, several *tele*-traditions had been invented, including coverage of national holidays and the inclusion of sports in newscasts, as well as the manner in which news anchors began the news by greeting viewers every evening with a *"muy buenas noches."*[47] Anyone who watches television news today knows that these traditions continue into the twenty-first century. Undoubtedly, the decision to cover certain national holidays grew out of a much longer tradition that began with independence itself. Holiday celebrations combined both print and performance to create an imagined community composed of those taking part in the holiday everywhere in the nation, and TV newscasts promoted national celebrations to solidify a sense of nationhood among citizens.[48]

Chapters 3 through 7 present and explain the qualitative content analyses of news reports regarding the five case studies in this book. The first case study is of the railway workers movement of the 1950s and the Cuban Revolution of 1959, both of which represented defining moments in the country's modern history. Mexican and Cuban dissidents emerged as major players on television news between 1954, the start of the Mexican railway movement, and 1959, the year Fidel Castro took control of Havana. The analysis shows that in their news coverage of Mexican railway "rebels" and Cuban revolutionaries, news producers hailed Cuban revolutionaries as champions who overthrew a dictator, while they deplored railway strikers as threats to the nation. The juxtaposition presented in this chapter illustrates the country's and media's inconsistent treatment of national and international dissidents. News coverage of Castro's regime would change as he aligned himself with the Soviet Union in the early 1960s, reflecting a dramatic shift in diplomatic relations among Mexico, Cuba, the United States, and the Soviet Union.

The quadripartite connections among Mexico, Cuba, and the two super powers take center stage in chapter 4. The Cuban Revolution of 1959, one of the most influential events in the Americas of the twentieth century, and Fulgencio Batista's ousting from Havana on January 1, 1959, marked Castro's triumph as well as brought into sharp relief tenuous relations among the four nations. News coverage of presidential visits abroad and foreign dignitaries' trips to Mexico serve as a window through which the state of diplomatic affairs in 1959 can be examined. The four visits include former president Lázaro Cárdenas's trip to Cuba on July 24–27; president Adolfo López Mateos's trip to the United States on October 8–18; U.S. president Dwight D. Eisenhower's trip to Acapulco on February 19–20; and Soviet vice-premier Anastas Mikoyan's trip to Mexico on November 18–28. The news reports highlight the country's contingent position during the first phase of the Cuban Revolution (1959–63). Furthermore, the chapter provides evidence of "television diplomacy," a more popular expression of diplomacy, in contrast to political practices that transpired in formal and elite circles. As television's popularity and power rose, high-ranking political officials increasingly began to use the medium to disseminate their distinct diplomatic agendas to the public.

Aside from meetings between heads of state, the Space Race between the United States and the Soviet Union provided another avenue in which international and national politicians could disseminate their Cold War agendas. Chapter 5 includes analysis of how television news reporters and producers portrayed major events related to the Space Race from 1957 to 1969. Focusing on events such as the launch of *Sputnik* on October 4, 1957; the Cuban Missile Crisis of October 1962; and the lunar landing on July 20, 1969, this chapter reveals that news reports function as another powerful audiovisual expression of Cold War politics. Viewers also learned about the country's attempts to enter the Space Race, as homegrown scientists launched their own rockets. Whether they were documenting domestic or foreign technological endeavors, news writers tended to portray space projects in ways that promoted the nation and modernity. News programs also illuminated the political tightrope that officials such as President López Mateos walked during episodes such as the Cuban Missile Crisis, at which time the president remained curiously out of the country on a visit to the Philippines.

Throughout the second half of the twentieth century, the country's and television executives' preoccupation with modernity were omnipresent, and this became dramatically evident in 1968 as the nation prepared to host the nineteenth Olympiad. On October 12, 1968, Mexico became the first country to broadcast the games live and in color to a worldwide estimated audience of 900 million people, the largest audience in the history of television.[49] The broadcasting of the Olympics represented a critical opportunity for government officials and television executives to beam the country's modern and economically successful face into the homes of viewers across the globe. However, ten days before the Olympic Games in Mexico City, special forces known as *granaderos* opened fire on thousands of demonstrators, killing more than three hundred students and bystanders at the Plaza de las Tres Culturas. This act momentarily dashed the dreams of television executives, who stood to gain millions from the broadcasts, as well as President Gustavo Díaz Ordaz, who three years before the games remarked proudly that "all the eyes of the world would be on Mexico in 1968 and that he hoped Mexicans would respond to their responsibilities in providing a warm and dignified reception for all visitors."[50]

Juxtaposing news coverage of the student movements and the Olympic Games held in Mexico City, chapter 6 describes the stark contrasts between the portrayals of two groups of youth—athletes and activists. Like the railway workers of 1959, student activists were portrayed as threats to the nation and order, while Olympic athletes were glorified as model citizens. Although news programs silenced the viewpoints of young activists, participants in the movement made their voices heard through alternative means of communication such as street theater, placards, and widespread demonstrations. The book culminates as these alternative forms of public information illuminated another hybrid way of framing the dramatic political events and issues that engulfed the nation.

News cameras returned to Estadio Azteca and sports in 1970, as Mexico City hosted the World Cup. At the same time, politicians such as Luis Echeverría, who served as secretary of *gobernación* in 1968, worked to restore PRI legitimacy after the massacre at Tlatelolco. The country geared up for a presidential election in which Echeverría was picked as the presumptive frontrunner. Chapter 6 examines coverage of the presidential elections and the World Cup in Mexico City, both held in July 1970. Thanks in part to the athletic prowess of Pelé, the Brazilian team won the cup at Estadio Azteca. While Pelé ran on the field waving a Brazilian flag, Mexican fans chanted in favor of their Latin American counterparts. Azcárraga Milmo claimed victory for having negotiated a very profitable deal for Telesistema Mexicano, for this was the first World Cup financed by private interests. A presidential campaign ensued on the airwaves along with the World Cup, but this chapter shows that election coverage paled when compared to the amount of time devoted to the World Cup. The amount of time given to opposition candidates was dwarfed by that devoted to the PRI candidate Echeverría. Once again, news producers chose to downplay the political in their efforts to let entertainment and sports take center stage.

By 1970 Telesistema Mexicano executives had severed contracts with the major capital newspapers, putting an end to the sharing of content between newspapers and TV news programs. This move ended a somewhat diverse era in television news in terms of production and content. With the dailies out of the picture, company executives sought to standardize and professionalize operations through the creation of a new corporate news division, with the son of former president Miguel Alemán Velasco at the helm. One of Alemán's first tasks as head of the news division was to design an hour-long national newscast. He created *24 horas*, a news program that aired for three decades. Although it had new features, the program carried with it many of the same tele-traditions of the earliest newscasts and solidified Jacobo Zabluvosky's position as the country's best-known news personality. It is to those earliest days of television that this book now turns.

"Muy buenas noches"

> I think that if the national government gave support toward the individuals interested in developing television in our country, in very little time Mexico could have television systems, equipment, and perhaps stations that would compare satisfactorily as the best in the world.
>
> Guillermo González Camarena

CHAPTER 1

The Rise of Television in Mexico

BROADCAST ENGINEER Guillermo González Camarena's visionary statement, written for President Miguel Alemán Valdés, was penned in 1948, two years before the official inauguration of television. On September 1, 1950, President Alemán beamed Latin America into the television age with his fourth address to the nation, broadcast on XHTV, Channel 4. The station was owned by his close friend and Puebla business owner Rómulo O'Farrill Silva, who also owned the popular Mexico City daily *Novedades*, his newly acquired radio station XEX, and an automobile manufacturing plant in the neighboring state of Puebla. O'Farrill's connections with the automobile industry would prove important to the early years of television news, as some of the first sponsors of news programming included companies such as General Motors and PEMEX (the state-run petroleum company). On the inaugural day of television, O'Farrill remarked proudly,

1

Today is a day of festivity for Mexico, as today our country will be the first in Latin America to have for the advantage and benefit of its inhabitants, the most important invention of modern times: television.[1]

O'Farrill's connections to President Alemán also proved useful, as he managed to beat fellow media entrepreneur Emilio Azcárraga Vidaurreta in the race to become the first station owner to receive a concession (similar to a license) to broadcast on television. O'Farrill had such close ties to the former president that some scholars argue that he acted as a front for Alemán in establishing the first television station. It is certainly curious that Azcárraga Vidaurreta did not receive a television concession until 1950, four years after he petitioned for it, as he had far more "cultural capital" in the late 1940s and early 1950s than his rival O'Farrill.[2] Since his arrival to the capital from Tamaulipas state, Azcárraga had amassed a large share of the country's commercial media landscape. Azcárraga owned both XEQ and XEW, the most powerful radio network in Mexico City and perhaps Latin America, and a majority of shares in Churubusco movie studios. Both XEW and XEQ enjoyed affiliations with the U.S. television networks, NBC and CBS, respectively. Indeed, by 1950 Azcárraga Vidaurreta had at least a quarter of a century of business dealings with U.S. media, beginning in 1925 with his work with the Mexico Music Company, an affiliate of Radio Corporation of America (RCA), a subsidiary of NBC.[3]

Meanwhile, surrounded by allegations of corruption, Alemán looked for a less direct route to influence television through O'Farrill, because "his immediate family would find it difficult to so nakedly use presidential power to profit from the new medium."[4] Alemán's decision to grant the first television concession to O'Farrill instead of Azcárraga Vidaurreta, "the czar of Mexican radio," remains important to understanding the medium's early years. Azcárraga Vidaurreta had been gearing up to expand his broadcast operations to include television since the 1940s, and in 1946 he launched a campaign to persuade potential television entrepreneurs in Latin America to establish commercial rather than state-run television systems.[5] By many press accounts, and certainly in Azcárraga Vidaurreta's eyes, he seemed like the natural candidate to receive the first television concession. President Alemán saw it otherwise, and in 1949 he granted the first concession to O'Farrill, who established Televisión de México, XHTV.[6]

This chapter examines more closely the first steps of the television industry, focusing on the first station owners, the decision to implement a commercial television model, and the laws set up to control the industry. Another first step included the consolidation of the three Mexico City network owners. These initial decisions help to explain the power relationships among foreign interests and the nation's media elite, the state and media, and the media elite and viewers. In addition, the chapter situates the development of the television industry into the larger context of society and illustrates how not long after the inauguration of the medium, through this new technology, citizens' daily lives had begun to change.

The first official public transmission was a live remote broadcast through a microwave link between the Chamber of Deputies and the National Lottery building. Officials from Alemán's administration had eight screens set up in public places for a "televisioning" of the event. Setting up a public viewing of the annual *informe* (address) was not a bad idea, considering there were only about one hundred television sets in the entire nation.[7]

O'Farrill, like Azcárraga, had business ties to U.S. companies. For example, he purchased the equipment for the transmissions from RCA at an approximate cost of US$2.2 million, and directors and producers from NBC helped with the first broadcasts. O'Farrill received financial backing from U.S. business owner William Jenkins. A well-established entrepreneur in Puebla and Mexico City, Jenkins owned a multitude of movie theaters. He and

Meade Brunet, the vice president of RCA, attended the station's inaugural ceremony the day before the official state inauguration of television.[8]

Despite his ties to U.S. business interests, O'Farrill exhibited a profound sense of national pride as he declared Mexico as the first country in Latin America to send television into the homes of its inhabitants. For O'Farrill, the birth of the television industry did not represent the deployment of a "U.S. cultural bomb."[9] He felt it was a symbol of progress and modernity. As a writer for his *Novedades* stated, "Television is the newest development that is now working in Mexico . . . a historic date for the country's progress."[10]

The official broadcast of Alemán's informe on September 1, 1950, thrust the country into a new cultural age. The venue for the first official transmission remains significant. That early television executives decided to unveil the technology with a presidential address shows that both the government and media worked together from the start.[11] With the inaugural transmission, Mexico became the first country in Latin America, the first Spanish-speaking country, and the sixth nation in the world to broadcast television.[12] This gave Mexican media moguls a bit of cachet over their counterparts in the region, especially in Brazil and Cuba, where television officially began just seventeen days, and a few months after Mexico, respectively.[13] Clearly, government officials as well as media pioneers understood the importance of developing this new form of mass communication for political and economic reasons, and Latin American business leaders and politicians raced to get their messages on the air.

Alemán, through the Secretaría de Comunicaciones y Obras Públicas (Ministry of Communications and Public Works), granted engineer Guillermo González Camarena the country's second television concession in January 1950. His company, Televisión González Camarena, established XHGC, Channel 5. The station was inaugurated on Mother's Day, May 10, 1950, but regular transmissions did not begin until August of that year. Channel

5's studios were located in El Teatro Alameda, a property on San Juan de Letrán Street, owned by Azcárraga Vidaurreta.¹⁴ The first program, a tribute to Mother's Day, was sponsored by the Mexico City daily *Excelsior*.

Although Azcárraga Vidaurreta seemed like the most obvious media entrepreneur to establish the country's first television station, his company, Televimex, would launch the third station, XEW-TV, Channel 2. At age fifty-six, Azcárraga Vidaurreta initiated regular transmissions, a year and a half after O'Farrill launched XHTV. The studios for XEW-TV, officially inaugurated in January 1952, were located in Televicentro, on Avenida Chapultepec, the site of Televisa's current news department and operations. A few months before the inauguration of XEW-TV, Azcárraga, in his typically arrogant but charming fashion, talked about his latest enterprise:

> I'm the biggest radio man in Mexico; I guess I'm no small-time operator in the movie business; and when Televicentro opens this month, there won't be any doubt who the TV czar of Mexico is.¹⁵

The inaugural program on XEW-TV was a baseball game transmitted by a remote signal from Delta Park (later called Parque Deportivo de Seguro Social) in Mexico City. The connection between sports and television was something that Azcárraga Vidaurreta developed from the incipient stages of the industry, and this tie would prove very lucrative in the decades ahead. Airing sporting events on television probably seemed like an obvious move, given that his XEW radio had been attracting listeners through sports since the 1930s.¹⁶

Getting television operations off the ground and on the air was not cheap. It required hiring engineers with specific technical knowledge and the purchase of broadcast equipment that General Electric and Dumont Laboratories sold to Azcárraga. By 1951 the total cost of construction was reported at some 11 million pesos.¹⁷

Although the fall of 1950 is considered the official start of television in Mexico, engineers had been developing the technology since the late 1920s. Guillermo González Camarena is often referred to as the technological father of national television, but two other scientists, Francisco Javier Stavoli and Miguel Fonseca, had been working on the medium years before González Camarena. Financed by the Partido Nacional Revolucionario (PNR, National Revolutionary Party), Stavoli and Fonseca traveled to the United States in 1928 and 1929 and returned with the country's first television equipment in 1930, the same year that Azcárraga Vidaurreta inaugurated his radio station XEW. In 1931, under Stavoli's direction, they set up a signal from the Escuela Superior de Ingenería Mecánica y Eléctrica (Superior School of Mechanical and Electrical Engineering) on Allende Street that beamed to Belisario Dominguez Street. After a few tests, they transmitted the first television image: the face of Stavoli's wife, Amelia Fonseca. She sat seventy centimeters away from the camera . . . for a while, then her photo replaced her, given that she could not remain seated for hours on end while the initial transmissions were underway.[18]

In 1935 Stavoli helped the PNR unveil the new technology to the public. At the PNR's office on 18 Paseo de la Reforma, with equipment acquired in New York, Stavoli demonstrated the new medium using a photograph of then president Lázaro Cárdenas.[19] Members of the press applauded as they saw the transmission: an image of the president.

Apart from the location of the first experimental television transmission, the PNR, which later became the Partido Revolucionario Institucional (PRI, Institutional Revolutionary Party), remained conspicuously out of the picture. In contrast to the government's direct participation in radio, through its own station, XEFO, officials played a less intrusive role in the television industry. Scholars have yet to explain fully the government's early ambivalence toward television in contrast to radio. For example, XEFO began as an arm of the PNR in 1931 and the PRM until 1946, when President Alemán sold the station to private interests in preparation for the arrival of television.[20] Although the government may have lacked the financial wherewithal to set up its own television stations, this only partially answers the question about the laissez-faire attitude of the Alemán administration, especially given the government's early participation in radio and experimental television.

COMMERCIAL VERSUS STATE-RUN TELEVISION

The state's hands-off attitude regarding television and the decision to implement a commercial television system was not a foregone conclusion, at least not until the so-called Novo report was published in 1948. In 1947 President Alemán commissioned the director of the Instituto Nacional de Bellas Artes (National Institute of Performing Arts), Carlos Chávez, to conduct a study of the new medium. Chávez selected Guillermo González Camarena and one of the country's leading intellectuals and authors, Salvador Novo, to lead the commission. In October the two traveled to the United States and Europe, meeting with technical and editorial experts in both countries. Novo praised the content and model of the British Broadcasting Company but offered no recommendation. González Camarena recommended that the country adopt a commercial model for technical and financial reasons. He argued that to date the televisions in Mexico followed U.S. specifications and that much of the equipment would be less expensive if imported from the United States.[21] Two years after the report, a decree published on February 11, 1950, in the *Diario oficial de la federación* stated that the country would follow González Camarena's recommendations.

Aside from the technical and economic aspects of the new medium, González Camarena and Novo's report discussed differences between radio and television audiences. Radio listeners, the report suggested, could sit for long periods and enjoy programming, and housewives could still manage to "cook while they listened to Mozart, Curiel, Panseco or Mendez Rivas," but this would not be possible with television viewers. As a result, the report concluded that it seemed probable that television transmissions would not be broadcast as frequently as radio programs.[22] It did not take long for it to become obvious that viewers had no problems at all sitting for long periods of time watching TV programming.

An assessment of the government's decision to adopt a commercial model must consider the influence of the radio industry. Experimental radio began in Mexico City in 1918, but 1923 is widely accepted as the first year of regular radio broadcasts.[23] That was the year that radio parts and equipment vendors, Luis and Raúl Azcárraga, established radio CYL. In 1930 Emilio Azcárraga Vidaurreta acquired CYL from his brothers to launch XEW radio. The owners of the cigarette company El Buen Tono started CYB (later XEB), the other major early commercial station.

Media families such as the Azcárragas and Palavicinis, who had holdings in both radio and print and who managed to maintain wealth by the end of the Porfiriato (1876–1911) and through the revolution (1910–21) represented the most likely candidates to initiate television. Félix F. Palavicini established the Mexico City daily *El Universal* in 1916 and in 1930 acquired the radio station CYJ, which became XEN. Prior to World War II, the family enterprises that grew into multimedia empires already had been entrenched in significant capital accumulation, which allowed them to pursue the expensive, but soon to be lucrative, television business.[24] Furthermore, the connections with U.S. radio networks had been established, and those continued with the advent of television. Indeed, Azcárraga Vidaurreta toured and trained at NBC radio facilities.[25]

Overall, the government chose to let private business owners such as Azcárraga and O'Farrill initiate the incipient industry, but it did make a few paltry attempts to directly influence the airwaves. In 1958 President Adolfo Ruiz Cortines helped to establish the country's first state-owned television station, Channel 11, located at the Instituto Politécnico Nacional (National Polytechnic Institute). The school held the concession, but because of the limited budget and resources, the station never came close to rivaling the programs produced by the country's commercial enterprises.[26]

The government's hands-off attitude toward television during its incipient stage seemed to be the result of two major factors. First, by the early 1950s radio was already a commercially viable enterprise. More than two hundred standard radio stations were in operation around the country, most of them privately owned. Second, the commercial model fit within the overall strategy of the Alemán administration, a strategy that fostered foreign investment, industrial development, and capital accumulation.

The government's decision to allow a commercial model over a state-run model would have lasting influence on the country's politicians and capitalists and consequently blurred the lines between the government and private business. For example, the Alemán family continued to benefit from large profits derived from the television industry well into the twentieth century.[27] In addition, this decision would directly impact all genres of programming, including television news. Within the commercial broadcast system, all programming, including news, depended on the revenue generated through advertising. Revenue to support television news first came in the form of sponsors such as General Motors, and later in the form of direct advertising through companies.[28]

TELEVISION AND SOCIETY

Today television touches the lives of nearly all citizens, but it took decades for it to rise to the level of national prominence. At several thousand pesos in the 1950s, the price of a television set was simply economically unattainable for many citizens. Even radios were costly for most, with a radio receiver in one out of every four homes.[29] Because so few people had television sets during the medium's first few years, often Mexico City residents would catch bullfights and soccer matches from outside a storefront, as many a public viewing stage was born. Bars and restaurants were another popular place to catch the news or a sporting event. Long before "Pay-Per-View," a literal cottage industry of selling television viewing time developed.

Those who managed to move into the category of the country's new middle class and who could afford to buy this new heavy box that transmitted images would often charge their neighbors twenty to fifty centavos to watch their favorite programs such as *El teatro Nescafé* (Nescafe Theater), *El programa de Max Factor* (Max Factor Program), Pedro Vargas, and *El conde de Monte Cristo* (The Count of Monte Cristo).[30] For television set owners, the apparatus functioned as a symbol of social status, and like other forms of conspicuous consumption, viewers often placed their new products in places of high visibility in their homes so that friends would be sure to see their new possession.

As a new luxury item, the television set tended to exacerbate social tensions between those who had TV sets and those who did not, as well as increase a family's financial liability. Anthropologist Oscar Lewis documented how some Mexico City residents were forced to pawn one possession to pay the monthly installment for another — the TV.[31] At least one member of the Gutierrez family had to stay home for fear that the television might be stolen if the entire family left the apartment. Less than a decade after the official inauguration of television, it appeared that the medium was transforming society. Viewer Rosa Gomez of Mexico City stated,

> Since the coming of television, people stayed up later. Previously, children and young girls had not been allowed out after dark and most families went to bed about ten o'clock. Now people no longer listened to their radios as much or went to the movies as often; children spent more time indoors. Girls dressed more in style and more things were bought on the installment plan as a result of televising advertising. People also had new ideas — a neighbor's daughter wanted to become a ballet dancer after she had seen a dance group on TV.[32]

Television directors and producers, many who had come from radio, theater, and film, learned quickly about the visual power of the new medium. Gonzalo Castellot recounted an anecdote about one of the first live fashion shows he directed. During the program, sponsored by Salinas y Rocha, one of the country's largest department store chains, a line of beautiful and scantily clad women walked down the runway, modeling the newest fashions in women's lingerie. The lighting proved so intense that the picture revealed not only the undergarments, but everything underneath! At once, Castellot cut to another, more appropriate image.[33]

The immediacy of television, as Castellot found out, was just one of the important differences between electronic and print media. The two media also depended on distinct technologies to disseminate information. Unlike privately owned newspapers, the airwaves that carry programming belong to the public domain — a situation established in the 1960 Ley Federal de Radio y Televisión (Federal Law of Radio and Television). The government has the right and obligation to approve station concessions, regulate the industry, and monitor broadcasting content. The technological nature of television transmission allows the government to intervene and control broadcasting in a much more direct way than it can with print media.

The technological limitations regarding transmission represent another difference between print and broadcasting. There exists a limited number of frequencies available to broadcast radio and television, which in turn restricts the number of individuals and companies who have been able to obtain concessions, with implications for the types of broadcast programming that emerged. The government granted concessions to an elite group of capitalists, and as a result, programming, including news, reflects capitalist and elite interests.

COMPETITION TO THE DEATH OR CONSOLIDATION

By 1955 the owners of Mexico City's three privately owned television stations — XHTV, XEW-TV, and XHGC — understood that although the upper and middle classes were growing, they had not yet reached a level capable of sustaining three separate commercial stations.

The three stations competed fiercely for the amount of advertising revenue available. At the same time, the enormous costs associated with television operations were forcing "the businessmen down a narrow road without an exit."[34] On March 26 Rómulo O'Farrill, Emilio Azcárraga Vidaurreta, and Guillermo González Camarena decided that instead of driving one another out of business, they would combine their economic efforts. The owners of XEW-TV and XHGC had already joined forces the year before.[35] Azcárraga Vidaurreta admitted to the press that the burgeoning television industry was losing millions of pesos a year.[36]

Numerous economic and social barriers all worked together to prevent each of the stations from turning a profit by itself. First, despite the country's economic growth, the peso suffered a 150 percent devaluation from 1947 to 1955. The drop in the peso's value made it more difficult for television entrepreneurs to pay for high operating costs. Second, because the medium was still in its incipient stages, advertisers were hesitant to invest in airtime. Third, government policies inhibited the growth of the country's television audience through quotas and high tariffs on the importation of TV sets. Business owners such as Azcárraga calculated that the country needed at least forty thousand television receivers in operation before a profit could be turned through advertising, but a government decree signed in 1951 declared that only ten thousand a year could be imported. In its first year of operation, just over thirteen thousand television sets were imported, including stand-alone and console television sets. Finally, the business of television competed with the movie industry, and those with a financial stake in film worked to hurt their competition by limiting the number and quality of movies that could be broadcast on television. In 1954 the film industry passed several protectionist measures that included the prohibition of airing any Mexican film for at least six years after its release.[37] The limitations placed on the television industry by the film industry and government quotas on the importation of television sets pointed to the various tensions that existed between media executives and other economic interests. The decree regulating the importation of television sets, illuminated the tension between state and private interests.

Citizens' complaints over programming, along with those of the government, brought to light the tensions between viewers and media executives. By the mid-1950s, groups such as the Liga de la Decencia (League for Decency) lobbied President Adolfo Ruiz Cortines to prohibit certain types of programming such as *lucha libre* (a form of wrestling) and behavior such as kissing on television.[38] On October 2, 1953, the president of the Federación de Asociaciones de Padres de Familias de las Escuelas Secundarias del Distrito Federal (Federation of Associations of Parents of High School Families of the Federal District) petitioned Ruiz Cortines to "moralize television transmissions" and requested the prohibition of lucha libre broadcasts and immoral magazines, such as *Pepin* and *Chamaco*, popular adult comic books published between 1936 and 1957.[39] In 1954 the president banned lucha libre for several years. Similar to bullfighting during the Porfiriato, lucha libre was thought to be a barbaric sport, an activity that threatened to further deteriorate popular behavior and attitudes.[40]

The public outcry against television programming was part of a larger effort to moralize a city and country in the midst of dramatic social and cultural change.[41] Criticisms about early television also reflect the tensions that existed between producers of the media and those who were watching and revealed that producers and viewers did not always share the same notions about modernity or *mexicanidad* (Mexicanness). But viewers did not criticize the many musical programs that aired on the television during its first decade. Programs featuring traditional music, such as mariachi, proved profitable for media executives and acceptable to viewers. Music as a part of culture began to become standardized through radio, and that process continued on television. Television programming in conjunction with other forms of media strengthened the *china poblana* as the iconic image of the Mexican woman.

1. China poblana and charro (cowboy) pose for the camera at XHTV, Channel 4, television studios, ca. 1950. Reprinted by permission from INAH, Fototeca Nacional, Fondo Casasola, no. 87604.

Although in practice Telesistema Mexicano functioned as a monopoly, legally, the company could not hold the concessions for the three stations. O'Farrill Senior retained the license for Televisión de México, Channel 4; Azcárraga for Televimex, Channel 2; and Guillermo González Camarena for Televisión González Camarena, Channel 5.[42]

The consolidation of the three capital stations meant that all television journalists would now be producing news under one parent company. The change in the company structure resulted in significant implications for the production of news, as the standardization of reporting and producing practices increased. For example, news staffs from the three stations began to share news content. Finally, the monopoly formed in the mid-1950s signaled a tendency to consolidate in the midst of economic or political pressure that would continue through the 1970s, with the eventual establishment of Televisa in 1973, when Telesistema Mexicano and Televisión Independiente de México merged. Therefore, the importance of the 1955 consolidation should not be understated and must be seen as part of a continuum that had a lasting impact on the production and content of news and, as a result, on viewers' interpretations.

LEGAL CONSIDERATIONS

Beyond the state-owned Channel 11, the government sought to influence television through legislation. The 1960 federal law governing television made it mandatory for stations to allocate free airtime to the government. Prior to the 1960 law, the 1940 Ley de Vías Generales de Comunicaciones (Law of Public Thoroughfares and Communications) controlled radio and television, giving the government exclusive regulatory control over the airwaves and the right to set advertising rates and establish rules for emergency transmissions. The government would pay 50 percent less than the rate-card cost to air official programs. The 1940 law had also established the Ministry of Communications and Public Works as the agency that granted concessions and permits, with the power to demand the correction or improvement of station services, suspend any station that did not meet standards, and levy fines for violations. Under the ministry's decree, no foreigner could own a radio station, nor could a station change ownership without approval.[43]

The 1960 law strengthened the principles of the 1940s legislation and added new provisions. One called for the government to participate in the television industry through privately owned channels. The law stipulated that the president, through the Ministry of the Interior, must act as a watchdog, ensuring that television promoted Mexican cultural and traditional values. Moreover, the law called on the Ministry of the Interior to produce educational, cultural, and social programs, and they were to be broadcast on the commercial stations free of charge.[44]

The new mass communications law attempted to counteract the onslaught of foreign, mainly U.S.-produced, programs. Although article 58 of the law stated that there should be no prior censorship of any broadcast material, certain provisions limited freedom of expression. One provision required that only Spanish could be used in broadcasts, unless prior permission had been obtained from the Ministry of the Interior. Another one prohibited broadcasts that could "corrupt the Spanish language, violate the accepted customs of the community, encourage anti-social behavior, denigrate national heroes, offend commonly held religious beliefs or discriminate on the grounds of race or color."[45]

These provisions of the 1960 law not only represented the government's increasing concern over television content but also illustrated an overt strategy to limit cultural flows from the north. That does not mean that cultural imperialism was underway, but that cultural production can be mediated from outside and inside a country's boundaries. Television executives had their share of input into the law. Indeed, media lawyers backed the law, but this should not seem strange at all. As Fernández Christlieb pointed out, by 1972 at least nine federal deputies were directly involved in the radio and television industry, either as station concessionaries or as media executives.[46]

The government's increasing role in television coincided with the rise in the number of viewers. At the outset of the industry only a hundred television sets existed in the entire country, but by 1957 that number had soared to three hundred thousand.[47] Watching the growing power of television must have caused Ruiz Cortines and members of his administration to look for subtle ways to implement their own legacy. While Alemán's regime wallowed in allegations of corruption and unbridled capitalism, Ruiz Cortines's administration sought to stamp out corruption. Ironically, Alemán campaigned under the same platform.

TELEVISION IN THE 1960S

Television's popularity soared in the 1960s, along with the nation's economy. The industry was becoming extremely popular and profitable. According to Luis Becerra Celis,

> A television set has become in Mexico an article of prime necessity. The urge of every Mexican home to get a TV set is so great that numerous poor families, living in houses not much better than huts pride themselves on a television set that is being painfully paid on the installment plan, peso by peso.

Clearly, by the end of the 1950s television had begun to change the cultural and physical landscape of Mexico City (see figure 2). The year 1959 was a record breaker for television sales, as 120,000 were sold nationwide, with large screens being preferred over smaller portable sets. By the beginning of the decade monthly viewership was estimated at 3,864,122, with about 780,000 television sets in operation. At the same time, television began to infiltrate regions outside of the capital. Television was being beamed into the homes of wealthy Tijuana residents. And in 1959 Guadalajara, the nation's second largest city, inaugurated its first television station.[48] Although Guadalajara media executives established the station,

2. Television antennae on Mexico City rooftops with the Latin American tower in the background, ca. 1957. Reprinted by permission from INAH, Fototeca Nacional, Fondo Casasola, no. 382613.

the monopolistic desires of the owners of Telesistema Mexicano would end up crushing regional ownership of television stations.

Beyond the entrepreneurial successes of capital city television executives, major technological advances in the 1960s assisted in the development of Telesistema Mexicano and the industry overall. First, the invention of videotape allowed for an easier and more economically efficient way to distribute programs. In 1959 *Puerta al suspenso* (Gateway to suspense) became the country's first program recorded on videotape.[49] Prior to videotape, television programs were recorded on sixteen-millimeter film through a kinescope. These recordings proved to be of inferior quality. Videotape dramatically changed news production by allowing news photographers to record events more cheaply and quickly than on film. Capturing news stories on film required a developing process, whereas a videotaped image could be brought back immediately to the news department for editing. The switch from film to videotape also allowed Telesistema Mexicano to begin to export its television programs to markets in Latin America and beyond. By the 1980s Televisa's programs were being exported to more than a hundred countries.

The advent of color television represents the second major development of the 1960s. Guillermo González Camarena patented his color television invention, called "kaleidoscope" in 1960, and by 1963 the first color program, *Paraíso infantil* (A child's paradise), was broadcast.[50] This was González Camarena's second color television patent. His first, in 1940, was a trichromatic system based on green, blue, and red. This second patent allowed viewers to watch their favorite programs without having to imagine what color their favorite actors were wearing. For advertisers, this meant they could market their products in new and exciting ways. For news producers, the ability to transmit images in color brought a whole new level of reality to the stories.

The ability to transmit television via satellite represents the third pivotal technological development of the industry in the 1960s. The first transmission was the launch of astronaut Gordon Cooper into space as part of Project Mercury in 1963. In November of the same year satellite technology beamed images of the assassination of U.S. president John F. Kennedy into the homes of U.S. and Mexican citizens. In 1966 the country became a member of the International Organization of Satellite Communications (INTELSAT), giving the country the right to use "spatial artifacts" belonging to the organization. By 1968, after six years of construction, the National Network of Telecommunications was completed, along with a National Microwave Network, a satellite communications center in Tulancingo, and a new telecommunications tower in Mexico City. Together these technological feats allowed Telesistema Mexicano to transmit the Olympic Games to the world via satellite. For the first time the Olympic Games could be reported and viewed live and in color by a potential audience of 900 million people around the world.⁵¹ This meant that a sports journalist in another country with satellite technology could see the event transpire in real time.

These developments had long-lasting consequences for news operations around the world. As satellite technology took hold, news departments recognized that they did not have to send their journalists to the event for the reporter to cover the story. Jorge Labardini, who for years enjoyed covering automobile racing, resigned after Televisa executives requested that he report the Indy 500 from his desk in Mexico City rather than report from the field. He found the idea disingenuous and said that "he would not lie to his loyal viewers."⁵²

Cable television represents a fourth important technological advance between 1950 and 1970. In 1969 the first cable concession was granted to Cablevisión, an affiliate of Telesistema Mexicano. Regular programming through cable started in 1970, more than fifteen years after the first cable television experiment was established in Nogales, Sonora. Through the underground system, U.S. television flowed south of the border for a community of English-speaking residents.⁵³ Cable television represented a significant departure from regular broadcast television in that companies could now charge its viewers for programs. Cablevisión benefited Telesistema Mexicano because the company garnered a tremendous amount of revenue from advertisers and on top of that acquired profits directly from viewers. Many early cable TV viewers found this practice of double-dipping unjust. They asked, why should viewers have to pay for programming and still have to watch commercials?

In the 1960s television through Telesistema Mexicano began to spin its web of influence in regional markets. The centralization of television in the provinces helps to account for Televisa's success.⁵⁴ The establishment of television in Guadalajara provides an example of the tensions that existed between regional business owners and interests. In 1956 Jalisco business owner Alejandro Díaz Guerra and Salvador López Chávez, one of the most powerful provincial capitalists in the country, formed Televisión Tapatía, with the goal of televising locally produced programming. The two struggled to come up with enough capital to establish the station and did not receive a government concession until 1960. In the meantime, the owners of Telesistema Mexicano, mainly Azcárraga Vidaurreta Sr., his son, and Rómulo O'Farrill Sr., had their own ideas of branching out to the provinces, and they created Televisora de Guadalajara in 1958. Their idea was to broadcast programming produced in Mexico City to the provinces. Aided by a newly established microwave network that covered the western states and that was constructed with government funds, the *capitalinos* (capital residents) in Jalisco achieved their goal. They began transmitting programming from XEWO, Channel 2, on May 14, 1960.[55] Televisión Tapatía managed to get on the air in the fall of the same year, after setting up its station, XEHL-TV, Channel 6. The Guadalajaran entrepreneurs operated at a huge disadvantage, given that Televisora de Guadalajara could count on production, content, and financial support from Telesistema Mexicano in Mexico City. Little by little the competition from Televisora de Guadalajara began to weaken Televisión Tapatía's position in the regional market, and the owners were forced to enter into a mutual contract with Telesistema by the end of the decade.

Another regional struggle unfolded between Mexico City and the "Monterrey Elite," in reference to long-standing business interests in the northern city of Monterrey.[56] Gustavo Díaz Ordaz's granting of a concession to Televisión Independiente de México on June 24, 1967, represented one of the president's attempts to create more competition in the industry.[57] Televisión Independiente de México was owned primarily by the Garza Sada family, who had well-established business endeavors based in Monterrey. Just as in Guadalajara, Telesistema Mexicano executives employed a similar conquer-and-consolidate strategy and suggested a merger with the Garza Sada family, which controlled XHTIM, Channel 8. The Azcárragas' and O'Farrills' cultural as well as real capital proved too much for their media rivals, and the two companies merged in 1973 to become Televisa, which stands for *televisión por satellite* (television via satellite). By the mid-1970s, Televisa owned seventy-eight out of the eighty-five stations throughout the country.[58] This owned-and-operated model is not unique to Mexico. It has been widely successful in the United States, Brazil, and other parts of the world.

By September 1970 Díaz Ordaz prepared for his sixth and final presidential address, which would be televised just as Miguel Alemán's had been twenty years before. But the television and political landscapes had changed dramatically in two decades. Whereas a few hundred residents in the nation's capital may have watched Alemán's fourth informe, citizens in almost all the states of the republic were able to listen to and watch Díaz Ordaz, who struggled to regain legitimacy after the massacre at the Plaza de las Tres Culturas. A microwave network, financed and constructed by the government, enabled coast-to-coast transmission of programming. The number of stations had grown from one to seventy-nine, seventy-seven of them being commercial and two cultural.[59]

The early development of television had serious limitations. During the first decades its penetration lagged in rural areas. Not until the administration of Díaz Ordaz and Luis Echeverría, did the government attempt to bring the medium into remote and rural areas. In remote areas radio continued to play a greater role in the daily lives of people.[60]

In 1970 Emilio Azcárraga Milmo appeared at Estadio Azteca along with Brazilian soccer star Pelé for the World Cup, which Brazil won. Within a twenty-year span, the electronic medium underwent enormous changes, especially with respect to technology, but there were also continuities, in particular with the way national holidays were covered and in the tendency to include sports as news. Additionally, in the early 1970s, under President Echeverría, the government began to increase its direct role in the development of television.

TELEVISION AND THE LARGER PICTURE

The second half of the twentieth century represents one of the most important periods in modern Mexican history, yet remains one of the least studied. As a whole, citizens experienced dramatic political, economic, social, and cultural changes. Miguel Alemán Valdés (1946–52), the nation's fifty-fifth president and eighth president after the revolution (1910–20), was the first president since the revolution who had not participated directly in the armed conflict. Being a civilian offered Alemán an opportunity to seek a different path than his predecessors. Indeed, he did, as his presidency has been characterized as one driven by foreign capital and corruption.[61] Clearly, Alemán departed from previous administrations, most notably, the *sexenio* (six-year term) of Lázaro Cárdenas. Loyal followers remembered well Tata Lázaro's (Cárdenas's nickname) signing of the decrees to nationalize the railroads in 1937 and expropriate foreign oil interests in 1938, but Alemán, in contrast, welcomed foreign investment. This, of course, had a bearing on Mexico's ability to become the first country in Latin America to broadcast television. Moreover, during Alemán's administration, the revolution took on an institutional character, as did single-party rule, as the PRM became the Partido Revolucionario Institucional (Institutional Revolutionary Party) in 1946. The changes that Alemán's administration brought arguably made him the most important president in the twentieth century.[62] Cárdenas, because of his personal and political popularity, has received a disproportionate amount of attention among presidents after the revolution, but Alemán's policies altered the material lives of citizens more than any other postrevolutionary president.[63]

The development of television and other mass media played a role in the institutionalization of the revolution as well as in the PRI. Leaders such as Alemán were able to get their messages about the memory and myths of the revolution to large groups of people from all sectors of society. And in a country with a high illiteracy rate and an affinity for visual media, television provided the perfect tool for winning the hearts and minds of citizens.

Alemán's administration sought to improve social and economic conditions through modernization and industrialization at an unprecedented pace. As a result, rural citizens flocked to the capital, creating a city with a deep divide between the rich and poor. Modernization and industrialization had another powerful result—more people moved into the middle class and were able to buy domestic and imported goods like never before, including radios and television sets.

Beginning in the mid-1950s the country's economy grew at a record pace of more than 7 percent annually.[64] In 1964 the economy grew by 10 percent. Paul Kennedy, who worked as a journalist for the *New York Times* between 1954 and 1964, called this period the "Cinderella Years."[65] The hallmarks of *alemanismo*—allying the state with moneyed interests, fostering industrialization, wooing foreign capital, continuing to bolster the economy from within the nation through manufacturing durable goods for a growing number of consumers, known as import substitution industrialization, and co-opting and repressing labor interests—appeared to be paying off.

The country's economic growth led to social advances for many citizens, but not all. The economy may have surpassed most other countries' levels of economic growth, but this did not translate into economic improvements for a large portion of impoverished citizens. In the mid-1950s the poorest citizens (bottom quintile) received 5 percent of the nation's income, and two decades later they earned proportionally even less, only 3 percent.[66] Residents living in the countryside suffered most.

As Mexican and U.S. business leaders increased their capital, the nation's population boomed. From 1950 to 1960 the capital's population increased by 27 percent. The number of inhabitants in the Federal District rose from 3,050,400 to 4,870,800 by 1960, or a percentage increase of 59.6.[67] By 1970 the country's population had risen to 50 million, a 157 percent increase from 1940.[68] The surge in population around the country had an effect on the "economic miracle." With more mouths to feed, the government's response to helping the indigent could go only so far.[69]

While the population and economy boomed, migration from rural villages to Mexico City increased significantly. The shift from the village to the metropolis was a result of both increased industrialization and the need to make a living. Rural migrants moved to the city to work in the growing manufacturing industry. In 1930 five thousand Mexico City factories existed, and that number grew to forty-five thousand by 1950. At the same time, agricultural production in the countryside diminished, as the gross domestic product from agriculture declined from 10 percent of the nation's economy to 5 percent by 1973.[70]

The two Adolfos, Adolfo Ruiz Cortines (1952–58) and Adolfo López Mateos (1958–64), who followed Alemán's presidency continued along the same economic and political path of their predecessor. Nevertheless, the two Adolfos should not be viewed as mere cookie-cutter successors of Alemán. If the broad economic policies of Alemán were in place, there were instances in which the two Adolfos demonstrated less conservative stances than Alemán.[71] With growing unrest in the labor sector, both Ruiz Cortines and López Mateos were forced to negotiate with labor to a greater extent than Alemán. Had they not, they may have led more citizens to call into question the mythology of the revolution much earlier than 1968. Perhaps Ruiz Cortines did not negotiate enough on the side of labor, as López Mateos inherited the labor problems of the two previous administrations, and the tensions culminated with violent labor strikes in 1958 as the second Adolfo took office.

As part of an attempt to quell unrest among popular sectors, Ruiz Cortines expanded the role of the Compañía Exportadora e Importadora Mexicana (CEIMSA, Mexican Exporting and Importing Company). Established in 1949, it controlled prices and subsidized basic food items such as milk, cornmeal, eggs, and grains. López Mateos replaced it with the Compañía Nacional de Subsistencia

Populares (National Company of Popular Subsistence Foods) in 1961 and greatly expanded the program through a network of government stores.

On the international front, López Mateos's sexenio began as one of the most significant twentieth-century events in Latin America unfolded, the Cuban Revolution of 1959. Throughout López Mateos's term in office, the Cuban Revolution would force him into a precarious position between reaffirming his country's revolutionary tradition against foreign influence (mainly the United States) and quelling U.S. concerns about communism and leftist tendencies in Mexico. At times, López Mateos managed to stand his ground. For example, in October 1962, during the Cuban Missile Crisis, López Mateos chose not to break diplomatic ties with Cuba despite U.S. pressure, which strained relations with the United States. These tensions often surfaced on the airwaves and were viewed by citizens watching television news.

Although the two Adolfos stood politically to the left of the more conservative Alemán, they stood only slightly to his left. A look at how the two viewed women's suffrage helps to illuminate their political positions. Both Ruiz Cortines and López Mateos supported the notion of women voting; however, they did not necessarily approve of the full integration of women into politics.[72] They both appeared to fall in line with earlier revolutionary rhetoric that women should be in the home to raise their children to become productive offspring for the nation, as seen in Ruiz Cortines's comments:

> They will continue to be the principal guardians of their homes as mothers, wives, and daughters; they will not be misled by mistaken assumptions; they understand well their obligations in order that they may dignify themselves as women and as citizens, for the autonomy of the family and the sovereignty of the nation.

During his campaign for the presidency, López Mateos took a similar stance:

The right to vote does not uproot women from family and home to lure them into politics. Rather, women's suffrage brings into the home a deeper understanding of great national issues, a daily inquiry on matters that are of concern to us all. This will prove once again that neither contentious preaching nor deceptive enticement can change women's most intimate sentiments or wean them away from their home and family.[73]

Women in Mexico finally did earn the right to vote in 1954. They were first allowed to vote in a presidential election in 1958, the year López Mateos became president. Television newscasts included this benchmark, but they did so from a male chauvinistic perspective. For example, elite women, such as the wives of high-ranking government officials, were mentioned as voters, but only in relation to their husbands.[74]

As the number of families in the capital boomed, it became obvious that the country could not provide enough jobs and opportunities for its citizens, so its citizens looked elsewhere, many in the United States. Between World War II and 1964, through the Bracero (from the Spanish word *brazo*, meaning arm) Program, 4.6 million Mexicans left the country for the United States to work in agriculture and in manufacturing.[75] Despite the end of the worker program, citizens continued to emigrate, essentially voting for the opposition with their feet by heading north. The large number of citizens who migrated altered the concept of Mexican national identity so that it included the growing number of compatriots and family members who lived and made a living north of the border. National identity began to be reconstructed and reinvented beyond the U.S.-Mexican border. Identity transcended the border, and the imagined community grew beyond *la frontera* to become greater Mexico.[76] In other words, as citizens headed north, national identity did not stop at Nogales or Tijuana. Instead, the diaspora living in the United States reconstructed and reinvented their identity in places like Modesto, Tucson, and Chicago.

On both sides of the border, television played a role in the reconstruction and reinvention of national identity through news and entertainment in Mexico, as images of national identity streamed north of the border into the United States. The level of Spanish-language penetration into the U.S. market corresponds to the growing number of Mexicans and other Latinos living in the United States. As a commercial enterprise both north and south of the border, the television industry followed the logic of the market.[77]

Gustavo Díaz Ordaz campaigned as a champion of the people, but his administration would be marred by political repression. Nevertheless, the events that occurred during his sexenio (1964–70) signaled new political, economic, social, and cultural changes. El '68 (1968), code for the student movements of that year and the subsequent massacre at the Plaza de Tlatelolco neighborhood, represented both the culmination of political and social struggle and a departure point for the long process of transformation from authoritarianism toward democracy.[78] The end to the "perfect dictatorship" was coming to a close, and by 1968 the mask of the revolution had been removed for everyone to see.[79] Television executives would scrutinize carefully what images it allowed to air, with the result of minimizing the shortcomings of social struggle, at least on *la tele*.[80]

Like all presidents, Luis Echeverría Alvarez (1970–76) inherited the problems of his predecessor, including continued social unrest. During the Echeverría years, the government applied a two-fold plan of repression and co-optation. Part of the co-optation strategy involved television, and the government sought to exert control over the industry while Echeverría was minister of the interior and during his presidential term. Echeverría supported a law passed on July 1, 1969, that taxed 12.5 percent of all airtime (one-eighth of daily programming).[81] Furthermore, during his administration the government took control of Mexico City's XHDF, Channel 13.[82]

Echeverría's regime continued the government's dirty war against dissident citizens, with one of the most significant events in the popular memory occurring on June 10, 1971. Known as the

Corpus Christi massacre, the incident involved an attack by the *halcones* (falcons, a paramilitary youth group) on student protestors. Trained at the Mexico City police academy, the halcones opened fire on the student demonstrators and assaulted them with clubs and sticks. Military troops prevented emergency workers from providing aid to the wounded. After the incident, an *Excelsior* journalist asked the mayor of Mexico City whether the massacre was similar to the violence at Tlatelolco two years before. The mayor denied any connection.[83]

As violence continued on the streets of the capital, Echeverría sought to curb its prevalence on television.[84] Echeverría deplored programs that contained violence, as well as the commercialization of the industry. As a result, in 1971 the president proposed the nationalization of television. In a presentation before a crowd of four hundred people, Miguel Sabido, Televisa vice president of research, explained that nationalization was not necessary, that the industry could garner profits at the same time it could educate. At the end of the speech, President Echeverría stood up and applauded, and consequently everyone else in the room did the same.[85] Whether transforming television from a commercial to a state-run model was a real possibility remains doubtful, given the country's previous media experiences, but the fact that there was discussion to nationalize television demonstrated a dramatic shift in media-state relations from Alemán to Echeverría.

Between 1950 and 1970 viewers grew familiar with watching the presidential *dedazo* (finger tapping, indicating the personal appointment of the presidential candidate by the PRI), but the ruling party had begun to shift away from Alemán's policies. Government officials understood that a certain level of incorporation and co-optation of the newly established middle class into the political sphere was necessary to avert another bloody revolution.[86] Television executives found themselves in the midst of pendulum shifts between right and left of center presidents, and as such they negotiated their interests accordingly. That included selecting carefully what wound up on the air.

CHAPTER 2

The Invention of Tele-Traditions

ON JANUARY 6, 1954, the Día de los Reyes Magos (Day of the Three Wise Men), thousands of Mexico City's poor children received presents from María Dolores Izaguirre de Ruiz Cortines, the wife of President Adolfo Ruiz Cortines. The children and their mothers had spent the previous night at Marte field and waited in long lines for a chance to receive a gift from the First Lady. An anchor for Noticiero General Motors commented that María Dolores was accompanied by the wives of the president's cabinet, as the happy and humble children accepted their presents on this much-anticipated holiday. A camera operator for XHTV, Channel 4, filmed the event, and it was reported that night on Noticiero General Motors, the nation's first television news program of record.[1]

The story about the First Lady's distribution of gifts, which aired as the fourth report in the newscast, after a report about a memorial service for deceased actor Jorge Negrete, brought to the fore several themes that run throughout this book. First, the annual distribution of gifts on the Día de los Reyes reinforced and reproduced an already existing tradition—that of presenting gifts to the children on January 6. The decision by early news producers to report on this day helped to establish a new *tele*-tradition (TV tradition) of incorporating popular religious holidays into television news coverage. Second, the report on the event highlighted several tensions within society: the conflict between the modern and the traditional, the government and private sector, and popular and elite groups, as well as the limitations of women's participation on the national political stage and the struggle between the construction of national identity and U.S. financial and cultural influences during the Cold War.

As this chapter demonstrates, producers and writers created numerous tele-traditions during the first five years of the industry. Another important tele-tradition included coverage of national holidays such as Día de la Independencia (Independence Day) and Día de la Revolución (Day of the Revolution). Government officials played a prominent role in the coverage of national and religious holidays, primarily as the subjects of news. Although these types of stories grew out of the older media traditions established by print and radio journalists, the ability to include images along with sound made them distinct and more powerful.

To explain the version of mexicanidad and tele-traditions that aired on television, this chapter analyzes some of the first programs and pioneering producers and then examines news coverage of Día de la Independencia celebrations. Over time, these types of news reports helped members of the PRI's authoritarian regime reaffirm aspects of national identity that they deemed important. The national identity broadcast on television reflected an elite view of mexicanidad, one that emphasized an official perspective of the nation. Television represented the medium through which media executives and government officials worked together to promote an elite national vision. Viewers did not always accept that vision, however; there were limits to cultural hegemony in this formative era of Mexican television.

When the Three Wisemen story aired in 1954, television news was still in its infancy. As a television director, Gabino Carrandi Ortíz helped construct some tele-traditions. The former radio producer spent much of his forty-year career working in television as both a producer and director.[2] He contends that until 1969 television did not play an important role in the information business and that "television news programs barely occupied a corner in the screen and in the studio." At that time television news was controlled by newspapers and merely provided a carbon copy of capital city newspaper coverage. This appears to be the standard line of many former television executives.[3] Yet most television executives made decisions about content independently of newspaper editors. Furthermore, while newspapers influenced the content of television news, broadcast news was very distinct from print. Television news reports were much shorter, and, more important, TV newscasts included audio and moving images. Azcárraga Milmo understood the strength of television and argued that people think in images, noting that while the word is limiting, the image is complete.[4]

For these reasons, it is imperative to examine the origins of television news. The space that this genre of programming occupied on the screen and in the studio may have been small, but it was significant. By examining early newscasts, specifically their production, content, and possible interpretations, and putting them into historical context, continuities emerge. Clearly, the road map created and invented in the first five years of television paved the way for television news production well into the end of the twentieth century.

These tele-traditions would have lasting impact far beyond the limits of Mexico City. Given the industry's tendency toward consolidation and centralization, the model of television news in the country's largest city would provide a blueprint for local news outside of the growing megalopolis. Beyond the country's borders, the television system in Mexico served as a model for the television industries in countries throughout Latin America.[5] After all, that was part of Azcárraga Vidaurreta's master plan, even before he established XEW-TV.[6]

Acting as gatekeepers and agenda setters, news executives made decisions about what would be included, as well as excluded, in news coverage. They also determined how events would be covered—in other words, how certain events and issues would be framed.[7] The decision to report on national holidays such as the Día de la Independencia would remain consistent throughout the first two decades of the television news industry, just as it does today. Archival news coverage of Día de la Independencia celebrations offers an intriguing opportunity to analyze the connections among popular culture, politics, and national identity.[8]

Coverage of sports as news, along with religious and national holidays, emerged as a tele-tradition during the first five years of television news production. The practice began with coverage of bullfights, boxing, and U.S. major league baseball scores. Sports coverage included international events such as the Central American Games of 1954 and the Pan-American Games of 1955, both hosted in Mexico City. These earlier events helped prepare and train news personnel as well as executives for larger, more prestigious events such as the 1968 Olympics and 1970 World Cup, also held in the nation's capital. Undoubtedly, audiences wanted to hear the latest about their favorite teams, and as audiences grew, sports coverage helped Telesistema Mexicano and its owners win over advertisers who had at first been hesitant to invest in the medium.

Like sports, business and capital enterprises won big on the small screen. A probusiness slant to news coverage that often favored the interests of media owners emerged as another tele-tradition that began during the first five years of the industry. As this chapter demonstrates, TV executives such as Rómulo O'Farrill often figured prominently in news coverage. If Mexican billionaire Carlos Slim remained "untouchable" by news reporters in the 1990s, the same could be said about the Azcárraga and O'Farrill families, who in the 1950s enjoyed positive news coverage.[9]

LIVE FROM A COMMERCIAL AND CAPITALIST WORLD

President Alemán's decision in 1950 to follow a commercial television model concretized the path of television news. If private interests were going to pay for the fledgling industry, they needed to generate funds to pay for programming, equipment, and personnel. They did so using their own capital as well as through sponsorship of programming and advertising. Sponsors bought blocks of time, which gave advertising agencies and newspapers powerful influence over the content of television news. For example, the Mexico City daily *Novedades* (owned by O'Farrill) generated the editorial content for TV news programs, and XHTV and NBC supplied the film that accompanied the scripts, which were written based on information gathered by the *Novedades* editorial staff.[10] The newspaper sold the news blocks to advertising agencies, also known as program brokers, that in turn placed commercials where the agency deemed fit.[11] Foreign and domestic companies had financial interests in the largest publicity and advertising agencies. New York–based agency J. Walter Thompson represented one of the most profitable agencies in the country.[12] The agency's clients included General Motors, the sponsor of the first newscast on record.

Commercial spots played a central role on-screen from the inception of the industry. On the official inaugural day of the medium, XHTV broadcast a commercial for Omega watches. Gonzálo Castellot functioned as both talent and narrator for the spot. Standing in front of a fireplace, Castellot emptied a pipe into an ashtray with his left hand, stating,

> Simply moving your hand to empty a pipe is enough movement to wind your watch automatically, "Omega Constelation," automatic . . . waterproof . . . and damage proof . . . .admire it![13]

The first commercials on television shed light on advertising agencies' attempts to create a mass market for consumer goods.

Because only the upper middle and middle classes could afford television, higher-priced goods, such as Omega watches, dominated commercials. Other goods advertised during this time included refrigerators and automobiles. As the medium grew in popularity, and viewership increased among citizens of lower socioeconomic status, cheaper goods began to be advertised. By the mid-1960s, Coca-Cola and Domecq, a wine and liquor company, were regular advertisers on television.

Although Castellot became the country's first news anchor through his *Leyendo Novedades* (Reading *Novedades*), he also appeared as talent beyond the newsroom, including participating in the first televised Christmas commercial. In the twenty-first century, journalists generally seek to create a distance from the financial aspect of the business (e.g., commercial production and selling of airtime) and the news-reporting side of the enterprise. Yet the standards of news professionalism were quite different in the 1950s, and Castellot's participation as both anchor of *Noticiero novedades* and talent in commercials provides an example of how lines often blurred between the business and journalistic sides of television programming.

Beyond the first commercials, the stories that composed the early newscasts demonstrated the close connection between producers and sponsors of the news. Stories often included uncritical and positive coverage of sponsors and advertisers. On January 17, 1954, on *Noticiero General Motors*, anchor Pedro Ferriz read a story about the invention of a diesel motor for trains. The following script illustrates how the lines between publicity and news overlapped:

> This morning the capital press got a demonstration of a diesel-powered auto trolley for the railroad. The trolley does not need a locomotive, because it has its own diesel motors — two diesel motors constructed by General Motors, with 275 horsepower per motor. It is manufactured by Budd Company, and it is known by its initials R-D-C. It has an eighty-nine passenger capacity, and

it's equipped with air-conditioning from Frigidaire. Licenciado Gustavo Arce Cano, representing Licenciado Amorós, manager of the railway system, attended the demonstration, along with Engineer Buenabad, accompanied by his daughters, one of whom steered the trolley during the long section . . . and Mr. Isaac Romero Malpica and Pierce Hunter.[14]

By mentioning three companies and emphasizing General Motors technological prowess, this story demonstrates the blurring of editorial content and business interests. Like other reports, this script illustrates the network's probusiness stance, which included national and international businesses, usually from the United States.

A direct line between high-ranking television executives and news writers also existed. Evidence of this connection appeared on the air, as television news executives often found themselves playing a prominent role in the newscasts. Rómulo O'Farrill Sr. and Emilio Azcárraga Vidaurreta, as well as their family members, often appeared as the subject of news stories. On April 7, 1954, for example, *Noticiero General Motors* (General Motors News) aired a story about Rómulo O'Farrill Jr.: "This morning, Mr. Rómulo O'Farrill Jr. departed for Paris, accompanied by his wife. Mr. O'Farrill will take a tour of Europe, observing television manufacturing plants in the Old Continent. Numerous friends and associates bid him farewell at the airport."[15] From the 1950s to 1970s television news became a prime mechanism to foment the interests of business and national development efforts. Moreover, from the earliest stages of television news programming, producers used news as an avenue to attract viewers and promote the interests of television owners and sponsors.[16]

The elder O'Farrill and Azcarrága Vidaurreta appeared as subjects of news reports, as they met for dinners and cocktails with leaders of various governmental officials and multinational corporations. On February 21, 1955, for example, both O'Farrills served as the focus of a report on *Noticiero PEMEX sol novedades* that provided details about a meal they hosted for Vernon Moore and J. J. McIntire of General Motors, as the two O'Farrills demonstrated "their sympathy and understanding" for the work of the GM executives before they headed for other positions. Avid automobile enthusiast Rómulo O'Farrill Sr., who functioned as the president of the Comité Directivo de los Congresos Panamericanos de Carreteras (Executive Committee of the Pan-American Highway Congress), appeared in the lead report in the same newscast. The report highlighted O'Farrill's leadership and assistance with the construction of the hemispheric highway and its "economic and social benefits" that would help all the countries of the Americas.[17]

A week later O'Farrill topped the news again, as *Noticiero PEMEX sol novedades* reported that he hosted a dinner at his house for delegates of the Pan-American congress. In yet another story, which ran on Christmas Eve of 1954, on *Noticiero General Motors*, both O'Farrills were hailed for distributing gifts among "all of the employees at XHTV, from the highest staff to the most humble positions."[18] The report mentioned that other businesses did the same throughout the country. Yet the fact that the newscast singled out XHTV and its owners illuminates the extent to which producers went to promote both. These types of reports served to improve the social standing of media entrepreneurs among the public, domestic and international business owners, and politicians who may have been watching the programs. In addition, the stories reflected the associated and dependent relationship that media moguls such as O'Farrill and Azcárraga maintained with foreign interests.[19]

The prominence of news coverage about television executives and their activities suggests that little distance existed between station owners, producers, and anchors. It appeared that those at the highest levels of station management directly influenced all levels of the operation, from the most important to the least. From the 1950s to 1970s Rómulo O'Farrill Sr. and Azcárraga Vidaurreta were in control. By the 1970s it was Azcárraga Milmo who would take over the helm of Televisa, after his father's death.

THE FIRST TV NEWS PROGRAMS AND PRODUCERS

Between 1950, the year of the first television newscasts, and 1969 newspaper owners exercised considerable influence over television news. From the start, editorial content for newscasts originated at the main newspapers in Mexico City. The owners of television stations did nothing to hide the close connections between print and television news: the first test newscast was even titled *Leyendo Novedades*, in reference to the daily newspaper owned by the O'Farrills. On July 26, during the final days of testing, before the official inauguration of the medium, Gonzálo Castellot tried to come up with a plan for filling five minutes of airtime. He picked up a copy of *Novedades* and told viewers that they were about to witness the premiere edition of *Leyendo Novedades*, and he began to read the news directly from the newspaper. For this broadcast, television sets were set up in several important offices, including those of President Miguel Alemán Valdés, secretary of communications Agustín García López, both O'Farrills, and Miguel Alemán Jr.'s office at the magazine *Revista voz* on the seventeenth floor of the National Lottery building, where the broadcast originated. *Leyendo Novedades* continued to air on Channel 4 from 7:45 to 8:00 at night throughout 1950.[20] It was soon renamed *Notícias del día* and then *Noticiero novedades* in 1957.[21]

By 1955 eleven news programs (four on XHTV and seven on XEW-TV) had been created, all with different names and sponsors. Despite the differences in sponsorship, evidence suggests that the producers of the various newscasts worked together, often sharing film and information. Much of the staff for the early news programs worked in the same building. In the early 1960s, for example, *Noticiero superior* and *Noticiero General Motors* were produced on Tolsa Street, Suite 301, according to the stationeries of the respective news programs. Handwritten notes on scripts show that newsreels were often used in one newscast and then handed off to producers of other newscasts. For example, on January 11, 1954, *Noticiero General Motors* aired a story about Viacheslav

Molotov, a "direct successor of Stalin," who was experiencing heart problems. A note on the script indicates that the film was given to Noticiero PEMEX on February 8, 1955, presumably for a follow-up report about Molotov.[22] These sorts of connections remained important for the formation of standardized reporting practices and tele-traditions.

Like Noticiero novedades, Channel 4's newscast, Noticiero General Motors, which began on December 5, 1950, received much of its content from the daily Novedades. This, of course, made perfect business sense, because O'Farrill owned both the network XHTV, Channel 4, and the newspaper Novedades. By 1968 television executives recognized they wanted more control over the production and content of the news, and through the urging of the country's president, they decided to form an independent news division. In 1969 as Telesistema Mexicano's contracts with the newspapers ran out, executives established the Dirección General de Información y Noticieros (General Division of Information and News), headed by Miguel Alemán Velasco, the son of former president Miguel Alemán. The show 24 horas was one of the first and most successful news programs initiated under this department. The program first aired on September 7, 1970, and was hosted by Jacobo Zabludovsky for twenty-eight years, making it the longest running news program in the history of television news. Its influence stretched beyond the nation's borders, as it was broadcast in many parts of the United States.[23] Until the 1960s most news programs were about fifteen minutes in length. Toward the end of the decade news programs were expanded to thirty minutes and up to one hour, as in the case of Café matutino, also known as Su diario Nescafé (Your Nescafé daily, also known as Noticiero Nescafé).[24]

Twenty years before 24 horas first aired, Jacobo Zabludovsky was on the ground floor of the television industry, helping to establish the country's first television news programs.[25] His influence on the development of television news has yet to be fully evaluated, yet it is well accepted that the role he played in the first twenty years of television news remains salient because, for better or worse, he would serve as a model for TV journalists across the country for forty years.²⁶ He interviewed hundreds, perhaps thousands, of politicians, intellectuals, entertainers, and economists on television. He witnessed and reported on most of the important events in the second half of the twentieth century, including eight presidential administrations from Alemán to Carlos Salinas de Gortari, Fidel Castro's rise to power in Cuba, the Cuban Missile Crisis, the 1968 massacre at the Plaza de las Tres Culturas, the 1985 Mexico City earthquake, and the Zapatista uprising in 1994. A controversial personality, he has been both lauded and lambasted. His supporters have followed him throughout his career, which has spanned more than fifty years. Critics liken him to just another "soldier of the PRI." In many ways, to understand Jacobo Zabludovsky is to understand television news in Mexico.²⁷

In 1945, as World War II drew to an end, Zabludovsky enrolled in law school, but he says he never had any intention of practicing. He thought that a degree in law would help his journalism career. A year prior to law school he had already begun working in broadcasting, playing commercials at XEQK radio, where he says he was paid 1.25 pesos an hour.²⁸ In 1950, as news editor, he helped establish *Noticiero General Motors*, which aired until 1962. Guillermo Vela served as anchor, and Pedro Ferriz served as commercial announcer. Newspapers supplied information for reports, and television camera operators gathered the images.²⁹ Zabludovsky wrote newscast scripts, and he also worked at *Novedades*.³⁰ His experience at the newspaper undoubtedly helped in preparing the newscast.

Although Zabludovsky was referred to as the editorial director of *Noticiero General Motors*, he was more than that. At the same time he functioned as editor and anchor of newscasts on XHTV, he worked as a chief radio and television consultant for presidents Adolfo Ruiz Cortines, Adolfo López Mateos, and Gustavo Díaz Ordaz.

The enduring question, of course, is, did Zabludovsky receive favors from either president for his favorable coverage of them? During a conversation with Elena Poniatowska, she told Zabludovsky that she had received a gift basket from President Adolfo López Mateos, after covering the inaugural train ride from Chihuahua to the Pacific Ocean. Zabludovsky remarked jokingly that he received so much that during Christmas he could eat 1,777 turkeys.[31]

If journalists such as Zabludovsky listened to and believed the official rhetoric of President Alemán, the press and individuals had the formal right to express themselves freely. In June 1951 the president delivered a speech to national newspaper and magazine directors, in which he emphasized that freedom of the press would continue to be an "indivisible part of human liberty."[32]

Yet limits to press freedoms existed. Through co-optation and repression, government officials sought to manipulate both print and broadcast journalists. In 1935 the government had established Productora e Importadora de Papel Paper Producer and Importer) a special agency that offered cheap newsprint to publishers.[33] As a result, publishers were less inclined to criticize the government for fear of losing the subsidy and consequently the newspaper. The widespread practice of *embutes* and *chayotes* (payoffs by government officials to journalists for favorable coverage) represented another carrot for reporters. Those who refused the bribes often found themselves unemployed. Government officials also purchased large amounts of space in newspapers so they could publish *gacetillas* (news items) on government events and activities. Written by government officials, these gacetillas undoubtedly placed the government and officials in a favorable light. When these more friendly tactics did not work to pressure journalists into putting politicians in a positive light, there was always the option of violence as a final resort.[34]

Article 7 of the 1917 Constitution protected freedom of the press and forbade prior censorship. The laws regarding freedom of the press date back to the reform period of the 1850s. Despite laws intended to protect journalists, what happened in practice was quite different. Forms of self-censorship and outright censorship controlled what eventually went on the air. Article 77 of the law that governed radio and television prohibited the broadcast of news items of a political or religious nature. Aurelio Pérez, who anchored the news in the 1950s and who rose to the highest levels of the company hierarchy, remembered how a representative of the Secretariat of Communications came to visit him and explained article 77. Pérez says the functionary gave him an example, saying that everything that has to do with Miguel Henríquez Guzmán (an opposition candidate for the presidency during the election of 1952) was political and, in accordance with article 77, was prohibited. Everything related to President Ruiz Cortines was civic and therefore not prohibited.[35]

A military officer and a member of the PRI, Henríquez Guzmán, started his own campaign when word circulated that President Alemán might favor Fernando Casas Alemán, the mayor of the Federal District and the president's cousin. Henríquez Guzmán had a diverse group of supporters from students and prodemocratic elements of the middle class to independent campesino groups and disenchanted workers.[36] This broad base of support did not help Henríquez Guzmán gain television coverage or Alemán's favor. In October 1951 Alemán picked a native of Veracruz, Ruiz Cortines, the fifty-five-year-old secretary of the interior, a more moderate candidate to lead the party. Veracruz happened to be Alemán's home state as well.[37]

TELEVISING INDEPENDENCE

National leaders began to celebrate the Grito de la Independencia (Cry for Independence) during the first decades of the nineteenth century, after Father Miguel Hidalgo de Costilla's early morning cry at Dolores Hidalgo on September 16, 1810. Since then, government officials, ordinary citizens, and television producers have used the day to help construct and define the meaning of mexicanidad. The formation of national identity has continued for more than two hundred years and perhaps has taken on greater significance in Mexico than in other Latin American nations.[38] Television programming, including news, allowed the majority of citizens to begin to see themselves as part of the nation.[39] The transmission of the Día de la Independencia ceremonies and celebrations reflected both the continuation of a long-standing ritual in the nation's history and initiated a new tele- tradition.[40]

Fourteen days after the first official broadcast of television, the first Día de la Independencia celebration was transmitted to the few who owned television sets and for the thousands who would watch the ceremony from publicly displayed sets. It gave Castellot great pleasure to see the headline in the newspaper that the ceremony would be aired on television.[41] The transmission began at precisely 10:30 p.m. from the Palacio Nacional (National Palace). The image of President Miguel Alemán and his wife, Doña Beatríz Velasco de Alemán, standing on the palace's central balcony appeared on-screen. The president then rang the historic bells, repeating the cry for independence, like Father Miguel Hidalgo de Costilla had done nearly a century and a half before.

DÍA DE LA INDEPENDENCIA, 1954

Four years after the coverage of Alemán's participation in Día de la Independencia festivities, news photographers covered the national holiday for *Noticiero General Motors* and *Noticiero PEMEX*.[42] Both newscasts aired on XHTV, Channel 4, the station owned by Rómulo O'Farrill. The coverage of Día de la Independencia events on these two newscasts were remarkably similar to each other as well as to coverage of the first televised Día de la Independencia activities in 1950.

Noticiero General Motors, Story 1

On September 16, 1954, *Noticiero General Motors* led the newscast with a crime story about two men whom the secret service had arrested in connection with the death of cinematographer Alfonso Mascarua Alonso. Following the crime story, the newscast included four stories related to Día de la Independencia celebrations and events. The first Día de la Independencia story focused on Mexico City's *zócalo* to celebrate the 144th anniversary of the Grito de Dolores. The anchor referred to the zócalo as the "spiritual heart" of the country, and an enthusiastic crowd convened there from the early morning hours to "happily celebrate one of our most beautiful traditions."

Noticiero General Motors, Story 2

Noticiero General Motors' second report about Día de la Independencia celebrations concentrated on the president and his wife's reception of foreign diplomats. U.S. general Matthew Ridgeway was the only other dignitary mentioned by name in the script. The decision to include General Ridgeway in the story provides evidence of the importance of U.S-Mexican relations. The general's placement in the story also reflected a tension between a desire to reinforce ideas and symbols of nationalism in the midst of the Cold War. The story also emphasized the station's contribution to the report, noting that XHTV achieved success with a perfect broadcast, in reference to Channel 4's transmission of the president's "grito" at eleven o' clock on the balcony of the Palacio Nacional, as the public stood by. An anchor read,

> In the main ballroom of the National Palace the president of the republic, accompanied by his honorable wife, Doña María Dolores Izaguirre de Ruiz Cortinez, received greetings from distinguished diplomatic officials before our government and representatives from industry, banking, commerce and art. The ballroom group intoned military airs of our anthem, which was heard solemnly by all who attended. General Matthew Ridgeway, on behalf of the U.S. government and military, offered his most sincere congratulations to the nation's head of state. XHTV cameras marked another success with last night's perfect transmission.

At eleven o'clock on the dot last night the president looked out of the central balcony of the palace eliciting the enthusiastic crowd that filled the Plaza of the Constitution. Happiness reached a high point when the president, with an emotional voice, cheered the heroes of our independence and rang the historic bell of Dolores. Later, he waved the national flag for more than two minutes, amid delirious cheers from the people.

Noticiero General Motors, Story 3

The third story on Día de la Independencia focused on the president's activities at the Columna de Independencia (Column of Independence) on Paseo de la Reforma. The anchor mentioned the president, accompanied by the heads of the Congress and the Supreme Court. During the ceremony, the president laid a flowered wreath in front of the column. State representatives from all over the country also attended. Adolfo López Mateos, then secretary of labor, read the official speech. López Mateos's involvement in the story provided him with face time and gave viewers a chance to become more familiar with the politician who would become the country's next president.

Noticiero General Motors, Story 4

The fourth story on Día de la Independencia ceremonies and celebrations summarized all of the day's activities with the president, from the Columna de Independencia to a show of public support at the central balcony of the Palacio Nacional and approval by the secretaries of state and the head of congress. The story again mentioned General Ridgeway. That paled, though, in comparison to the number of times reporters referred to the president. Ruiz Cortines was mentioned by name five times in the four Día de la Independencia reports on *Noticiero General Motors*. To say that Ruiz Cortines received positive coverage would be an understatement. Governmental officials were heralded as keepers of the nation's heroes and hailed as models of the nation's ideals.

The television industry benefited as well from this type of new coverage. News producers used the opportunity to promote XHTV and its staff, as the script hailed the "magnificent visual reporting" of the details of the "extraordinary military parade and extraordinary visual reporting of cameraman, Angel Cabrera."

In addition to the focus on Día de la Independencia celebrations and government officials, the newscast included eight stories that treated international events, three of which either centered on or mentioned the United States. The writer placed the international stories below national news. The first report featured John Foster Dulles, the U.S. ambassador to Mexico, meeting with German chancellor Konrad Adenauer at a conference in Bonn. The report included a statement from Adenauer, who said that the "satisfactory" meeting produced "fruitful discussions" and that details about the event would be publicized the next day. President Dwight Eisenhower was the focus of another international story. Eisenhower "sent greetings to Don Adolfo Ruiz Cortines," congratulating him on the Día de la Independencia. The third international story focused on U.S. major league baseball, calling attention to the latest New York Yankees win over the Detroit Tigers, by four to one.

Aside from the United States, international reports focused on events in France, Italy, China, and the Soviet Union on the *Noticiero General Motors* newscast on September 16, 1954. The story on the Soviet Union was attributed to its official news agency, TASS, which reported a recent testing of a new atomic weapon. Reports such as this signaled the country's, as well as the rest of Latin America's, precarious position and somewhat dependent political and economic position in relation to the United States and the Soviet Union.

Noticiero PEMEX-Novedades, Story 1

Día de la Independencia celebrations topped the newscast produced by *Noticiero PEMEX-novedades* on September 16, 1954. Four of the six stories that aired surrounded the celebrations and ceremonies.

Like *Noticiero General Motors*, *Noticiero* PEMEX-*novedades* was broadcast on Channel 4. The Día de la Independencia stories on both newscasts were similar visually as well as textually.

The first story focused on activities at the main square, where a "patriotic euphoria" unfolded with the presence of the president and his wife, Doña Maria, who received a host of dignitaries. At the same time, "the contrast was notable outside" of the Palacio Nacional, where "the people with unbridled happiness" enjoyed the fireworks. The wording suggests an attempt by producers to separate high and low cultures, and elite and mass participation in events. As the script indicated, dignitaries inside the palace participated in the traditional greeting of the president, but both those "outside and inside had the same thought, Mexico."[43]

The juxtaposition between those celebrating outdoors and indoors provides an interesting window into the attempts by members of the country's elite to separate themselves from popular groups. The final statement of the story brought the two sectors together in an effort to demonstrate that the modern nation embraced both popular and elite sectors of society. Somewhat contradictory, the story illustrated tensions between the upper and lower classes, as well as efforts to create one national identity in which all "thought of Mexico" and which encompassed all socioeconomic sectors of society.[44]

Noticiero PEMEX-*Novedades*, Story 2

The second story focused on the traditional laying of the wreath at the Columna de Independencia "at the foot of the monument of the heroes of our independence." The story mentioned that Don Adolfo carefully guarded the principal of "faith in our heroes" of independence. The images used resembled those used in the *Noticiero General Motors* story, but they were edited together in a slightly different way. The story began with a wide shot of Ruiz Cortines and an entourage of men walking up to the Columna de Independencia. In the second shot, the group of men walked past the camera toward the column. The next shot (medium shot) showed Ruiz Cortines from behind, laying down a traditional flowered wreath at the foot of the column. The final shot was a pan down from the "Loor a los Héroes" flowered arrangement to the president and a group of men standing in front of the column.

Noticiero PEMEX-Novedades, Story 3

The third story centered on the annual military parade. The story began by mentioning the "traditional" September 16 parade, but this event was "more brilliant than in previous years." According to the script, the morning parade was "without precedent." The event, "the best that they have seen," was better organized, larger, and equaled those in "other more powerful nations."[45]

The wording of the story demonstrates a tension among producers of news to both preserve the traditional as well as provide evidence of progress, development, and newness. Phrases such as "best that they have seen," "without precedent," and competitive with "other more powerful nations" helped to set apart the 1954 celebrations from previous years, yet they were woven into a traditional discourse of the nation and national symbols such as the bell, the flag, the Columna de Independencia, and the balcony of the Palacio Nacional.

EL GRITO ONE YEAR LATER, SEPTEMBER 16, 1955

A year later both *Noticiero General Motors* and *Noticiero PEMEX sol* aired stories on the independence celebrations. In 1955 ambassadors from Guatemala, Honduras, El Salvador, Nicaragua, and Costa Rica participated in the ceremonies as they stood at the Columna de Independencia.[46] They laid down flowered offerings at the monument, given that, as *PEMEX sol* stated, September 15 "is also a national holiday for the five Central American countries." *Noticiero General Motors* reported the story in much the same way, but beyond naming all of the Central American countries, the writer named the diplomats: Díaz Loarca of Guatemala, Hernández Irias of Honduras, Sevilla Sacasa of Nicaragua, Alfaro of El Salvador and Gonzalo Solorano of Costa Rica.

CONSUMING TELE-TRADITIONS

During the first five years of the industry having a television set remained a privilege of the economic elite, as so few citizens owned them. As each year went by, more citizens had access to the medium in their homes, but for many early viewers, television news was a public event. For those who remained inside their homes to watch the celebrations, September 16, perhaps became more of a private affair.

Ethnicity, class, and gender informed an individual's reception and interpretation of Día de la Independencia stories. For the poor mestizos and indigenous groups, who could not afford to purchase a television but watched the celebrations standing in front of a window of a department store, it was clear that they were not included in what government officials and news executives thought should be part of the national celebration. The film clips by-and-large focused on national and international dignitaries. In one story, a large multitude of people reveled in the streets, while "in contrast" a more subdued celebration in the Palacio Nacional occurred, illuminating the popular masses from an elite and cultured group. In short, the stories discussed in this chapter in large part depicted Día de la Independencia as a top-down affair.

Similar to poor mestizos and the indigenous, women remained sidelined in the coverage of Día de la Independencia events, calling attention to their lack of political participation.[47] The only woman given space in the Día de la Independencia coverage was Doña Maria, the president's wife. News clips show her standing beside the president, in a formal dining gown, shaking the hands of dignitaries.

By the end of the decade, Telesistema Mexicano produced about six hours of daily news-related programming, a considerable amount for that period.[48] Five years after the first Día de la Independencia celebration aired on television, the tele-tradition regarding how to cover this national holiday had taken root. By 1963 the national holiday was still being covered in much the same way. On September 16 *Noticiero diario de la tarde aceptaciones* led its newscast with Día de la Independencia activities. The ceremony of the Grito de Dolores was led by President López Mateos, along with members of his personal staff and others from various cities in the United States and Guatemala. The ceremony hailed "the history of the continent, unanimity, law, sovereignty, and self-determination."[49]

More than ten years after the first televised broadcast of Día de la Independencia events, stories continued to focus on presidential and official ceremonies rather than local and provincial events. The manner in which producers and journalists covered the events resulted in a new and far-reaching platform for politicians, who then, along with television producers, used the medium in an attempt to create a sense of national unity like never before. As a result the coverage over time helped to legitimize the regime.

At the inception of television, because so few citizens owned television sets, celebrations continued to be a public affair; people watched events on the street or on televisions located in public spaces, installed either by the government or their neighbors. Just as they watched their favorite *tele-teatros* (television dramas), they watched their president sound the bells at the Palacio Nacional in remembrance of the Grito de Dolores. Over time, as the medium gained popularity and televisions became more affordable, opportunities were created to celebrate independence individually and in the home. Through the broadcasts of Día de la Independencia events, a new public sphere beyond the zócalo was in the midst of development.[50]

Yet because television journalists tended to ignore local and nongovernment-sponsored events, viewers saw only the official perspective of the nation's holidays. Watching how others celebrated could lead citizens to follow similar patterns of behavior, thereby "generalizing" a tradition.[51] The televising of Día de la

Independencia celebrations in some ways helped to unify and define what it meant to be Mexican. At the same time, it could also reaffirm what it meant to be part of a certain segment of society.

The Día de la Independencia stories between 1950 and 1955 also reflected the numerous tensions within society and in the world. Watching Doña María Dolores standing by her husband, President Ruiz Cortines, as the couple shook the hands of dignitaries, demonstrated that elite women could occupy a space on television news, but their presence was limited. No women marched to the Columna de Independencia or spoke from the balcony of the Palacio Nacional. In addition, no women reported on the Día de la Independencia events. Poor mestizos and the indigenous found themselves on-screen only when they held out their "humble" hands to receive gifts from the First Lady. In contrast, the owners of television stations and sponsors of news programs often appeared in the scripts and on-screen. The tendency of television news to exclude poor and popular voices and include elite and official voices continued through the rest of the 1950s and for decades to come.

CHAPTER 3

Rebels and Revolutionaries

"THIS IS the beginning of the end," declared Ernesto Betancourt, Fidel Castro's agent in Washington DC. "Victory has been secured."[1] And so began 1959, a defining year for twentieth-century Mexico and the hemisphere. Betancourt's statement on January 1 referred to the downfall of Cuba's dictator, Fulgencio Batista. The ousting of Batista signified the rise of Fidel Castro and brought into sharp relief tenuous relations between Mexico, the United States, Cuba, and the Soviet Union. Decades later historians and political scientists would view the Cuban Revolution of 1959 as one of the most significant and influential events in Latin America.[2]

Between 1959 and 1963 Mexican politicians, and in particular President Adolfo López Mateos, struggled to maintain the country's revolutionary image by supporting the Cuban Revolution and at the same time they wanted to preserve relations with the United States in the midst of Cold War events. The fact that former president

Lázaro Cárdenas openly supported the Cuban revolutionaries, took trips to the island nation, and in July 1956 had worked to get Fidel Castro released from a Mexican prison only complicated matters for López Mateos.[3]

Mexican and Cuban insurgents had a history of mutual support, dating back to the countries' independence wars with Spain in the nineteenth century.[4] From two countries with long histories of battling first the Spanish, then U.S. imperial powers, Cuban and Mexican insurgents found opportunities to motivate as well as mobilize each other's causes. The Mexican Revolution provided a source of inspiration for Cuban revolutionaries, including Castro, who stated to a journalist for *Siempre!* magazine, "You could say the Mexican Revolution influenced the Cuban Revolution very much."[5]

During the 1950s and 1960s the U.S. public and government viewed Mexico-Cuba relations with increased interest. Beyond news coverage in daily newspapers, government committees such as the Senate Judiciary Committee held "inquiries" to investigate Cuba-Mexico connections. The U.S. interest about the relations between the two countries, as Christopher M. White argues, "indicates just how relevant Third World actors had become on the Cold War stage."[6]

Politicians, activists, and television producers understood the importance of the events, and they all sought to frame them in various and conflicting ways. Television news projected international and national tensions on-screen. Putting news coverage into historical context helps to illuminate the intersections between international and national politics.

The connections between the national and the international unfolded on television, as 1950s newscasts often led with reports about national news and then concluded with a series of international stories. Depending on the day's events, sometimes writers began with international events and then segued into the day's events around the country. The combination of national and international reports in the same newscast provided viewers with daily examples of tensions between domestic and foreign influences. Moments after viewers watched a report about Mexico City railway strikers, they saw stories about U.S secretary of state John Foster Dulles's trip to Brazil and a meeting between the leaders of communist China and the Soviet Union, Mao Tse-tung and Nikita Khrushchev.[7]

This chapter places Mexican railway strikers and Cuban revolutionaries at the center of discussion and juxtaposes television news coverage of the two dissident groups. Like the other case studies in the book, news coverage of Mexican and Cuban rebels enables an investigation of the central question of this study—the limits of cultural hegemony—from a domestic and international perspective. An examination of the portrayals of Cuban revolutionaries and railway strikers or "rebels" of 1958–59 allows a complex picture of national politics and international relations to emerge. On the one hand international events certainly influenced domestic politics, news, and society, but the decisions regarding how to respond to international events were made locally to achieve a set of national goals, which might have reaffirmed or contradicted the goals of the Cuban Revolution and U.S. Cold War policies.[8] For example, some news reports emphasized Castro's upper-middle class background, which might have served to undermine the efforts of supporters of the Cuban Revolution, but the same reports might also have stressed Mexico's support of the movement.[9]

In contrast to Cuban rebels, news producers tended to portray railway strikers in a much less favorable manner, demonstrating that in the news and in government circles, the two dissident groups received distinct treatment. Although both dissident railway organizer Demetrio Vallejo and Castro fought against authoritarianism, the former was labeled as a threat to the nation, while the latter was painted as a champion of democracy.[10] Despite negative portrayals on television and in the printed press, railway workers spread their positive and idealized messages through alternative means of communication, much like their compatriots would do a decade later in 1968 (see chapter 6).[11] These counterofficial messages, what I call *hybrid frames*, offered evidence that there were limits to the cultural hegemony imposed on popular groups such as railway workers, even at the height of PRI dominance.

UNREST ON THE RAILROADS

Railway workers had been disgruntled for a decade by the time López Mateos took residence at Los Pinos (the official residence of the president) on December 1, 1958.[12] A look at the incomes of railway workers helps to illustrate their plight. Their real wages had declined steadily since the late 1930s. According to some estimates, during the 1950s they earned less than 75 percent of their 1939 wages.[13]

President Miguel Alemán's probusiness political stance affected workers' lives negatively in several ways. First, Alemán's Plan de Rehabilitación Ferroviaria (Railroad Rehabilitation Plan) allocated funds to modernize the railway system but did not include money for wage increases. In October 1948 the president thwarted workers' attempts to redress their concerns by replacing elected union officials with government-appointed ones. The action became known as the *charrazo*. Government-appointed union leaders and those who sided with the government were called *charros*. *Charrismo* was the name given to the widespread practice of government control over unions, in lieu of independent labor organizations. The term was coined after President Alemán appointed Jesús de León, who dressed as a charro (cowboy), as head of the railway workers' union.

The clientelistic relationship between unions and the government prompted the *tortuguismo* (turtlelike or worker slowdown) movement in 1954, which represented the first large-scale challenge to the government-controlled railway union, Sindicato de Trabajadores Ferrocarrileros de la República Mexicana (Mexican Railway Workers Union). The peso had dropped 150 percent between 1947 and 1955, affecting the working class as well as media moguls. Workers took action in response to a 1954 peso devaluation that decreased their buying power, on top of the reality of declining wages and inflation. Workers argued that they had to slow down production to remain in compliance with federal transportation and security rules. The movement led to a six-hour strike on September 21, which in turn resulted in the arrest of six leaders and the firing of fifty-nine workers.[14]

The conflict between progovernment unions and independent unions ensued in the context of a wider anticommunist discourse that prevailed throughout the Cold War.[15] The official line argued that railway workers were first citizens and then laborers. Charros argued that workers' rights were contingent on the interests of the nation. News writers often embraced this nationalistic argument and included it in reports about the railway strikes.

By June 26, 1958, a chasm had developed between dissident leaders and the rank and file, and the official railway union. Dissident union leader, Demetrio Vallejo, set a deadline for the railway company to meet workers' demands of a 350-peso monthly increase and to recognize new dissident leaders elected in Chiapas. If the government failed to meet the demands, workers threatened to initiate stoppages, beginning at ten in the morning on June 26. Each day the company failed to meet workers' demands, the stoppage would increase by two hours. Railway workers' demands were not met, and they went on strike until President Ruiz Cortines conceded, giving them a raise of 215 pesos per month. Yet that did not quell the workers' unrest, and by August they organized another stoppage, demanding the creation of an independent union. That same month, shortly after Adolfo López Mateos was elected to the presidency, the rank and file voted in Vallejo as secretary general of the national railway union.

On the eve of Holy Week in March 1959, three months after Castro's arrival in Havana, Vallejo staged a second strike that the government quickly repressed. Vallejo was imprisoned, brought to trial, and in 1963 convicted of conspiracy and sabotage under the law of social dissolution. He remained in jail for sixteen years.

Vallejo's imprisonment would become a source of inspiration for the student protestors of 1968, whose demands included the release of the dissident railway leader.

RAILWAY "REBELS" ON THE AIRWAVES

The railway strikes figured prominently on *General Motors* newscasts between June and August 1958. Analysis of news reports revealed that producers portrayed the railway conflict and strike in a way that privileged official perspectives over the voices of the rank and file. In general, the voices of dissident leaders and rank-and-file members remained off the air. The tendency to report the labor dispute from the top-down provided evidence of a news mentality that embraced capitalist and elite attitudes but did not necessarily signify an unequivocal embrace of the political regime. In other words, news executives downplayed dissident voices to emphasize other groups and voices; in this case, those perspectives that aided in the capitalist enterprise of garnering viewers and, in turn, creating advertising revenue. This pattern and logic would continue well into the twenty-first century.[16]

During the late 1950s and 1960s television journalism as a profession was still in its infancy. As one of the first and one of the most successful television reporters, Jacobo Zabludovsky became the exemplar for other journalists to emulate. But his role on television blurred with his political life. At the same time he wrote and anchored the news, he functioned as a special consultant to presidents López Mateos and Díaz Ordaz on matters related to radio and television. In addition to Zabludovksy, print journalists and newspapers influenced greatly what appeared on television. Several of Mexico City's top newspapers helped generate content for TV newscasts. For example, *Novedades* provided editorial material for *Noticiero General Motors*.

On June 27 *Noticiero General Motors* began its newscast with a national report about the railway worker stoppage, then in its second day:

The problem with the railway workers continues tonight without any resolution. Men of the railway today staged a four-hour work stoppage, and they announced that tomorrow they will stop from ten in the morning until four in the afternoon. Licenciado Roberto Amorós, the manager of the railway system spoke today with the rebel railway workers. It is repeated in this union, as in others, that there are large groups of workers who do not recognize the union leader. A supporter of the law, Licenciado Amorós will deal with the legal leaders. At eight in the evening Licenciado Amorós will meet with journalists to make a statement.[17]

The report provides a clear example of how the news tended to focus on management's rather than workers' concerns. The first phrase of the report placed blame on workers by stating that they were the source of the conflict. The report made no reference to company policies and abuses, which prompted labor to take action and informed their demands.[18] By labeling disgruntled workers as "rebels," the producer suggested to viewers that railway dissidents were outsiders. As a result, the report created additional political and social distance between workers and the company, thereby delegitimizing the workers' role in the conflict. Additionally, the report legitimized Roberto Amorós's role by placing him in opposition to rebel workers who operated outside the legal system in contrast to Amorós, an insider who followed the law. Finally, the report placed Amorós above workers as the most important participant in the conflict, because he was going to offer a statement, while viewers heard of no workers' comments on the issue. The absence of dissident leaders' and workers' names or voices downplayed their role and emphasized Amorós position of power.[19]

The second story on June 27 on *Noticiero General Motors* focused on a fire that ignited at the San Lázaro railway station two hours before airtime. The most intriguing part about this report was that the writer made no mention of a possible connection to the ongoing labor dispute: "Two hours ago an impressive fire broke out at the old San Lázaro cargo station. A railway tank carrying paint thinner caught fire. Its cause is unknown. Beneath the cool sprinkles of rain, firemen deployed their forces to isolate the inflamed tank. Fortunately, there were no victims, no deaths, no injuries, but the material damage is considerable. The firemen asked that volunteers not help them because it could endanger their lives. Thousands of onlookers, residents of the neighborhood located at the beginning of the Calzada Mexico-Puebla, gathered on the sidewalks."[20]

The fact that the report made no connection between the labor dispute and the fire could be interpreted in a variety of ways. First, since the investigation into the fire had just begun, it could be seen as good journalistic practice not to speculate or jump to conclusions about its cause. Another possible way to view the treatment of the story could be that by not mentioning the coincidence between the strike and the fire, producers could have been attempting to downplay the seriousness of the strike.[21]

During the railway workers' movement, government officials and charro leaders often described dissident workers as extremists and sometimes as having communist ties. If the ties were so strong between the government and television producers, then this would seem like an excellent opportunity for the media to discredit the workers' movement. The fire may have been started by workers loyal to the company who did not agree with dissident workers, since such an action could have been used to discredit the movement.

On June 28, the third day of the strike, the workers' movement received second billing, following a report about the kidnapping of U.S. and Canadian citizens in Cuba and the signing of a trade agreement between Mexico and Argentina. Two brief strike updates aired consecutively. The first brief report stated, "The railway workers staged their third day of work stoppage today on the entire system. Today's stoppage lasted six hours and began at ten in the morning." The second story, which was really a continuation of the first report, added, "At noon, the railway workers started to concentrate in the garden of San Fernando, and from there they began to protest until the main square (zócalo) passing by Juárez and Madero Avenues. In front of the National Palace, they staged their meeting in which they insisted on their petition for a 250-peso salary increase for workers."[22] The two brief reports gave viewers scant information on the movement. On the third day of the stoppage, viewers were informed of at least one of the workers' demands, a salary increase. News producers also failed to mention any motivations, except that workers wanted more money. Writers omitted essential facts from the story, failing to note that real wages for railway workers had declined since 1939 and that job conditions put worker safety at risk, and the report neglected to mention that fatalities on the job were common.

The conspicuous omission of such facts had intriguing implications. The less middle-class viewers knew about the on-the-job conditions and real wages for workers, the less likely they would have been to side with railway employees. Perhaps more important, if working-class men and women from other labor sectors saw these reports, they too might have been less inclined to support the railway workers because the report offered such scant information about the reasons behind the labor conflict. The ability of railway workers to garner support from other labor groups would prove vital for the success of the 1958–59 movement. Early on, workers acknowledged the importance of having laborers from other sectors participate in the stoppage.[23] Government officials recognized the importance of worker solidarity and attempted to divide it through various carrot and stick measures.

Examining more closely what facts were omitted from reports provides more evidence that producers wrote reports from an economically elite perspective. Still unresolved by the fourth day, the strikes led the newscast on June 29, as an anchor stated, "This afternoon, Licenciado Roberto Amorós, manager of the FNM [Ferrocarriles Nacionales de México (National Railways of Mexico)] held a press conference in which the General Motors news team was present. He declared that his conciliatory mood ends with the beginning of patriotic interests, that his obligation as manager is to ensure good service and the economic future of the railway system. He says that the workers who placed themselves outside of the law when the talks were going magnificently are causing serious damage to the national economy, that the workers are intransigently insisting on unacceptable demands."[24]

Similar to previous strike-related reports, this one favored company concerns over workers' demands, but this story took the issue a step further and presented the conflict in blatant nationalistic terms. The report posited Amorós as spokesman for the nation, while workers moved beyond being labeled as "rebels" and outsiders and were now working against the country's economic goals. Amorós was depicted as responsible for and in favor of securing the nation's economy, and in contrast dissident workers were presented as a threat to the nation's economy and the nation itself. The final sentence of the report paraphrased Amorós's statement that characterized workers as extremists who made outrageous demands.

The railway workers movement arrived at a crossroads on August 4, 1958. Solidarity among workers from other sectors increased, as Mexico City school teachers joined the strike. The Union of Electricians aligned itself with the movement by calling for the release of arrested railway workers. Mounting support from other labor sectors assisted in changing the railway company's position. Amorós accepted the railway workers' demand that dissident leader Demetrio Vallejo run as a candidate for the general manager of the workers' union. Vallejo was elected on August 23 and took office five days later. A month later the company cracked down on the mounting mobilization. Police killed three workers and numerous others were fired.[25]

On August 3, 1958, the day before Amorós conceded to the dissident leaders' demand to hold an independent election of officers, *Noticiero General Motors* aired the following lead story:

At this moment at the railway management offices on Cinco de Mayo Street, Senator Roberto Amorós is finishing up a press interview, in which he reports that the activity on the nation's railway system is being reestablished. Also, he is informing us about the sanctions that will be imposed on the workers who continue with the general stoppage. Tonight at seven o' clock is the deadline that management has given to workers to return to their jobs. The railway management made an appeal to the patriotism of the workers that they stop their actions and return to work. Workers who do not will be fired and will not be paid for the time that they've been off the job. Whatever is necessary will be done to find capable personnel to fill the vacancies.[26]

In this report, management clearly wielded more power than labor. The report began with Amorós as the spokesperson for the dispute. Similar to some of the other reports aired in June, no workers' perspectives or comments were broadcast. In addition, producers put Amorós on the "correct" side of national concerns, and as a result placed workers who did not return to their jobs in opposition to national interests.

The newscast's second story continued in the same vein, although the report did mention Vallejo by name. The report painted strikers as violators of the law, relaying that they were removed from the union offices and that the secretary of national defense ordered troops to guard the railway stations to prevent sabotage. Nowhere in either of the two reports were workers' demands or perspectives mentioned.[27]

Despite the silencing of railway workers on Telesistema Mexicano newscasts, dissident workers disseminated their messages through a variety of other means. In the streets they spoke with their feet through widespread marches in public squares such as the zócalo. Workers also rewrote popular folk songs such as "La Rielera" (The railway lady) to air their viewpoints to the public. Dissident workers published their demands in newspapers through editorials and on placards.[28] At times railway "rebels" criticized the news media, condemning what they called "the reactionary press."[29] As one scholar has noted, through these diverse communications outlets "railway families articulated an alternative workers' narrative that served to idealize their value to the country's political process and economic development."[30] Workers' messages, including songs and handwritten signs, represented hybrid frames that centered on the railway strikes of 1958 and 1959, but from the bottom-up. The workers' overt criticisms of the government and the press provided clear evidence that the cultural hegemonic project of the PRI had its limits.

CUBAN REVOLUTIONARIES HIT THE AIR

While railway workers fought to change the country's authoritarian labor practice of charrismo, Cuban rebels struggled against its dictator Fulgencio Batista. The events of 1959 in Cuba forever changed Latin America. January 1 represented a watershed in U.S.-Mexico-Cuban-Russian relations, and the decision to lead the newscast with a story on the fall of the Batista regime as well as to devote the entire newscast to events unfolding in Cuba signaled the importance of this international story over national events. Television news reports in 1959 demonstrated that news writers and producers, including Zabludovsky, subtly denounced the Batista dictatorship, while they romanticized and favored Fidel Castro. At the same time, Castro charmed U.S. journalists who followed his rise to power.[31]

Castro seemed keenly aware of the power of the new medium and how it could further his political goals. Acting as his own publicist, he often made sure he was available for interviews with foreign journalists. Reporters of print and electronic media seemed enthralled by the new leader's ability to rally a crowd and inspire individuals. He even wound up as a guest on the Ed Sullivan show. Sullivan traveled to Matanzas to conduct the U.S. exclusive interview with Castro. Much to the chagrin of CBS News executives,

3. Fidel Castro addressing a crowd of several hundred thousand persons gathered in the park in front of the presidential palace in Havana, Cuba, January 1959. AP Photo by Harold Valentine, 06080301039.

Sullivan announced, "It was Castro Day on CBS." His interview with Castro aired between a dog act and an interview with comedian Alan King.³² In short, Castro became one of the first to use and develop television diplomacy. This new type of diplomacy, discussed further in chapter 4, began to diminish the power of traditional political diplomats and created a "populist Cold War."³³

During the 1950s news producers often led their newscasts on the first day of the new year with a montage of the previous year's most significant events. January 1, 1959, was an exception.

Political changes in Cuba made up the entire newscast on *Noticiero General Motors*:

> Today the president of Cuba, Fulgencio Batista, fell. A military junta presided over by General Eulogio Cantillo assumed power. General Cantillo was the chief of operations against the rebels in the eastern province that had its headquarters in Santiago de Cuba. Afterward Cantillo announced that the magistrate Carlos Manuel Pedra, dean of the Supreme Court, had taken oath as the provisional president of Cuba. Ernesto Betancourt, Fidel Castro's agent in Washington, said that the rebels will never accept the junta that has assumed power in Cuba, because it is a false government. "This is the beginning of the end," said Betancourt. "Victory has been secured."[34]

Although this lead story began by mentioning Batista and Castillo, it is clear that Fidel Castro wielded power. The tone of the report legitimized Castro's cause and discredited Batista. As one of the first stories about Castro's ousting of Batista, the report remained crucial for the newly empowered leader in his effort to establish credibility. The writer's decision to use a direct quote from Betancourt, in which he claimed victory for the movement and the end of Batista's regime, helped to further legitimize the emerging Castro administration.

The following report focused on Batista's side of the story. This story included film of Batista and his followers at a party before he fled to the Dominican Republic:

> President Fulgencio Batista and forty companions fled to the Dominican Republic, where they are now. Upon arrival Batista declared, "I was hoping to visit the Dominican Republic under circumstances less *embarazo* [pregnant or disturbing], and then smiling he corrected himself saying, "Pardon, I think I should have said, less embarrassing." Here we see him at a party in Cuba, accompanied by some military officials that are now with him

in Santo Domingo. Batista's children arrived in New Orleans. Three other children of his landed in Jacksonville. In Miami numerous functionaries of Batista arrived by airplane, being received by Cuban exiles that threatened him, saying that "they wanted him dead." Among the persons that accompanied Batista in his exile, include the president-elect, Andrés Rivero Agüero; the ex-minister of the interior and senator-elect Santiago Rey; the colonel of the police, Conrado Carretala; and the presidents of the Chamber of Deputies and Senate. The fall of the government occurred at the same time as military troops and rebel forces sustained an intense struggle for the fifth consecutive day for control of Santa Clara. This struggle is developing with great losses on both sides. One of the refugees in New Orleans, Agustin Lavastida, has been singled out by the rebels as "assassin number one of the fallen regime."[35]

This second story, although it featured Batista's activities, portrayed him and his followers in a negative light. First, the writer's decision to include Batista's "embarrassing" quote served to frame the deposed dictator as somewhat of a buffoon and made him appear less than presidential. Second, the story focused on the president's flight and served to further subvert the power that Batista once had as Cuba's leader.

Four other reports concentrated on events unfolding in Cuba before the newscast shifted its focus to Cuban exiles in Mexico. A lengthy report, it was the only story included in the second block of the newscast. Most stories written at this time occupied between one-quarter to one half of an 8½" x 11" page. This report took up almost two pages. Newscasts are divided into blocks or segments, usually separated by commercial breaks. In this case, the commercial promoted products by Frigidaire.[36]

Aside from reporting the story from a local angle, the story provides clues to several salient issues.[37] First, the length of the report revealed the importance that *Noticiero General Motors* placed

Rebels and Revolutionaries 67

on the activities of Cubans in Mexico. This particular report also may have been longer than others because of the availability of news film. A televised report of this length, even in this early stage of the industry, would have been less interesting without images, and from a producer's perspective may not have been able to sustain itself. The report focused primarily on the transition of power. Within the text, the report did not overtly question the legitimacy of the rebel leaders who took control of the Cuban embassy. The main figures mentioned in the story were those who handed over power and those who assumed power. Castro and his followers, according to the report, were clearly in control. The report mentions that photographs of Batista were burned, which served to place the rebel leaders above the outgoing administration.

Despite the favorable treatment of the rebel leaders, the report criticized the movement indirectly midway through the story: "One radio station, Rebel Radio, could be heard, and it limited the broadcast to certain information, such as the information that we [*Noticiero General Motors*] have already given you." The fact that the news writer decided to report that the new regime was limiting information to its citizens demonstrated that the writer saw it as noteworthy and negative.

Two of Fidel Castro's sisters were also included in the report, which provided a window through which questions regarding how news writers portrayed women could be answered. For the most part, women were absent from scripts that treated political matters. If writers did choose to incorporate women into news programs, they often were merely mentioned (see chapter 2). In addition, only upper-middle class and elite women appeared in news reports. Wives, sisters, and daughters of male political figures and businessmen were included only in relation to the male news maker.

The writer's decision to include Lidia Castro Ruz and Emma Castro Ruz in the January 1, 1959, newscast was an exception to most reports that included women. If viewers paid close attention, they might even have begun to understand the politics of Lidia Castro Ruz and Emma Castro Ruz, Fidel Castro's youngest sister. Lidia Castro told the reporter that the rest of her family was still in the Sierra Maestra, a sign that the family politically aligned with Fidel. The report suggests some interesting, yet contradictory, ideas. First, Lidia Castro thanked Mexico for the hospitality it had shown the rebels. The statement emphasized the alliances between Mexico and Cuba during the struggle. At the same time thanking *el pueblo mexicano* could also be seen as traditional protocol for a woman whose family member was in a high political office. Her last comment was perhaps the most telling, as she stated that the victory was for everyone. Clearly, this statement indicated that she sided politically with her brother. The writer's treatment of the Castro Ruz sisters provided a rare chance for viewers to see women as political actors. More often, during the 1950s they appeared as mere window dressing.

Aside from providing evidence of the politics of Castro's younger sibling, the January 1 story illuminated tensions between foreign and domestic influences. The report attributed the content of the newscast to its own "special services" and two foreign news agencies, United Press International (UPI) and Agence France-Presse (French Press Agency).

During the Cold War, these two international news agencies made up two of the Big Four world news agencies. The other two were the British agency, Reuters, and another U.S.-based news agency, Associated Press (AP). The Soviet Union's TASS represented another source of foreign news, but was not used as frequently as the other four. During the early phase of television, producers relied heavily on information and film from international news agencies. That does not necessarily mean that the television news coverage would automatically translate to a direct reproduction of the images and information obtained from non-Mexican sources. The editorial directors of a news program had the final word when it came to how a story would be reported. In addition, producers and writers edited and translated foreign reports to Spanish before airtime. Moreover, it has been shown that although the AP and UPI, for example, set up bureaus in Latin America, the majority of news staff members were hired locally. These staff members often wrote for domestic news consumption and certainly informed the decisions of foreign correspondents, who often wielded more control over information at the news agencies' foreign bureaus.[38] By the 1980s dependence on news from foreign news services in the region waned as Latin American companies such as Televisa developed and created their own national and international news-gathering agencies.[39]

On January 7, 1959, six days after the fall of Batista, Cuba's Rebel Radio announced that Fidel Castro Ruz had reached the city of Matanzas and could arrive in Havana at anytime. But before Castro set foot in Havana, the anchor of *Noticiero General Motors* announced that Jacobo Zabludovsky, the editorial director of the program, had flown to Havana to interview other principal leaders of the movement while he awaited the famed revolutionary's arrival. The anchor read the following lead report:

> The U.S. Department of State announced today that the country has recognized the new government of Cuban president, Manuel Urrutia. In Havana Rebel Radio said today that the chief of the revolution, Dr. Fidel Castro Ruz, arrived in the city of Matanzas, 101 kilometers east of Havana. The Cuban revolutionary is about to arrive in the island's capital at any moment. But before him, yesterday Mr. Jacobo Zabludovsky, the director of this newsgroup arrived, with the object of interviewing the principal directors of the movement that just culminated with the triumph of the revolutionary forces against the Batista regime. As such, *Noticiero General Motor*, conscious of its responsibility to serve all of the Republic of Mexico, contracted the best services in order to give truthful and up-to-date information about the situation in the Republic of Cuba.[40]

This report touched on three central issues: U.S. influence in the region, the favorable portrayal of Fidel Castro, and the use of television news to further station owners' interests. The report began by helping to establish the legitimacy of the Urrutia administration. That the United States recognized the insurgent leader bestowed credibility on the new president and the administration, as well as highlighted the U.S. dominance in the region. In other words, because the newscast did not include any other countries that did or did not recognize the new leader, it suggested that the United States acted as a political barometer for the hemisphere.

The report also helps explain how television producers tended to portray Castro. By referring to him as "doctor," the report gave him heightened social status. In a subsequent report on the same day a writer described him as the son of a wealthy landowner, "a cultured person who possessed high levels of university knowledge." The report then distinguished Castro from the official rhetoric of the Mexican Revolution, calling attention to Castro's announcement that his revolution was "political, not social." Moreover, the writer's decision to omit any reference to Batista served the dual function to further discredit the former leader and legitimize the new one.

The final part of the report served to strengthen Zabludovsky's and the station's position as leaders in the production of television news, as it highlighted Zabludovsky's role as interviewer of major news makers and touted the General Motors' news team as firm believers in truth in journalism. This report, similar to many others produced during this time, illustrated how frequently producers took up newscast airtime to promote a station's talent and news-gathering services, always with the goal of increasing viewership and profit.

During Zabludovsky's half-hour long interview with Castro in Matanzas, the rebel leader again thanked Mexico, because it was "exactly where we found shelter when we had to abandon our country until we could return to begin this fight." Zabludovsky probed Castro further, asking him about the countries that sold weapons and arms to Batista to quell the rebel movement. Castro replied sarcastically, "We are the happiest with the English because they sold [Batista] airplanes and tanks that are now in our hands. We are very happy with the Italians because they sold good arms that are now in our hands. [We are] indignant with [Dominican dictator Rafael] Trujillo because what he sold to Batista is not worth anything—some of the worst machine guns."[41]

After a break, which featured a live commercial for Frigidaire, the newscast returned to the subject of Zabludovsky and Castro. An anchor reported that Zabludovksy had interviewed several principal persons in the movement and they all declared immense gratitude to the Mexican government and people. By allowing others to give thanks to Mexico, as Lidia Castro had done, these reports offer more evidence of the close political and cultural ties between the two Latin American nations.

In subsequent stories on *Noticiero General Motor*'s January 7 newscast, the writer mentioned that Zabludovsky got a glimpse of unrest in the streets of Havana. He and his news team interviewed José Alberto Iñíguez from Free Radio of Cuba, which had been Batista's official radio station, as well as the staff from the newspaper *Revolución*, formerly *Alerta*. The reports focused on the fact that the news team had the opportunity to speak with the "famous Ernesto Ch. [sic] Guevara" at the Fortress of Cabaña. The final report in the newscast about the events in Cuba concluded by announcing that telephone service to the provincial capitals of Santa Clara and Camagüey had been restored and that it seemed that calm would soon be restored to the "beautiful country of Cuba."

The last report brought several interesting points to the surface. First, referring to Che Guevara as the "famous" revolutionary helped to foster the myth of Che, a popular and modern day "savior of the people." The reference to him as famous also served to romanticize the movement. The myth building and romanticizing of Guevara grew more intense after October 9, 1967, the day he was killed by Bolivian soldiers trained by CIA operatives and U.S. Green Berets.[42]

Second, referring to Cuba as a beautiful country evoked a sense of timelessness and offered an audiovisual expression of the kinship that many Mexican felt for its Caribbean neighbor.

INCONSISTENT DISSIDENTS

If both railway workers and Cuban revolutionaries fought for democratic reforms and social justice, why were they portrayed so differently on television? In the news, railway organizer Demetrio Vallejo became a symbol of antinationalism and a threat to democracy, while Castro and Che were glorified as men who triumphed over a dictator and championed democratic principles. There are at least three reasons for the stark contrast between the framing of railway strikers and Cuban rebels. First, the television executives who controlled what went on the air represented the country's economic elite. Newscast producers viewed railway strikers as a threat to the corporate structure and the ideology of economic development through modernization. If railway workers impeded the flow of goods and services, they impeded the country's development and modernization. Editorials written by newspaper journalists criticized railway workers in the same way.[43] During this period Castro maintained that his revolution was a political, not social one.[44] In other words, he wanted to oust a despot and restore democracy. In addition, news writers might have perceived Castro, whose family owned a sugar plantation, as a member of their socioeconomic group, as they highlighted his class position and university training.

Second, both print and broadcast journalists seemed fascinated by Castro's personality. His charisma worked to rally a crowd as well as to develop a following of foreign reporters. Through his actions and availability to the news media, Castro went beyond being able to generate a media following. In some ways, he helped to manipulate the way reporters framed him as a heroic revolutionary. The tendency to portray the Cuban leader in a positive light demonstrates the flexibility within the construction of frames. While reporters and news managers made decisions about whether to cover Castro, he too played a significant role in shaping what and how reporters and producers would eventually write about him.

A third reason for the glaring difference in portrayals of the two groups is related to the close political and cultural connections between Mexico and Cuba. By 1959 politicians had grown familiar with and had institutionalized the revolution in Mexico.[45] Politicians used the rhetoric of the Mexican Revolution in an attempt to foster national unity and pride. The revolution, it was argued, helped to improve the lives of the country's citizens. The reality was, however, that revolutionary policies had not increased the standard of living for all, in part because the country's population continued to soar at an unprecedented level along with economic growth. Supporting the Cuban Revolution showed Mexican citizens that its leaders had not turned their backs on their promise to adhere to revolutionary goals. Anti-imperialism, mainly against the United States, one of the tenets of the Cuban Revolution, certainly appealed to those who supported the goals of the Mexican Revolution. By the time the Cuban Missile Crisis unfolded in 1962, the manner in which writers depicted Castro and his revolution changed shape, as Mexico found itself caught between an attempt to remain neutral as well as to support the United States.

The decisions by producers to portray railway strikers and Cuban revolutionaries in distinct ways had real cultural and political consequences. By disseminating the official line, without critically assessing the government's actions, Telesistema Mexicano in effect sent a signal to viewers that it approved of the regime. The exclusion of statements from dissident union leaders such as Demetrio Vallejo and the rank-and-file members eliminated opportunities for viewers as citizens to hear alternative perspectives. In the meantime, the glorification of Che and Castro contributed to the myths of both revolutionary leaders.

Reports in print media also tended to portray domestic dissidents in negative ways. Journalists often attempted to link railway workers to foreign agitators and communist activities. Connecting domestic dissidents with radical elements from abroad did two things: it downplayed the strength of local discontent and blamed the country's unrest on outside forces. This may appear somewhat contradictory, given the favorable coverage of Cuban rebels on Mexican airwaves, but in 1959 Castro had not yet declared himself to be a communist. Furthermore, positive portrayals of the Cuban insurgents began to change dramatically after the Cuban Missile Crisis. What did these stories about the railway strikes and the Cuban Revolution mean to viewers of early television? The ways viewers interpreted reports on the railway strike and on the Cuban Revolution depended on several political, social, cultural, and economic factors. A wealthy man of European descent who owned a business in Mexico City might have a drastically different interpretation of the events than a rural indigenous woman who recently came to the capital from a remote village in Chiapas. Participants in the railway strikes of 1958–59 most likely interpreted coverage of the railway movement and Cuban movement much differently than those who produced it. Certainly, the messages delivered along the capital city streets during workers' protests included discussion of labor's demands and concerns, and members of the public could discuss the issues one-on-one, something viewers could not do with their TV sets.[46] As they took to the streets, workers and the students who joined them began to create their own frames of a mid-twentieth century Mexico, and theirs often contrasted with those aired on TV.

Railway workers and other citizens expressed their political ideologies about the Cold War and the Cuban Revolution on the streets as well. In the spring of 1960 Cuban president Osvaldo Dorticós arrived in Mexico City. At the airport, about fifteen thousand people showed up to greet the new head of state.[47] Hundreds of those in attendance shouted, "*¡Cuba sí, yanquis, no!*," as Dorticós walked alongside President Adolfo López Mateos. Intellectuals, like popular individuals who marched in the streets, contributed to a small but significant counterweight to members of official media who, through their pro-American business practices, seemed to be shouting, "Yankee, don't go home!"⁴⁸ *New York Times* correspondent Paul Kennedy quoted painter and intellectual David Siqueiros, who attended the rally: "The Cuban Revolution has been the most important social movement in all Latin America. The defense of this revolution by Mexico is fundamental to the struggle against North American imperialism."⁴⁹

That was the last time the public saw Siqueiros with President López Mateos. By August 1960 Siqueiros was in prison, after being charged with violating the country's law of social dissolution, the same law that officials used to imprison Vallejo and student activists in 1968.⁵⁰ That the country's citizens supported the Cuban Revolution might be more of a reaction against the United States than a vote in favor of Fidel Castro. At the same time, support of the Cuban Revolution could be viewed as a reaffirmation of the nation's own revolutionary goals. Certainly, López Mateos walked a fine line in supporting the Cuban Revolution, because on the one hand it fell in line with following Mexico's revolutionary tradition, but on the other it could strain relations with the United States.

Railway strikers who watched news about the labor dispute undoubtedly viewed the coverage much differently than railway officials. For railway strikers, television coverage must have seemed to echo the government's official line. In contrast, railway officials may have recognized that reports put them in a privileged position, but railway executives might have also thought that news writers did not go far enough in support of the government.

When looked at collectively, several conclusions can be drawn with respect to strike coverage. First, news writers tended to favor the government railway company's concerns over workers' demands. Second, coverage tended to place the conflict within the larger scope of national goals. The reports that posited the strikes in national terms implied that company representatives were responsible individuals concerned with the national economy, in contrast to dissident workers who symbolized a threat to the nation. Third, news reports described workers as outsiders and irrational, and they depicted company and dissident union representatives in contrasting lights. The conclusions presented here seem to reflect the government's arguments at the time. Nevertheless, this did not signify that the print and TV news reports served as blatant government-supported or initiated propaganda, such as embutes and chayotes or gacetillas. The manner in which *Noticiero General Motors* covered the strikes was more a reflection of the common business objective of the television industry and the railway system to strengthen the country's economy. In essence, the goals of a commercial enterprise such as television and television news could coincide at times with the goals of the government, but they were not one and the same.

Nine years after the first television transmissions, the number of citizens who could watch the news on TV had grown dramatically. A record number of 120,000 television sets were sold that year, and the previous year had also been a record seller. Viewership had soared to 3.8 million, with 780,000 television sets plugged in around the country.[51] Television had reached other major cities, including Guadalajara, and the signal from Mexico City through repeaters could be watched in parts of the southeast and southwest, from the gulf to the Pacific Ocean. Citizens in states such as Guanajuato, Michoacán, Tamaulipas, San Luis Potosí, and Querétaro also were able to view Mexico City programming via repeaters.

How people watched and interpreted television depended on their social positions. Many could not afford to purchase a television set, but they could pay their neighbors a few centavos so that they could watch their favorite programs, which may or may not have been *Noticiero General Motors*.[52] Others simply watched on the streets, standing outside large department stores. For at least some viewers who watched Castro take over Havana and listened to Zabludovsky's interview with the rebel leader, it must have forced them to question why reports tended to hail Cuban rebels but assail their homegrown dissidents.

The reports televised in 1959 centered on two of the most pivotal events of the twentieth century for the nation and the hemisphere—the railway strikes of 1958 and 1959 and the Cuban Revolution. Telesistema Mexicano's news coverage of the events gave its viewers a top-down and capitalist perspective of the events. On the international front Castro received favorable treatment in news coverage, something that homegrown rebels did not enjoy. On the national front the network towed the line with the government by privileging official opinions and silencing the rank-in-file railway workers. Nevertheless, workers got their messages out through a variety of other news and public outlets. Their hybrid frames of the events showed that the boundaries of cultural hegemony appeared to stop at long-standing public squares such as the zócalo.

CHAPTER 4

The First Television Diplomats

PRESIDENT MIGUEL Alemán traveled to Washington DC and Manhattan Island to meet with U.S. President Harry Truman in the spring of 1947. The U.S. and Mexican press extensively covered Alemán's official visit. *Time* magazine's Latin American edition featured a photograph of expatriate men and women dressed in "native" costumes as they greeted the president in Manhattan. A journalist covering the visit wrote, "The big *viva* was far from being synthetic. President Alemán, tanned and affable, carried with him a kind of movie-star glamour. He smiled a big, beaming smile, waved boyishly at the crowds. People liked him — especially the girls. 'He's cute,' they said."[1] In a special report to the *New York Times*, Virginia Lee Warren gushed over Alemán: "Handsome, smiling President Miguel Alemán of Mexico swooped down out of the sky this afternoon in President Truman's personal plane, the Sacred Cow, and was hailed by one of the largest and most enthusiastic throngs Washington has ever turned out for any foreign guest."[2]

An embarrassing cultural faux pas occurred when the U.S. State Department had its staff throw into Alemán's parade route 650 of what staff members thought were miniature Mexican flags. It turned out that they were Italian flags. John O'Donnell's report concluded, "The Mexicans are as polite as our State Department is stupid. It's one of those ghastly social horrors that all present ignore, and keep on talking and smiling just as if nothing happened."[3] Alemán's visit to Washington was the last official trip by a sitting president to the United States until twelve years later in 1959, when Adolfo López Mateos met with Dwight D. Eisenhower (1953–61).[4]

News coverage of presidential visits abroad and foreign dignitaries' trips to a host nation provide a unique window through which the state of diplomatic affairs can be examined between one country and another. During some of the most tenuous years of the Cold War (1959–63), Mexico occupied an important and influential, but not fully understood, role in shaping the events that would define the second half of the twentieth century. After serving time for the attack on the Moncada barracks, Fidel Castro traveled to Mexico to train guerillas who would eventually overthrow Batista's regime. López Mateos was the first world leader to recognize Castro's government after the fall of Batista. These and many other Cold War events and activities were covered by television journalists. The way reporters covered these events, including presidential visits abroad and foreign dignitaries' visits to Mexico, helps us to appreciate both the complexity of the time as well as understand how government leaders began to use television to further their Cold War agendas.

By 1959, less than a decade after the inauguration of Mexican television, leaders such as López Mateos, Cárdenas, Castro, Eisenhower, and Soviet leader Anastas Mikoyan may have held different political views, but they all recognized the growing significance of television news and its connection to their roles as international diplomats. More than a half a century after the emergence of television, it remains clear that these figures were indeed the first television diplomats.

López Mateos's trip in October 1959 was momentous because it represented the first time television news reporters accompanied their print and radio counterparts to cover a presidential visit to the United States, signaling the increasing role that the medium played in society. His visit became part of a new phenomenon known as "television diplomacy," a more popular expression of diplomacy, in contrast to past diplomatic practice that occurred only in elite circles.[5]

From 1950 to 1970 political figures across the globe increasingly began to use television as a tool to disseminate their political agendas. Since the emergence of satellite communications in the 1960s, numerous terms have been coined to refer to the increasing influence of electronic media on international relations, such as "tele-democracy," "new diplomacy," and "CNN effect." News reels shown at movie theaters, like television news, offered diplomats an earlier audiovisual format through which they could deliver political messages to popular audiences.[6]

This chapter examines television news coverage of presidential visits abroad and visits by foreign heads of state to Mexico in 1959. The four visits include President Lázaro Cárdenas's trip to Cuba, July 24–27; Adolfo López Mateos's trip to the United States, October 8–18; U.S. president Dwight D. Eisenhower's trip to Acapulco, February 19–20; and Soviet deputy premier Anastas Mikoyan's trip to Mexico, November 18–28. Although the length of the four 1959 visits varied, which created an imbalance in the amount of news produced related to each visit, I create a balanced analysis by giving equal time in this chapter to each political figure.

Given that 1959 represents one of the most significant years of the twentieth century for Mexico, the United States, the Soviet Union, and, of course, Cuba, analysis of this category of news coverage enables the reconstruction of a complex picture that elucidates the contingent situation that existed during the first phase of the Cuban Revolution (1959–63).[7] News coverage about the four visits illuminates the tensions that existed among the four nations. López Mateos and Cárdenas, along with Eisenhower and Mikoyan, all understood the growing importance of television, and they used the new medium to promote their distinct diplomatic agendas among their respective constituents.

Beyond illuminating the increasing role that television would come to play in international relations, the news reports brought to the fore the competing, yet sometimes complementary, strategies of containment during the Cold War. While the United States attempted to thwart and contain communism in Latin America, Mexico sought to contain political dissidents and dissonance within its national boundaries, as well as stave off U. S. imperialistic efforts in the region.[8] This particular case study of state visits within and outside of the country is another area of news coverage that allows for an examination of the limits of cultural hegemony from the "colossus to the north" as well as the "colossus from within"—the PRI. Regarding U.S. hegemony in the region, Cárdenas, López Mateos, and Mikoyan showed there were checks against foreign influence. Similarly, Cárdenas showed members of the waning left that PRI hegemony had its limits as well. In addition, it became evident that international political figures, such as the four men discussed in this chapter, began to understand the salience of television and its critical connection to diplomacy three decades before the "CNN effect."[9]

PRODUCING THE PRESIDENTIAL

Television news, by 1959, had been on the air for nine years. Jacobo Zabludovsky's role in the nascent medium is difficult to overstate, as he was an editor of one of the most important Mexico City news teams. In addition to his newsroom duties, Zabludovsky worked as a consultant to the president's press office, blurring the lines between the government and television news. He covered the most significant events of the time, from the fall of Batista to presidential trips abroad and visits by foreign dignitaries. His interpretation of events and style of reporting, including his newscast's opening line, "*muy buenas noches*," would have a lasting impact on the way news would be produced throughout the rest of the century. Hundreds, if not thousands, of journalists worked under Zabludovsky's tutelage. Lolita Ayala, the first woman to anchor her own news program, remarked, "Jacobo was, and continues to be, a principal figure in Mexican journalism. So, when they called me to work with him [in 1974], it was an honor, but at the same time a challenge because Jacobo was and continues to be a very strict person."[10]

Zabludovsky has downplayed his extracurricular role as consultant to the president. He argues that his position as radio and television adviser for both López Mateos and Díaz Ordaz was an honorary post more than anything else and that he made a clear separation between his job as a journalist and his job as presidential adviser. When asked about a conflict of interest, he remarked only that those were different times. The former television anchor maintains that the government did not attempt to directly influence the news. Zabludovsky's recollection of those different times fails to include the government's carrot and stick measures that were meant to keep the press in line.

Print journalists had long grown accustomed to payoffs from government officials seeking to ensure favorable coverage, but during this time López Mateos took the practice of embute and chayote to new levels with television and print journalists. During his term in office he created press departments in all major levels of government. Social communication officers in each government department had the responsibility to watch how reporters covered their departments as well as offer them so-called financial aid.[11] The term represented not only a euphemism but a necessity, as by the 1980s seven out of twenty-five Televisa reporters worked second jobs to support themselves and their families. Frequently, government officials made payments to journalists on a monthly basis. The quantity of the payments depended on the size of the ministry or department. Zabludovsky, and other higher-level journalists, did not have to take on extra work to pay the bills, although he did work for both the government and private industry. The anchor disputes that Televisa reporters had to take on secondary employment to make a living. He claims that by 1970, with the formation of 24 horas, they made a decent living.[12]

By 1959 television news programming had increased dramatically, compared to the incipient days of the medium, in terms of both the quantity and the length of programs. By the end of the decade at least four television stations produced news programming (see table 1). Through the course of the decade, the length of newscast scripts increased from about three to four pages to six to seven pages. The increase in the length of the newscasts, as well as the number of news bulletins, suggests that there were more people involved in the daily news-gathering process, as well as an increasing demand for news content.

By the start of the Cuban Revolution, Telesistema Mexicano continued to consolidate its position both in Mexico City and in the provinces. By 1960 four stations operated in the capital city, with fifteen more throughout the country. Just over 1,013 people worked in the television industry, with 76 percent of the workforce concentrated in the capital. In Guadalajara the country's second largest city, three stations transmitted television, and 118 people worked to bring programming to residents of the state of Jalisco.[13] The number of repeaters to outlying areas increased, allowing viewers to see events reported on television for the first time, although the news came through a capital and predominantly elite male lens.

By the end of the decade, the federal government passed and put into place a law specifically designed for television. When television began it was regulated by the 1940 Ley de Vías Generales de Comunicaciones, signed by the then president Cárdenas. In 1960

TABLE 1. Television newscasts produced in 1959

XEW-TV, Channel 2	XHTV, Channel 4	XHGC, Channel 5	XEIPN, Channel 11
Noticiero celanese mexicana, 1959–64	Noticias del día, 1956–62	Noticiero celanese mexicana, 1957–59	Noticiero estudiantil
Noticiero excelsior, 1954–70	Noticiero General Motors, 1950–62	Cuestión de minutos, 1957–59	
Cine mundial (film news), 1955–63	Noticiero novedades, 1957–63, 1966–70	Cuestión de sociales, 1957–59	
		El eco del día, 1957–59	
		Instantaneous TV (news commentary), 1959–61	

Source: Huesca Rebolledo, "Cronología de noticiarios televisivos."

López Mateos signed the new Ley Federal de Comunicaciones (Federal Law of Communications). The law in part reflected an attempt to improve the quality of television programming, which had recently been the target of much popular criticism. Article 58 of the law guaranteed freedom of expression for electronic media and prohibited censorship of radio and television programming, as it stated specifically, "The right to information, expression, and reception through radio and television is free, and consequently it will not be subject to judicial or administrative inquiry, nor limited in any way, or be subject to prior censorship, and the terms and laws of the Constitution shall be exercised."[14] Although the law had been passed, in practice, self-censorship and government intervention through the embutes and chayotes continued to influence content.

Technologically, getting the images on the air, which were still in black and white, from the United States back to Mexico was much more difficult than after the advent of videotape and establishment of satellite communications. Once a camera operator shot the film it had to be processed, which would take several hours. The film then had to be flown to Mexico. For that reason, viewers often received information a day or sometimes two days after the event.

By December 5, 1959, *Noticiero General Motors* had been on the air for nine years. The news-team producers did not hesitate to promote the newscast's ninth anniversary, and in its lead story, producers included the fact that it had been in operation for 3,285 continuous days and that its staff had done so "without eulogy or attacks and through objectivity and straightforwardness."[15] After almost ten years of production the tele-tradition of self-promotion had taken hold. The program remained on the air until 1962. The practice of self-promotion continues in the twenty-first century.

By the end of the decade the popularity of television had skyrocketed. The year 1959 became a record-selling year for companies such as RCA, as 120,000 sets were purchased.[16]

CÁRDENAS AND LÓPEZ MATEOS TRAVEL ABROAD

By July 1959 Fidel Castro had been in power for just over seven months, and he used the sixth anniversary of the attack on the Moncada barracks in 1953 to stage numerous media opportunities.[17] On July 26, 1953, Castro had organized an attack on the Cuban army's garrisons at Moncada and Bayamo in hopes of sparking a movement to overthrow Batista. It became known as the Movimiento de 26 de Julio (26th of July Movement). One media opportunity involved the arrival of former Mexican president Lázaro Cárdenas. In office from 1934 to 1940, Tata Cárdenas has been portrayed as Mexico's most left-leaning president after the Mexican Revolution until Luis Echeverría took office in 1970.[18] Between 1959 and 1963, the country's policies toward Cuba both strained and strengthened U.S.-Mexico relations, and Cárdenas often wound up in the middle of the conflict.

Like his leftist Cuban counterpart, Cárdenas took advantage of media opportunities to promote his own political agenda. The former president became adept at using radio and news reels during his presidency, especially in times of crisis, so it should not have come as a surprise to his opponents that he would turn to television to continue to further his goals.[19] The news reports show Cárdenas invoking revolutionary rhetoric and highlighting the similarities between Mexico's revolution of 1910 and Cuba's 1959 movement. Ironically, Cárdenas's support of the Cuban Revolution coincided with official attempts to quell (through both co-optation and violence) leftist activity within his own country.[20]

Cárdenas's political activities in 1959 remain essential to understanding the diplomatic scene for two reasons. First, his involvement in political and diplomatic affairs helped give guidance to members of the Left and signaled its resurgence, which had waned since he left office. Second, his increased visibility in politics had a positive (though undesirable on Cárdenas's part) effect on the presidency of López Mateos. By igniting polemic arguments, Cárdenas wound up functioning as a political lightening rod for criticism that otherwise may have been aimed at López Mateos.[21] The former president's dual role became evident in news reports between July 24 and July 29.[22] The first script that focused on his visit to Cuba aired after a story on the Basilica de Guadalupe and was simply a promotion for Zabludovsky, who was on his way to Havana to cover the events. Five stories later, Pedro Ferríz read this report about upcoming celebrations scheduled for July 26.

TATA CÁRDENAS IN HAVANA

All of Havana's newspaper dailies on the 26th of July will be printed on paper made from sugarcane pulp, produced by Cuban manufacturing plants in the town of Cárdenas.[23] Fidel Castro will play baseball tonight to generate funds for his agrarian reform program. With his long beard, his campaign uniform, and high boots, the revolutionary leader will pitch for at least the first five innings of the game, during which soldiers and police will face off. Castro today arrived at the palace at three in the afternoon for an unexpected visit that constitutes his first appearance at the presidential palace since the resigning of the ex-president, Manuel Urrutia, last Friday.[24]

The day before the anniversary of the Movimiento de 26 de Julio, *Noticiero General Motors* aired a report that featured Cárdenas' scheduled visit to the island:

> We just received the first report from our special envoy, Jacobo Zabludovsky, editorial director of *Noticiero General Motors*. Jacobo interviewed General Lázaro Cárdenas, who arrived in Havana shortly before three this afternoon. General Cárdenas, who was invited by Fidel Castro, told our special correspondent, among other things, that "the Cuban Revolution was an example for all countries in the Western Hemisphere." He expressed his solidarity with the Cuban Revolution and his sympathy toward Castro's politics. Speaking about agrarian reform in Cuba and drawing a parallel with the agrarian reforms of our nation, General Cárdenas stated that the politics of Licenciado López Mateos in that respect is directed to the best paths, that it is encouraging to all observers, [and] that Mexico has land for all. General Cárdenas thinks he will return to our country this Tuesday. The ex-president of Mexico finished by saying that [his visit to] the Cuban island will be very pleasant and that the enthusiasm of its people everywhere has awakened old feelings in him.[25]

In the second of these two reports, Cárdenas used the television opportunity to draw connections between the Cuban and Mexican Revolutions. At the same time, the former president praised López Mateos's push for agrarian reform. For viewers who stood on the left of the political spectrum, Cárdenas's words, "the enthusiasm of its people everywhere has awakened old feelings in him," may have amounted to a call to action or least offered a glimmer of hope to *cardenistas* that the Mexican Left was not dead.

On the sixth anniversary of the attack on the Moncada barracks, *Noticiero General Motors* aired three reports related to events in Cuba. The lead story focused on the use of Cuban arms in a failed attack in Nicaragua; the second and longest report treated Cárdenas's visit and 26th of July celebrations; and the third (the eighteenth story in the newscast) mentioned U.S. involvement in counterrevolutionary activities in Cuba. When looked at together, these reports reveal the national and international importance of the Cuban Revolution.[26] On a national level Cárdenas's visit and comments helped to strengthen López Mateos's popularity among the country's political Left, which supported land reform. During his administration López Mateos redistributed more land than any other president, including Cárdenas.[27] That Cárdenas, a champion of agrarian reform, linked López Mateos to Castro, served to bolster the sitting president's image among his popular and rural constituencies. On an international level, the Cárdenas visit strained relations with U.S. officials, who would begin to work to undermine, although unsuccessfully, Castro's regime.

The content and placement of the three stories highlighted existing tensions among Mexico, the United States, Cuba, and Eastern Bloc countries. The first story suggested that the Organization of American States recognized that Cuba and its leaders could play a larger role in Latin America, as well as a fear of leaders such as Ernesto Guevara in exporting the revolution. Furthermore, the decision of news directors to make this item the lead story suggests that they thought it was more important than all the other reports that followed. The story on Cárdenas's visit to Cuba served to stem criticism from members of left-leaning groups who may have started to think that López Mateos drifted away from the tenets of the Mexican Revolution. At the same time, U.S. government officials working in Mexico may have viewed this report differently. They might have seen the report as evidence of dangerous ties between Cuba and Mexico. Indeed, U.S. envoys met with Cárdenas during his trip to the island nation.[28]

The last of the three reports that mentioned Cuba called attention to anticommunist discourse that often permeated television news and reflected the politics of the Cold War. This story focused on a "communist" East German newspaper that alleged that the United States was backing counterinsurgency efforts to overthrow Castro's government. The report subtly discredited the information by labeling it a communist paper. The tendency of news executives to be more critical of information coming from Eastern Bloc and communist countries applied also to other Cold War–related stories.

LÓPEZ MATEOS IN THE UNITED STATES, OCTOBER 4–19

By the fall of 1959, three months after Cárdenas's trip to Cuba, López Mateos traveled to the United States, stopping in Washington DC, Chicago, and New York. News about the visit filled *Noticiero General Motors*'s airtime for almost a week before his aircraft departed for Washington on October 9. Again, Telesistema Mexicano sent editorial director Zabludovsky to cover the historic events. On October 6, 1959, three days before he left for the U.S. capital, López Mateos held a news conference with the directors of the major newspapers and news outlets in Mexico City at the Palacio Nacional. It was a chance for him to inform the news media and the public about the nature of the visit. The lead story signaled the political balancing act that López Mateos and other leaders performed both domestically and abroad:

> President López Mateos told the press today that his desire for Mexico and Mexicans on the eve of his departure to the United States was that everyone continues to work in peace. Mr. President affirmed that the main concern during this visit

to the American Union will be to solve some economic matters. He signaled that concrete problems related to the economy will be tackled, especially our natural resources. With respect to the visit that ex-president Lázaro Cárdenas paid to political prisoners, he signaled that he considered it a humanitarian act of generosity and that if General Cárdenas makes a petition for them, as he announced in the press, the president would help him as he would any other citizen, because all have a right to petition.[29]

By making a connection between national and international events, the president clearly attempted to stress that the main objective of the visit would favor national objectives. In the first sentence, the report emphasized López Mateos's concern for Mexico and its citizens. That the president stated he would be working on economic matters demonstrated to citizens that this trip might be good for the economy, a significant issue for the nation's development.

On the international front, the report illuminated the president's concern that officials work in a peaceful manner, which would become part of the discourse of Latin American leaders throughout the Cold War. The primacy of peace in news coverage, both in electronic and print media, reflected official and unofficial attempts to have a voice in the discourse on the nuclear arms race and participate in the events shaping the Cold War.[30]

The tensions between López Mateos and former president Lázaro Cárdenas also surfaced in the report. Although the script excluded any reference to which political prisoners Cárdenas had gone to visit, other news sources detailed that the former president stopped at the state prison in Aguas Calientes to talk with railway strike leaders such as Demetrio Vallejo, as well as other prisoners and their families. Cárdenas was reported to have said he would try to do what he could to negotiate the prisoners' release.[31] This was just one of the latest political bombs the former president dropped on López Mateos. Cárdenas's visit to Cuba and support of the Castro regime in July represented another. *New York Times* correspondent Paul Kennedy summed it up well when he wrote, "Whether his [Cárdenas's] trips are planned to demonstrate his political influence or not, they have exactly that effect."³²

By October 14 López Mateos's trip to North America was well underway (see figure 4). *Noticiero General Motors* led the newscast with a report about a speech that the president delivered before the United Nations General Assembly in New York. As the report revealed, his message focused on the Cold War. The speech and the way that producers chose to report it emphasized that government officials, as well as news producers, saw the country playing an important diplomatic role in the search for a solution to the threat of nuclear war:

> President Licenciado Adolfo López Mateos said today in front of the United Nations General Assembly that the world should unite not only against the horror of war but in goodwill to achieve progress peacefully. The chief executive was received with a grand ovation as he entered the assembly hall, escorted by veteran Peruvian diplomat Andres Belaúnde and the UN secretary general, Dag Hammarskjeld [sic]. The topic of disarmament and peace was the focus of the speech given by the chief executive. Peace signifies cooperation between countries to resolve world problems, and the achievement of dialogue, classic of all the nations that are working together to achieve the best solution possible.³³

In addition to talking about the primacy of peace, the president drew a connection between inequalities among the most powerful and least powerful countries and war. López Mateos also mentioned that Mexico, as a founding member of the United Nations General Assembly, was within its right to call for nuclear disarmament and that smaller, weaker countries were at the mercy of the larger, more powerful ones.³⁴

Meanwhile, as the president was in New York working to improve U.S.–Latin America ties, it appeared that Cárdenas was attempting to unravel López Mateos's efforts. Cárdenas continued to speak out

4. President López Mateos arriving with his family in Chicago and greeting expatriate children in traditional dress. *Noticiero General Motors*, October 14, 1959. © Grupo Televisa.

about political affairs, going against previous protocol established by other former presidents, who once they left office remained out of the political sphere. In Huichapán, Hidalgo, Cárdenas delivered a speech before a group of agricultural workers. In the speech, he praised the People's Republic of China and at the same time denounced leaders of his government for falsely imprisoning railway workers.[35] In addition, the former president decried businesspeople who garnered wealth, such as bankers, merchants, and speculators, during the Mexican Revolution.

In a capital newspaper advertisement, a Mexico City lawyer lambasted the former president's critiques as well as his timing. Mario Guerra Leal remarked, "When anyone like General Cardenas [sic] takes advantage of a patriotic mission abroad to create during the president's absence unnecessary problems [he] is betraying Mexico."[36] *Noticiero General Motors* excluded the controversy in its coverage of national events.[37]

After ten days in the United States and Canada, the president returned to Mexico City on October 19, 1959. *Noticiero General Motors* estimated that a crowd of a half-million people rallied at the Palacio Nacional to welcome him home.[38] The news report mentioned that manufacturing plants, workshops, and offices let workers off so that they could attend the event. The newscast overlooked a critical piece of information—that government-backed unions had threatened members with reprisals if they did not attend.[39] Clearly, the conflicts between the government and labor had not been resolved in López Mateos's absence. And, television news executives, through their decision to exclude information about union leaders' threats toward workers, sent a signal to viewers showing where *Noticiero General Motors* stood politically—on the side of the government.

IKE IN ACAPULCO AND MIKOYAN IN MEXICO CITY

One month after the Cuban Revolution of 1959, and prior to López Mateos's trip to the United States, Dwight D. Eisenhower embarked on his third official visit to Mexico. His first trip in an official capacity happened in 1948, when the country presented him with the Orden Mexicana del Águila Azteca (Mexican Order of the Aztec Eagle) that, said López Mateos, singled him out as a distinguished friend of Mexico.[40] Shortly after taking the oath of the presidency in 1953, Ike returned during the Ruiz Cortines administration, when he traveled to the small U.S.-Mexico border town of Nueva Ciudad Guerrero. Six years later, Eisenhower was set to return. The day before his arrival to Acapulco, on February 18, *Noticiero General Motors* led its newscast with a report about the U.S. president's visit, in which Eisenhower stated there was no set agenda for his trip:

> President Eisenhower declared today that the basic purpose of his visit to Mexico is to pay his respects to President Adolfo López Mateos and extend his friendship toward the neighboring republic. Eisenhower expressed that there was no set theme

for his conversations with the Mexican president, but that both would discuss numerous matters of common interest. President Eisenhower left at 2:13 p.m., local time, in his airplane, *Columbine III*, on his way to Acapulco to be interviewed with Licenciado López Mateos, who was believed to be leaving on the road today in the afternoon, but he postponed his trip until eight in the morning tomorrow. The president will leave in the presidential plane, accompanied by his close advisers.[41]

The stories included in the February 18 newscast, when looked at as a whole, illustrate Cold War tensions during the late 1950s and early 1960s. What follows is the show rundown of the reports aired that day:

1. Eisenhower press conference
2. Acapulcans prepare for presidents
3. Duchess of Kent
4. Manufacturing industry
5. Issac Stern in Houston, Texas
6. 20–30 Club Luncheon
7. Journalists head for Acapulco
8. Bullfights
9. News Wrap
   - Archbishop Makarios versus Greek government
   - Eisenhower on Berlin
10. Commercial-Super-Motors
11. Eisenhower on Guatemala versus Mexico dispute
12. John Foster Dulles hospitalized
13. Archbishop of New York Francis Spellman in Central America
14. Summary of other presidential visits to Mexico
15. News Wrap
    - Suspension of livestock trade between Mexico and the United States
    - Execution of Cuban war criminal by firing squad[42]

This list shows how news producers stacked the newscast on February 18, that is, in what order they placed news reports. Eleven out of the fifteen stories (73 percent) focused on international news. Of these, seven focused on the United States, one on England, one on Greece, and two on Latin America (Guatemala and Cuba). Eight stories could be viewed as having a national focus, although they may have had an international twist, such as the eleventh report, which mentioned the role that Eisenhower would play in resolving a dispute between Mexico and Guatemala.[43] Two stories focused on religious events. Three reports fell into the business category.[44]

On February 19 López Mateos greeted Eisenhower in sunny Acapulco. The decision to choose Acapulco as a meeting place remains unclear, but the visit occurred during a period of increased government investment, through the assistance of former president Miguel Alemán to develop tourism in the coastal and former colonial city.[45] At three points in his brief speech, the president stressed the friendship between Mexico and the United States. In closing, he welcomed Eisenhower to a country that "fights tirelessly for freedom of men, justice for the people, and for peace within countries."[46] The issue of friendship between the two countries became a central theme in the news scripts as well. The lead story on February 20 illuminated the point: "Mexican–North American relations are culminating with President Eisenhower's visit to Acapulco, whose people have received him with true friendship. This word [friendship], a sincere sign of the cordial reception that Eisenhower receives wherever he goes. Grand posters could be read throughout the town, in trees, on polls, and even on the rooftops in the welcoming summerlike city of Acapulco."[47]

Noticiero General Motors devoted most of its newscast to the meeting between López Mateos and Eisenhower on February 20. Three of the ten stories in the newscast treated the presidential encounter:

1. Presidents' arrival in Acapulco
2. Presidents on yacht, greeting crowds, dining
3. End of meeting
4. Cuban embassies
5. Italian prime minister
6. Mailie Salassie, Ethiopian emperor
7. Castro named prime minister of Cuba
8. U.S. satellite technology
9. Randing [sic] Turpin, English boxer
10. News wrap: thanks to Arturo Somoza Solís, head of Mexican airlines Aeronaves, for help getting film back to Mexico City to give viewers up-to-minute coverage.

While *Noticiero General Motors* touted its visual storytelling abilities, viewers got little more than superficial coverage. News reports focused on the happy time that the two presidents seemed to be having and their cordial and friendly relationship. In the second story on Eisenhower's visit, the anchor stated the most important thing noticed so far was that "every time cameras focused on the faces of the presidents, the men were quick to express smiles of satisfaction."[48]

Similar to the newscast rundown on February 18, the February 20 rundown, when analyzed together with the scripts, reveals competing interests. In other words, the newscast gave viewers a picture of Cold War events, how the country (albeit from an elite perspective) understood its position, and how producers constructed reality. Writers portrayed the United States as powerful both politically and technologically. Aside from highlighting Eisenhower's positive reception, the first report mentioned that the two heads of state would be discussing important financial matters, such as North American quotas on Mexican imports of zinc, lead, and coffee, as well as the possible funding of a new dam near the Río Bravo (known as the Rio Grande in the United States). The content of the report emphasized U.S. influence on Mexico's economic development.

The second story, also focusing on Eisenhower's visit, demonstrated the close relationship among the country's business and television moguls and the government. As the report revealed, Rómulo O'Farrill Sr. and his son were invited guests at a banquet for both presidents.[49] The O'Farrills owned XHTV, Channel 4, the station that aired *Noticiero General Motors*.

Beyond reports about Eisenhower's visit, the newscast included two reports about Cuba. The first mentioned that representatives from the Latin American embassies would be given safe conducts to leave the country. The second story on Cuba focused on the naming of Fidel Castro as prime minister by Manuel Urrutia. While televised reports on *Noticiero General Motors* in January 1959 focused on Castro's victory and signaled news leaders' support for the revolution, this particular February 20 report offered a more critical portrayal of the leader.

As the following script shows, news writers mentioned that Castro has controlled the country since the fall of Batista, yet the new prime minister faced serious problems: "Last Monday, provisional president of Cuba Manuel Urrutia named Fidel Castro, the leader of the Cuban Revolution, as prime minister of the new government of Cuba. Since the revolution, Castro has been the strongman on the island, and now he will be able to govern it. The principal problem is the economic repercussion (of the revolution) on Cuba, the redistribution of land to the peasants; other problems that he faces will be resolved in the future, as Castro himself has declared on various occasions."[50]

MIKOYAN IN MEXICO CITY, NOVEMBER 18-28

On November 18, eight months after Eisenhower's trip to Acapulco, Anastas Mikoyan, Soviet Union deputy premier, paid a visit to Mexico City. A look at how television news reports portrayed the Soviet official's visit helps to further illustrate the contentious quadripartite relationship between Mexico, the United States, Cuba, and the Soviet Union. Mikoyan was scheduled to visit for ten days on November 18–28. The timing of Mikoyan's visit remains significant, given that he arrived during the height of Mexico's week-long celebrations of its 1910 revolution. Mikoyan toured Mexico City on the Día de la Revolución and was with the president on November 20, partaking in celebrations commemorating the national holiday.

MIKOYAN'S ARRIVAL, NOVEMBER 18, 1959

The following report on the vice–prime minister's arrival led *Noticiero General Motors* on November 18:

> Today at noon the vice–prime minister of the Soviet Union, Anastas Mikoyan, arrived in Mexico City, after connecting in Canada on the airplane *Illusion 18*, with one hundred passengers landing on the central airport's runways. The number 2 man of the Soviet Union was received by foreign relations secretary Donato Miranda [sic], economy secretary Raúl Salinas, and education secretary Jaime Torres Bodet.[51] Russian ambassador Mr. Vladimir I. Bazikin was also there. Mikoyan will be received tomorrow by the president of the republic. His trip will include the inauguration, this Saturday, of the Russian exposition. During his ten-day trip, he will visit Alto Hornos, Ciudad Pemex, the city market [rastro] and many other places. Shortly after his arrival to Mexico City, a reception was offered at the Russian embassy, which members of the diplomatic corps and representatives from various sectors attended.[52]

The Russian Expo mentioned in this report was a first. The event lasted twenty-three days and was attended by more than a million visitors.[53] Events such as the expo offered another example of the country's propensity to "double deal," as well as highlighted the important diplomatic position that Mexico held for the Soviet Union at this critical time during the Cold War.

After a first commercial break, a report (item 16 in the newscast) focused on the Soviet press. Placed late in the newscast, as if unrelated to Mikoyan's visit, the news brief subtly criticized the Soviet system. The report claimed that "the Soviet press is still very insipid and at times one is tempted to throw away the newspaper after having looked it over and frequently even without having read it."[54]

NOVEMBER 19, 1959

The day before Revolution Day, *Noticiero General Motors* led its newscast with the following story, which did not include images:

> The vice-prime minister of the Union of the Soviet Socialist Republic, Mr. Anastas I. Mikoyan, in one of his first official visits to our country, greeted Licenciado Adolfo López Mateos, president of the republic. Mr. Mikoyan arrived accompanied by the secretary of foreign relations, Mr. Manuel J. Tello, and Russian ambassador, Mr. Valdimir I. Basikin. The vice-prime minister handed over a Soviet message to the Mexican leader that says that this message continues a greeting from the Russian government and an invitation to Licenciado López Mateos to visit Russia. Mr. Manuel J. Tello has stated that it is fitting for Mr. Mikoyan to make announcements about the meeting and Licenciado López Mateos's response, which will happen in the next press conference.[55]

Within the same newscast three other stories reported the vice-prime minister's activities of the day. A brief report focused on the Soviet official's stop at the Columna de Independencia. He was accompanied by Vladimir Basikin, the Russian ambassador and a member of the ministry of foreign relations, who laid a flowered wreath before the Columna de Independencia in honor of Mexico's Revolutionary heroes.

That Mikoyan was invited to place a wreath at this important national and historical landmark demonstrated the significance that Mexican officials assigned to his visit. In contrast, the short shrift that news writers gave to this event shows that perhaps television news executives were not as excited about his arrival as were the country's high-ranking government officials. López Mateos was noticeably missing from the event, and consequently no images of the president and vice-premier standing in front of the Columna de Independencia aired. Another brief report about Mikoyan's visit followed the story at the Columna de Independencia. The report focused on an hour-and-a-half meeting between Mikoyan and President López Mateos. During his visit, the story went on, he had a chance to meet with the minister of industry and commerce, Licenciado Raúl Salinas, and the minister of public education, Jaime Torres Bodet. The Soviet vice-premier stated, "direct personal contact is the best possible means to maintain good relations between the two countries."[56]

Analysis of news coverage of Mikoyan's ten-day visit resulted in three main observations. First, news writers depicted Mikoyan in a respectful but cool manner, in contrast to the warm language used to discuss Eisenhower, who was always "quick to smile." Mikoyan received an even cooler reception in the city's most prominent dailies. Some print journalists disagreed with a part of Mikoyan's speech before the Senate, in which he drew parallels between the Mexican and Russian Revolutions.[57] Second, although television news reports did not directly criticize Mikoyan or his activities, other stories questioned the legitimacy of the Soviet system. For example, the story regarding the quality of journalists in the Soviet Union cast a stone against the Soviet press. This contrasted with the stories that focused on the United States during Eisenhower's trip to Mexico and López Mateos's trip to the United States. The reports that focused on the United States during those two visits made no criticisms of its press or political system. Third, television news executives for *Noticiero General Motors* decided not to cover every day of Mikoyan's ten-day visit. This is in sharp contrast to the coverage of Eisenhower's February 1959 trip, although he was in the country for fewer than ten days. Finally, stories on Mikoyan aired on November 18 and

19, but not on November 20, the Día de la Revolución. Curiously, news coverage on the Soviet minister's activities resumed the next day on November 21, when he and the president inaugurated the Russian Expo. The omission of Mikoyan on November 20 could be seen as a subtle criticism or at the very least an attempt by television news writers to distance their country's revolutionary past with that of the Soviet Union.

COLD WAR TENSIONS AND TELEVISION DIPLOMATS

During 1959 Zabludovsky interviewed Castro on at least two occasions: once in January in Matanzas as Castro marched toward Havana and another time on July 26, during former president Cárdenas's visit to the Caribbean island nation. In both interviews, the questions Zabludovsky's posed to Castro concentrated on agrarian reform, Cuba's relationship to Mexico, and the United States. In the July interview that took place at close to midnight and lasted more than an hour, Zabludovsky asked Castro about statements in Mexico and abroad that showed growing opposition to his government. Castro replied, "I invite those who are of that opinion to come here to Cuba, so they can see where the opposition is and, above all, so that they can do any kind of survey. There is absolutely no opposition, because support for me is so huge that a nucleus of opposition is imperceptible—that is, one point fortieth or so percent. Less than two percent is against the revolution."[58] Of course, criticism of the Castro regime from the outside would swell by the mid-1960s, especially after the Cuban Missile Crisis.

Noticiero General Motors's coverage of the four state visits discussed in this chapter highlighted domestic and international political conflicts that characterized the Cold War. Reports provided evidence that former president Cárdenas invoked Mexico's revolutionary rhetoric and linked it to Cuba's 1959 revolution in an effort to gain favor among his own country's left. Just as he had used radio news while he was president, Cárdenas used television as a tool to promote his own diplomatic agenda. In addition, news reports on Cárdenas's trip to Cuba helped to illuminate how his attempts to invigorate the country's Left and inspire Cuban revolutionaries could have also resulted in straining relations between Mexico and the United States.

News coverage of López Mateos's trip to the United States worked to smooth diplomatic relations as well as helped to create recognition of the shifting nature of political boundaries.[59] Reports revealed domestic conflicts between Cárdenas and López Mateos. While López Mateos was abroad, Cárdenas visited Mexico's political prisoners, calling attention to the fact that the current president had not resolved serious problems between the government and the country's dissidents. TV news reports also showed how López Mateos used television news as an opportunity to disseminate his message of peace and Mexico as peace broker in the region.

News coverage of López Mateos's visit to the United States excluded critical discussion of the issue of the country's diaspora. Reports did not mention the political and economic factors that drove citizens to leave the country, such as the Bracero Program and the limitations of the "Mexican miracle," which did not provide enough jobs for all its working-class citizens, who then sought employment north of the Río Bravo. Moreover, the conviviality between U.S. and Mexican citizens highlighted in news coverage did not reflect the reality of all ex-patriots living abroad. Five years prior to the president's visit, Operation Wetback, a U.S. Immigration and Naturalization Service program, forced the deportation of hundreds of thousands of Mexicans. Perhaps as many as a million Mexicans were rounded up throughout the United States and expatriated.[60] That issue did not enter the news picture during López Mateos's visit.

Positive television coverage of Eisenhower's visit to Acapulco just a month after the Cuban Revolution demonstrated the alliances and appeal of the United States for television news executives. Glowing reports on the World War II hero's visit provided evidence of the capitalist as well as political interests of those who controlled television news. The positive welcome and news coverage of Eisenhower certainly was a contrast to the violent reception that U.S. vice president Richard Nixon received the year before on the streets of Caracas, Venezuela, at the end of an eighteen-day goodwill tour in Latin America. On May 13, 1958, an angry mob of students and citizens shouted "Get out, Nixon," as they threw rocks at the vice president's car, forcing the driver to take an alternative route and to cancel plans to stop at the statue of Simón Bolivar.[61] A year later, with the images of the cracked windows of Nixon's car still on Eisenhower's and his advisers' minds, it is no surprise that the meeting between the U.S. and Mexican president would take place in sunny and calm Acapulco instead of Mexico City. Furthermore, the Caracas incident reminded Eisenhower of the growing power of global media, and how he should use them in his favor to promote his political position by touting his visit as a gesture of goodwill toward Mexico.

In contrast to the warm tone of reports about Eisenhower, cool coverage of Anastas Mikoyan's ten-day visit pointed to television news executives' political and economic stances. His visit was perhaps too big to ignore, but news directors carefully placed his activities below reports about President López Mateos. The decision to not cover Mikoyan's activities on November 20 (Día de la Revolución) revealed that news producers sought to distance the Mexican and Soviet Revolutions, at the same time that Mikoyan attempted to draw a connection between the two.

Aside from illuminating the quadripartite tensions that existed between Mexico, the United States, Cuba, and the Soviet Union, news coverage about official visits demonstrated the extent to which producers relied on international news to fill airtime.[62] In addition, coverage that focused on Latin America tended to take on a secondary role, whereas reports on the United States provided the focus of most foreign news. Exceptions include the suicide of Brazilian president Gétulio Vargas in August 1954, the first days of the Cuban Revolution, and the Bay of Pigs invasion in April 1961.

By 1959, with the growing importance of television and news programming, Mikoyan, Cárdenas, Eisenhower, and López Mateos all looked to television to foment their distinct Cold War agendas. Mikoyan found himself at the Columna de Independencia, as he affirmed the significance of Mexico's revolutionary heroes. Yet López Mateos's absence at the event showed that he applied the strategy of "double dealing" on-screen as well as off. Cárdenas attempted to woo the waning Left at home and abroad by appearing on television, something from which most former presidents tended to shy away. Eisenhower stood in balmy Acapulco on a trip of goodwill, a much better photo opportunity than his vice president, who had to cut his trip short because of anti-American sentiment in the region. Undoubtedly, all these figures had different political agendas, but they all understood that to get their messages out to a wider audience, they needed also to be television diplomats.

CHAPTER 5

Hot Rockets and Cold War

ON OCTOBER 4, 1957, a potential audience of six hundred thousand Mexico City residents tuned in to watch Channel 4's nightly newscast, *Noticiero General Motors*.[1] The program began with a bulletin that originated from the Soviet Union. Based on information gathered from Radio Moscow, the newscaster reported that the Soviet Union had launched the first satellite from Earth.[2] The satellite became known as *Sputnik* 1, Russian for "traveling companion or satellite." The full name of the extraterrestrial object was Iskusstvenniy sputnik zemlyi (ISZ), literally, "artificial Earth companion." Former *Newsweek* journalist Albert L. Weeks claims that he was the first to coin the name *Sputnik* and that other news organizations followed.[3]

This same newscast included a story about another first, the inauguration of WEM, Channel 3, in Baja California.[4] The report stated the new station demonstrated economic progress in the northern state. Another story that day focused on three Telesistema Mexicano executives, Emilio Azcárraga, Rómulo O'Farrill Sr. and his son. The three men had attended a banquet hosted by radio and television journalists in honor of Telesistema Mexicano and its successful transmission of Día de la Independencia activities, such as President Ruiz Cortines's grito on September 15.

The three reports broadcast on October 4 illuminated Cold War and regional tensions, as well as tele-traditions. Reports on the launch of *Sputnik* provided examples of the technological race between the United States and Soviet Union. The report on the inauguration of WEM in Baja California brought to the fore regional tensions between capitalinos and those from the north. Because the story mentioned that television signaled economic progress in Baja California, it implied that capital residents were ahead of their northern compatriots when it came to modernity. The third report offered an example of the influence of television news on preserving and creating traditions, such as Día de la Independencia celebrations. Finally, aside from the tele-tradition of covering national holidays, the report that mentioned network executives provided another example of the tele-tradition of network promotion on news programs.

This chapter examines television news coverage of the Space Race, beginning with the launch of *Sputnik* through the U.S. *Apollo 11* lunar landing on July 20, 1969. As with the other case studies in the book, Space Race coverage serves as a window to investigate the process of cultural hegemony on several levels: international influence on the nation and television executives, domestic (the state's) power over national media, and the national media's influence on citizens as viewers. The analysis demonstrates intriguing similarities between Latin American print and Mexican television news coverage of the Space Race and the Cold War. A comparison with print journalists remains salient during this period, because until 1969 newspapers sponsored and influenced content of television news.⁵ In addition, the period signals the standardization of the occupation of television journalist. Until 1969, because television producers acquired much of their editorial content from the capital dailies as well as wire services, photojournalists covering national news functioned as both on-the-scene reporters and photographers, which consequently emphasized the importance of the photojournalist until the beginning of the 1970s. This process of what others call "professionalization" was happening in other parts of the world at around the same time.⁶ Comparing how print and television news producers framed the Space Race sheds light on the relationship between newspaper and broadcast news and on the emergence of the professional TV journalist.

An examination of TV news coverage revealed Mexico's role in the Space Race, nuclear arms race, and the Cold War. Outer space and the powerful images that accompanied the subject through television caused viewers to reconceptualize their connection to the world. Once they actually saw the planet from a distance, it helped people to see themselves as part of a global village for the first time.⁷ Moreover, reports on the arms race emphasized the planet's fragility and the possibility of global annihilation.

Like the TV diplomats López Mateos, Cárdenas, Eisenhower, and Mikoyan, TV producers, as cultural authorities, contributed to the ways in which the Cold War was expressed and as a result strengthened the connections between television and diplomacy. News reports suggested that TV executives walked a fine line as they attempted to appeal to and attract a growing, yet diverse audience. As the medium became more accessible to everyday citizens, programmers had to be concerned about attracting a wider variety of viewers. The "miracle" of economic growth increased the standard of living for thousands of citizens, and they could afford to purchase television sets for the first time. As a result, new members of the middle class and upper middle class parented the first generation of youth raised on television. Many young members of the middle class grew disenfranchised with the shortcomings of the revolution, and they had far different views than another important audience to which television executives catered: domestic and international business interests.

Aside from demonstrating how television producers and writers grappled with changing Mexico City demographics and world politics, news coverage revealed how the country's political leaders wrestled with multiple obligations of appeasing the growing number of discontented youth, as well as the business elite and foreign interests in the United States, Soviet Union, and Cuba. For example, López Mateos may have supported Fidel Castro's revolution and criticized the Bay of Pigs invasion, but by the Cuban Missile Crisis in October 1962, his stance toward the Castro regime had begun to shift.[8] Furthermore, although political leaders may have supported U.S. technological feats in space, they also participated in the Space Race. As the news reports showed, the country's engineers provided assistance for U.S. aerospace projects as well as launched their own hot rockets.[9] Television reports emphasized Mexico's role in the Space Race and its homegrown technological advances. In other words, although the United States certainly imposed its Space Race activities, Mexico and other Latin American nations found ways to limit the powers of their northern neighbor both through accords and airwaves.

The Soviet Union's launch of the satellite, known in the 1950s as a "man-made moon," inaugurated the Space Age for the viewing public. Although *Sputnik* has commonly been described as the spark that ignited the Space Race, the competition between United States and the Soviet Union had been well underway by 1957. Space-related events and activities between 1957 and 1969 composed a large part of television news coverage. Jacobo Zabludovsky, along with Miguel Alemán Velasco, head of Telesistema Mexicano's incipient news division, had a keen interest in the subject. In July 1969 the two traveled to Cape Kennedy to cover the launching of *Apollo 11*, the spacecraft that landed on the moon.[10]

Similar to the launching of a rocket, broadcasting images of Space Race events involved an enormous undertaking. Television broadcasts of these events required planning, *plata* (money), and persistence. Audio recordings of the first artificial satellite were not broadcast until three days after the launch on October 7. Five days after the launch, images still had not appeared on television. Over time television producers used more advanced technology to improve coverage of space-related events.

For anchors and announcers, who previously may have been unfamiliar with astronomical terms and the latest in space technology, preparing for rocket launches required a great deal of work. Prior to the 1969 lunar landing, for example, announcer Jorge Labardini studied for weeks.[11] Alemán Velasco, who had a passion for understanding space technology and who wrote his thesis on the laws of space, was perhaps the most knowledgeable of announcers.[12] His interest in the subject would pay off as Telesistema Mexicano and later Televisa would become global media leaders by using satellite communications to disseminate the network's programs, including news, across the planet.

Network producers created special programs that focused on the Space Race, such as a 1961 "infotainment" program titled *La verdad del espacio* (The truth about space). Hosted by Zabludovsky and Alemán Velasco and directed by Gabino Carrandi Ortiz, the show featured the latest technological developments in the Space Race. After several years, the show's producers changed the program's name to *Telemundo* (TV-world), which ended in 1969, the year of the lunar landing.[13] By 1969 television executives had more than a decade of experience covering the Space Race. The technological feats that allowed the astronauts to communicate with mission control also catapulted television news coverage to new heights.

SPUTNIK, OCTOBER 4, 1957

The first television story about *Sputnik* aired on *Noticiero General Motors* on the same day as the launch and led the newscast: "We begin this newscast with a bulletin coming from Moscow. Radio Moscow announced today that the Soviet Union has launched the first satellite in space around the earth. At the same time, TASS, the official information service, announced tonight that the Soviet Union launched a satellite. It added that this object is revolving around the earth, following an orbit located 893 kilometers above the planet. The news arrived just minutes ago to our editors and at this time we do not have more information."[14] At this early stage in reporting on the first satellite, the name *Sputnik* had not yet become part of the media's or the public's terminology. Early reports refer to the object either as a satellite or an artificial moon. Whether viewers comprehended the meaning of an artificial moon was doubtful. In the United States, shortly after the launch of *Sputnik*, most citizens did not yet understand the term.[15]

How TV producers treated the sources they used in the stories about *Sputnik* helps explain the Telesistema Mexicano news staff's attitudes toward different foreign news agencies. Depending on the news agency and type of story, writers chose to either attribute information to the agency or not. When it came to information from North American and Western European news sources, writers most often chose not to attribute information. Only in the most controversial or significant reports did producers and writers choose to attribute sources directly. For example, after the massacre at the Plaza de las Tres Culturas in 1968, news writers attributed information about the death toll to foreign news sources. Yet that was the exception, and often stories were "ripped" from wire copy, but once writers created the television report, the information was not attributed. News writers, however, did attribute information that came from TASS, the Soviet Information Agency, and Radio Moscow. This was the case with information about *Sputnik*. Certainly, given the political situation in the Soviet Union at the time, there existed a great difference in the level of credibility between UPI and TASS; at the same time attribution or the lack of it remains critical for understanding the relationship between news producers and foreign influence.

A second story aired after the newscast's first commercial break that advertised Pontiac cars distributed by Cornejo Automotive. The report offered a few more details than the first, but neither of the two reports appeared with accompanying images, which did not air until three days later.[16] In addition, the second report provided clues as to how news writers and politicians outside of the Soviet Union would begin to interpret the Space Race: "The latest information on the launch of the Soviet satellite: Observers believe that the secrecy with which they launched [the satellite] was a premeditated move to provoke surprise and a display of propaganda. The Russian satellite is spherical. It contains radio equipment. It measures fifty-eight centimeters in diameter and weighs eighty-three kilos, six hundred grams. It is understood that the Russians are planning to launch various satellites during the year."[17]

The tone of the report treated the launch with a degree of skepticism. Throughout the Cold War, news scripts tended to portray Russian space-related activities in a more negative and critical light. The writer's decision not to attribute this information, in contrast to the previous report, remains significant. The report mentioned that observers contend that the satellite was launched to provoke surprise and as a "show of propaganda," but just who made these observations remained unclear. It is probable, given the tone of the story, that the information came from a U.S. source.

Foreign interests influenced the content produced on television news through wire service reports. News coverage, scripts analyzed, the existing literature, and interviews indicate that it was more common for news writers to use information and images from the AP, UPI, Agence France Presse, UPITN (UPI's television news services), and Visnews (Reuters' news service) than TASS.[18] The critical nature of the previous report makes it improbable that the report came directly from TASS. Furthermore, the failure to attribute in this case was consistent with other reports taken from more frequently used news services, in which writers and producers translated the information without attributing the news source. This reliance on foreign news services demonstrated the important role that these agencies played in deciding what was going to be covered (agenda setting) and how the events would be covered (framed) during the Cold War. One study showed that three times during the Cuban Missile Crisis news-agency reports functioned as the first source of information for Washington on Moscow developments.[19]

The practice of not attributing information to North American and Western European news agencies might be partially explained by the business agreement between Telesistema Mexicano and the news agency. For example, if Telesistema Mexicano subscribed to AP and UPI, Telesistema Mexicano paid for the right to use the information without attribution.

The critical tone of the story resembled reports on Soviet space technology published by news outlets in other parts of Latin America. Newspapers often criticized the Soviet Union for operating in secrecy, while they commended the United States for acting openly. Frequently, editors argued that because the United States let the world know about its actions, the possibility of sharing knowledge beyond U.S. boundaries increased. Hence, if the Soviets acted covertly or did not disclose to the world its activities until after the fact, this diminished the chances of providing the world with new knowledge.[20]

Beyond providing details about U.S.-Mexico–Soviet Union relations, the story alluded to tensions between government officials and media moguls. The tone of the report indicates a pro-American stance on the part of television news writers. That television news relied heavily on information and images from the United States and that companies forged financial agreements with businesspeople to the north would understandably make news managers more inclined to support the United States over the Soviet Union. In contrast, government officials seemed more apt to play both sides of the Cold War fence by catering to the communist bloc countries as well as the United States, as was the case during López Mateos's administration in 1959, when he hosted Dwight D. Eisenhower in February and Anastas Mikoyan in November. The fact that at least two factions had developed within the PRI further complicated matters. On one side were the *alemanistas* (Alemán supporters), who favored national as well as international business, and on the other were the López Mateos supporters and *cardenistas* (Cárdenas supporters), who stood less on the side of big business and more on the side of improving the country's education system and increasing the state's interests in development through the nationalization of industries, such as electric power.[21]

Aside from attribution, something else remained missing from the story on the launch—the name *Sputnik*. Why wasn't the name used in the reports? Evidence suggests that international news agencies such as Associated Press and United Press International had not yet settled on a name for the space object, and therefore it did not appear in the first reports. The delay in the establishment of the name provided another clue into the relationship between international news services and early television news writers—that the writers seemed to be following the lead of the news agencies.

Sputnik topped the news on *Noticiero General Motors* for the next three days. The October 5 newscast included three stories about the artificial moon. The October 6 newscast included three reports about *Sputnik* and another about the United States' plans to launch a satellite. The following day the newscast included five stories about *Sputnik*, along with images and sound transmitted from the satellite.

Noticiero General Motors' second story on the subject on October 5 aired after a commercial for Oldsmobile distributor O'Farrill (the same family that owned a large interest in Telesistema Mexicano). The story focused on the White House's response to the satellite. As the report demonstrated, U.S. officials clearly attempted to downplay the significance of the world's first satellite: "The White House, by way of its spokesman, James Haggerty, [said] that the launching of the Russian satellite from Earth will contribute a lot to scientific knowledge, and he emphasized that the United States [space] program is advancing satisfactorily. Haggerty repeated [several] times that the United States does not consider its satellite program to be in competition with that of the Soviets. He also affirmed to journalists that the small Russian moon was not a strange surprise for the White House staff." This story contrasted a report that aired immediately before, which touted the launching of the satellite as a historic event that reached the front pages of newspapers all over the world, highlighting its global significance.[22]

At the same time, Haggerty's attempts to downplay the event echoed remarks made by other U.S. officials. The day after the launch, U.S. admiral Rawson Bennett, chief of naval operations, called the satellite, a "hunk of iron almost anybody could launch."[23] The article went on to report that the admiral made the statement on an NBC broadcast. Clearly, broadcast and print journalists began "borrowing" information from each other.

WE INTERRUPT THIS NEWSCAST

While the previous story and the lead story on this day focused on global technological feats, other reports in the newscast concentrated on two long-standing popular traditions: bullfighting and religious pilgrimages. The fourth story in the October 5, 1957, newscast focused on a labor dispute between matadors and *novilleros* (apprentice bullfighters): "Last night in the offices of the CROC [Revolutionary Confederation of Workers and Peasants], a group of apprentice bullfighters met to form an association of matadors of young bulls independent of the association of matadors, because the apprentice bullfighters think that the matadors do not pay them any attention and that they do not recognize them, nor do they defend their interests. Nacho Treviño, who a few days ago resigned his membership with the association of matadors, was at the assembly. The new group is headed by Rodolfo Garcia, Alberto Juárez, Ramón Villegas, and Antonio Belmont."[24]

The report on the conflict between novilleros and matadors demonstrated that labor disputes in the 1950s stretched well beyond disgruntled railway workers, and the news called attention to three important points. First, the report illustrated that workers, even within a given profession, are not monolithic. The same could be said about the railway workers who struck for better conditions and pay. In this case, novilleros felt that their demands were not being addressed by more experienced matadors and decided to branch off, taking their professional matters into their own hands. Second, bullfighting remained an important subject for a critical mass of producers and viewers. Third, and perhaps more important, stories on bullfighting gave the newscast entertainment value and emphasized aspects of *mexicanidad*. Foreign news and agencies certainly influenced television news content, but stories on bullfighting revealed that *Noticiero General Motors* remained a truly Mexican product, geared for a Mexican audience.

Another popular cultural event, semireligious pilgrimages, found their way onto the airwaves. Pilgrimages to the Basilica de Guadalupe should be viewed as more than religious events. Frequently, various branches of the government, businesses, and even individuals sponsored pilgrimages. Because they were accepted as national and cultural events, television news journalists were able to report on the processions. Under the provisions of the law that governed television, religious events were not to be covered. Emilio Azcárraga successfully argued in favor of televising images of pilgrims at the basilica on the Día de la Virgen de Guadalupe (Day of the Virgin of Guadalupe; Mexico's patron saint, December 12), because, as he stated, this was a "cultural," not religious affair.[25] This brief report provides an example of how business practices and religious tradition intersected in society and on television: "This morning the traditional pilgrimage of the employees of Celanese Mexicana to the Basilica of Guadalupe took place. Year after year, ever since the company was formed, they have been holding the pilgrimage."[26]

Established in 1944, Celanese Mexicana (CelMex) was one of the country's largest producers of synthetic fibers. Although the *Sputnik* launch led the news on October 5, it did not compose the entire newscast. Reports on national and local events and activities such as bullfighting and pilgrimages showed viewers the familiar and quotidian, along with the new and unfamiliar.

The day that news broke about the *Sputnik* launch, television news writers framed the launch in two important ways: as an example of Soviet technological prowess and as an example of Soviet propaganda. The two distinct frames had the dual effects of both praising and criticizing the Soviet Union.

Two days later, *Noticiero General Motors* gave its most comprehensive coverage of *Sputnik* in one lengthy story (1½ pages on 8½" x 11" paper), followed by two additional reports on the subject. Newscast highlights included an audio recording of the satellite transmission, by scientists from the Universidad Nacional Autónoma de México (UNAM, National Autonomous University of Mexico) and a detailed description of how the satellite worked. Because the news team did not have images from the Soviets, it used images received from U.S. satellite developers, along with the sound of the Soviet satellite. This must have been confusing for viewers who saw images of a U.S. satellite, while the report flipped back and forth, referencing both the Soviet and U.S. artificial moons. The following abbreviated version of the first report gave viewers a chance to hear the reasons behind the Soviet satellite launch:

> The most commented-about news continues to be the satellite launched by the Russians. Moscow today announced that they are conducting preliminary studies to send rockets to the moon. This and the underground explosion of a newly constructed powerful hydrogen bomb, on Sunday in the Arctic Circle, are events

of notable importance. How was the satellite launched? Surely the Russians did it in a way very similar to the one planned by the United States. The most arduous problem that researchers have had to face is not the structure of the satellite, but how to control it. Within an object only fifty centimeters in diameter, there are powerful instruments and radio transmitters to communicate with observers on Earth. To put the satellite in orbit, they are constructing a large rocket with parts or better yet, three rockets in one. Among the three it measures twenty-five meters and can travel more than eight kilometers per second. To follow the small moon on its voyage, so-called minitracking stations have been installed, whose ultrasensitive antennae allow it to be followed despite its great velocity. Aside from the minitracking [station], there will be many other radio and visual observation stations that will concentrate in Washington, but they will come from various parts of the world.[27]

The report revealed that the Soviets launched the satellite as a first step toward a future lunar landing and indicated that the images corresponded to a satellite in the United States still in the development stage.

Although the anchor's copy focused on *Sputnik*, the decision to support a story about a Soviet satellite with U.S. images and technology had the effect of emphasizing U.S. advanced technology. Based on the news report alone, it is unclear why the writers chose to use U.S. images. More than likely, news producers wanted to include some visual support (although not necessarily visual proof), and they used what they had available at the time; in this case it was film of a U.S.-engineered satellite. Whatever the intention, their attempts to make the story visually interesting favored the U.S. position in the Space Race, although the Soviets had obviously won this round.

The report that followed provided viewers with a chance to hear a transmission from the satellite. Like the previous story, this might have been a bit disconcerting for viewers, because while they listened to an audio recording of the satellite transmission, they watched a shot of the turntable on which the recording played and then the director cut to an image of a satellite, presumably the same image that came from the United States. Undoubtedly, producers wanted to give viewers an idea of what a satellite looked like, but the fact that it was not the Soviet satellite might have led to some confusion among viewers who had a difficult time comprehending what a satellite was in the first place. The newscaster read the following words while viewers listened to the audio recording of the satellite transmission: "The radio-receiver station of the Geophysics Institute of the National University captured and recorded the satellite signal and lent it to *Noticiero General Motors*. Engineer Eleazar Erazo tuned in the satellite at 20005 megacycles. They were able to tune in over the Atlantic, just before the satellite flew over American soil and [the signal] was lost as it flew over the Pacific. It [the satellite] is transmitting continually the letters "T. W." The secretary of communications' stations also are tuning in to the satellite."[28]

Between 1957 and 1969 viewers would become more familiar with new technological terms related to outer space, and television helped them acquire this knowledge. At the same time, especially given the magnitude of the event being discussed, the way information was presented might have created more questions than answers.

As was the case with television news, *Sputnik* triggered a wave of coverage among print journalists across Latin America. Although Dwight D. Eisenhower attempted to downplay the competition, newspapers were quick to emphasize the race between the United States and the Soviet Union. Press coverage of the Space Race evolved and became more sophisticated over time. In 1957, for example, editorials tended to focus on the realization that sending a satellite into orbit could result in the destruction of humankind. Shortly after the launch, newspaper journalists in Mexico and Brazil acted as agenda-setters for the rest of Latin America, as they began to see the race as a "balance of terror."[29] Reports among Latin American journalists stressed that if both the United States and Soviet Union were capable of sending a satellite into orbit, they were both capable of annihilating each other through intercontinental ballistic missiles.

MEXICO JOINS THE SPACE RACE

While the United States and the Soviet Union included the main "conquerors" of space, other countries also participated in space exploration. In Latin America, Mexico, Argentina, Brazil, and to a lesser extent, Chile, Peru, and Ecuador began to research and launch rockets between the 1950s and 1960s. By 1968 almost three hundred Latin Americans in Chile, Ecuador, Mexico, and Peru worked at tracking stations that had been set up through joint projects with the United States.[30]

Mexico's entrance into the Space Race served three purposes. First, it helped bolster the country's image as a leader in Latin America. While the United States and the Soviet Union raced to put a man on the moon, Mexico, Brazil, and Argentina competed on a secondary level. Second, Mexico's rocket-building program served as an example to the nation that the country continued to modernize. Third, it helped strengthen diplomatic relations with the United States, as the two countries worked together on several space projects, including Mercury. Consequently, televised reports on the country's participation in the Space Race fomented all these objectives.

As Mexico's secretary of communications and transportation, Walter C. Buchanan helped the nation enter the Space Race. In October 1959 he coordinated the launch of the country's first rocket. Buchanan, who was an engineer as well as the son of an engineer, established a formal area of study in communication and electronics at the Instituto Politécnico Nacional.[31] Later he devoted almost fifteen years of his life developing the nation's public works and communications infrastructure. He served as secretary of the Secretaría de Comunicaciones y Obras Públicas (Ministry of Communications and Public Works) between 1955 and 1958 and of the Secretaría de Comunicaciones y Transporte (Ministry of Communications and Transportation) from 1958 to 1964.[32]

For Buchanan, October 24, 1959, must have been a proud moment. On that day the Secretaría de Comunicaciones y Transporte launched the country's first rocket, SCT-1, in Buchanan's home state of Guanajuato. After more than a year of research, engineers set off the rocket in the northern part of the state in an area known as Charcas. The rocket weighed two hundred kilos and measured four and a half meters long and thirty-five centimeters in diameter. Although "strong winds" prevented the rocket from reaching the attempted altitude of forty kilometers above the earth's surface, it managed to perform according to calculations and predictions.[33]

Three weeks after the event, on November 17, 1959, *Noticiero General Motors* led its newscast with news of the launch.[34] Two stories treated the subject. In the first one, the anchor read without any images; in the second, which focused on Buchanan's participation, there were accompanying images:

> Engineer Walter C. Buchanan, secretary of communications and transportation, reported the information this morning. He showed a film he took the moment of the launch. He added that a new rocket model is already under construction, in which they will try to eliminate defects. Thanks to the technicians and enthusiasm of the railroad administration, who worked without rest, this launch cost less than forty thousand pesos. The rocket was named SCT-1, [and] the operations were directed by engineer Porfirio Becerril. The rocket blasted off from a tower 10 meters tall and after forty seconds of flight reached a velocity of 660 meters per second. Engineer Buchanan has judged this effort as modest research work, to obtain practice in this area.[35]

Reports such as this one provide examples of the country's concern, almost obsession, with technology as a symbol of modernity and progress. The rationale went that if the country was technologically advanced enough to launch a rocket, then it was certainly on its way to creating a more developed and modern society.

This love affair with technology and modernity did not start during the mid-twentieth century, nor was it unique to Mexico. It stemmed from an intellectual tradition led by Auguste Comte that began during the nineteenth century. His philosophy of positivism held that through progress and order a nation could overcome social ills. During the Porfiriato (1876–1911) the so-called *científicos* (scientific ones) applied a strategy of modernization in an effort to improve the country's economy and, therefore, society. Technocrats in the country's government have waxed and waned since.

The 1950s to the 1970s marked the apogee of modernism, some calling it high modernism. It was in this environment that state officials and business leaders sought to solve the nation's problems through modernization, and those efforts included improving mass communications. Obviously, there were limits to the benefits of technological improvements for the country's poor. Often, various development schemes failed because they ignored the very populations they attempted to help.[36]

The information that the government released about its first rocket provided an example of the supremacy of technology. The anchor's comment about the exact height to which the rocket soared as well as its speed attested to the country's scientific progress. Buchanan was also careful to announce the cost of the launch and the research behind it, a mere forty thousand pesos, thanks to the hardworking railway workers.

Informing citizens about the rocket's cost would perhaps quell criticism of the government's decision to spend money on space technology rather than focus on social ills such as hunger and unemployment.[37] That railway workers were included in the story might have been a signal on the part of the government to appease those workers who felt disenfranchised.

PROJECT MERCURY

A year after the country launched its first rocket, engineers had an opportunity to participate in an international space project. On November 18, 1960, as government officials, citizens, and television producers prepared for the fiftieth anniversary of Francisco Madero's call to arms on November 20, 1910, a group of scientists worked to establish a tracking station in Guaymas, Sonora, for the United States' Project Mercury. Initiated in 1958, the project, whose primary goal was to put a man in space, ran until 1963. Through an agreement with the United States, the Mexican government entered the international Space Race by allowing the tracking station to be built on its territory.

The third and fourth reports in the newscast described, with pride, the country's involvement in the Space Race. Accompanied by images taken in Guaymas, the stories were read as follows:

> **Report 3**
> These are pictures of the city of Guaymas, Sonora, taken by our cameraman, Julio Cámara, yesterday. An installation of Project Mercury is located near this port and made possible by the Mexican and United States governments.
>
> **Report 4**
> The Project Mercury station has been set up a little more than sixteen kilometers from Empalme-Guaymas. It is one of eighteen stations established in strategic places around the world. Around June or July of next year, the rocket *Atlas* will be launched from Cape Canaveral. It will carry with it the first human to fly through the stratosphere. The function of the Project Mercury tracking station installed on our territory will be to follow the trajectory of the rocket and transmit information that will be concentrated in this telemetric building, where the center of the

radar station is located. Information from the pilot's capsule will be captured on electronic recorders, as well as information regarding pressure during the space voyage and the pilot's state of well-being, all in less than six minutes from its location at the radar stations to its reception antennae.[38]

The uncritical tone of these two reports suggests that television reporters and producers supported the country's participation in the Space Race. Of course, the television industry stood to gain directly from the development of satellite technology.

While the two reports certainly demonstrated U.S. technological prowess, the writers carefully couched the country's participation in nationalistic terms. The writers made sure viewers heard that involvement was contingent on a bilateral agreement. In addition, the fourth report set Mexico apart as one of less than twenty countries around the world that participated in this space mission. Fully aware of anti-American sentiment and the criticisms of U.S. involvement in Latin America, producers managed to support U.S. technology as well as their country's involvement in an international project, which at the same time helped to bring the nation prestige and strengthen its image as a country that was increasingly more modern.[39]

By framing the Guaymas tracking station in a positive light, producers omitted a critical part of the story. Not all citizens approved of the nation's involvement in the Space Race. Earlier in 1960 fierce challenges to the project surfaced as opponents attempted to derail plans to include Mexico in Project Mercury. For opponents, participation in setting up a tracking installation went against the country's long-standing vow to remain neutral in the face of international conflict. Moreover, opponents of the project expressed concerns that the station would be used for military purposes. Clearly, not all citizens viewed the tracking station as a benefit for the nation. Opposition forced foreign minister Manuel Tello to request clarification and concessions from U.S. ambassador to Mexico Robert C. Hill, who agreed that newspaper journalists would be allowed to view the facilities when they were completed and, in addition, special planes would be available to bring them to the site.[40] The U.S.-Mexico accord was signed by the Mexican government and the National Aeronautics and Space Administration (NASA) on April 12, 1960, in Mexico City. Construction on the US$2.5 million station began shortly after the agreement was signed.[41]

A year after the signing of the agreement and four days before the inauguration of the tracking station, *Noticiero aeronaves* aired this report: "This Monday, the Guaymas tracking station in which Mexico will participate, through the U.S. Project Mercury, to launch a manned rocket around the earth, will be inaugurated. In agreement with the Mexican–North American accord, the station's objective is to observe and maintain communication with the manned vehicle that would be launched into extraterrestrial space. The station forms part of a worldwide network of observation points. Experts and newspaper and television directors have been invited to the inauguration of this station."[42]

Similar to the two previous stories, this report illustrates how writers framed the upcoming inauguration of the tracking station in nationalistic terms by emphasizing the country's role in the project. The report touted U.S. technology (second sentence), but it also reassured viewers that the country's involvement in the project happened because the United States had agreed to Mexico's terms. Pressure to depict the events in this way stemmed from deep-seated sentiments against the United States, harkening back to the country's history of being invaded physically and economically by its neighbors from the north.[43] Moreover, television news producers' tendency to posit the country's involvement in international affairs in nationalistic terms began before the country's participation in the Space Race.[44]

The propensity to frame events within a national perspective did not apply only to Mexican television news between 1950 and 1970.

The same phenomenon occurs today in Mexico and throughout the world, including in the United States, where the news media (print, broadcast, and online) tend to portray events perhaps even more myopically than in other parts of the world.[45] This tendency among reporters across the globe to explain international events through a national lens reflects the power of the idea of the nation among citizens of various countries and how they find it useful for understanding events and issues.

JUNE 26, 1961

The day of the tracking station's inauguration, *Noticiero aeronaves* aired the following lead report: "Today in Guaymas, Sonora, the tracking station constructed by the U.S. government was inaugurated, as part of Project Mercury, and based on a scientific accord of cooperation between the two countries. The highest official from the Secretaría de Relaciones Exteriores (Ministry of Foreign Relations), Mr. Carlos Dario Ojeda, representing the Mexican government, unveiled a plaque that commemorated the event. The official indicated that Mexico has cooperated and will cooperate with the United States on this project, because it does not have any other end than to serve the human species, without any warlike intention."[46] This story provides another example of news writers' attempts to cater to multiple audiences. On the one hand, the story highlighted Mexican and U.S. involvement. This served to appeal to political and business interests. On the other hand, the report addressed opponents' concerns by stating that officials announced that Project Mercury had no "warlike" objectives.

The day after the inauguration of the tracking station, *Noticiero aeronaves* aired a report about the station. It was the third item to air in the newscast. The program led with an update on national and international affairs, including a conflict between a U.S. union and Mexican workers, who, according to the report, crossed the border on a daily basis to seek employment in the United States. U.S. workers argued that their counterparts south of the border forced them out of their jobs.[47] The report on migrant workers shown in conjunction with a story on the tracking station demonstrated to viewers the complex relationship between the countries. Historically, relations with the United States have been marked by both conflict and cooperation, and the two reports—one on migrant workers and the other on the tracking station—provide another example of the complexity of Mexico-U.S. affairs.[48] State and national leaders were present at the inauguration to show that this was as much a Mexican as well as U.S. affair. An anchor read the following report:

> In Guaymas, Sonora, the Project Mercury station was inaugurated. It is one of eighteen across the world that will serve to track U.S. astronauts when they are in orbit. This station was constructed with the cooperation of the Mexican government, and knowledge that will be gained will be placed at the disposal of scientists around the world. The deputy secretary of foreign relations, Carlos Dario Ojeda, inaugurated the tracking station, [along with] the governor of Sonora; U.S. officials; engineers Jorge Suárez Díaz, Eugenio Mendez Docurro, and Ricardo Monges López; and other men of science. It is said that Aland [sic] Shepard, the leading U.S. astronaut, will be one of the directors of the station installed in Guaymas. The electronic brains of this station will register almost all the physical and emotional responses of the astronaut in orbit.[49]

Again, this report illuminated television journalists' tendency to frame international events by emphasizing the nation's participation in the project.

RISING TENSIONS AMONG MEXICO, CUBA, AND THE UNITED STATES

The timing of the inauguration, June 27, 1961, must be considered when analyzing the tone of coverage on Project Mercury. The failed U.S.-backed invasion of Cuba's Bay of Pigs, which occurred just two months before the inauguration of the tracking station, helps to explain how journalists covered Project Mercury. U.S. involvement in the Cuban invasion clearly provided viewers and politicians with an example of U.S. imperialistic endeavors. Although Kennedy seemed to garner support among Mexicans like no other previous U.S. president, his decisions regarding Cuba's leader Fidel Castro served to curb his popularity. Large protests in cities throughout the country, including Mexico City, Guadalajara, and Morelia, indicated the level of anger over the invasion.[50]

Two months after the Bay of Pigs invasion, television news writers found themselves in a precarious position: on the one hand, favorable coverage of the United States could help maintain strong business ties with U.S. advertisers; on the other, negative coverage of the invasion could strengthen support from viewers, a growing number of them younger and more inclined to be supportive of Castro and the Cuban Revolution. A critical view of the invasion could also put a strain on Telesistema Mexicano's relations with U.S. and Mexican business interests.[51]

Television news coverage of the Bay of Pigs invasion revealed the diverse interests news directors attempted to attract. *Noticiero aeronaves* led its newscast with a report about Fidel Castro based on information from UPI. The report focused on Castro's claims that he, along with assistance from Soviet tanks and airplanes, managed to thwart the attack.[52] The newscaster then read a report about a protest in front of the United Nations building in New York against U.S. involvement in the invasion. The same day Mexico City students from the Instituto Politécnico Nacional staged a protest against the invasion in Cuba. A logical placement for a report on the Mexico City protest would have been immediately after the New York protest, but the producer put it in tenth place, following a story about a new road between Apizaco and Tlaxco and before a report about U.S. crooner Frank Sinatra. The report on the Mexico City protest read as follows: "This morning another student demonstration from the Instituto Politécnico Nacional, of youth [going] through the streets of Mexico City. The protestors arrived at the zócalo and expressed their support for Castro. In an attempt to prevent all acts of violence, the Mexican police are guarding the U.S. Embassy. The demonstration was orderly and at no time did it result in unfortunate incidents."[53]

The content and placement of this report served to appeal to the diverse audiences of television news. To ignore the student demonstration completely would have most likely caused young viewers to criticize news producers and perhaps caused a protest against Telesistema Mexicano. The third line in the report functioned as a subtle warning to students of a police presence. As students were well aware, police and government troops used violence to repress social movements. The most immediate example was the force that the government used against railway workers in 1958 and 1959. The fourth sentence of the report also served to placate foreign business and political interests that might have been concerned about anti-American sentiments.[54] Furthermore, by burying the report in the newscast, producers sent a message about the relative importance of the demonstration. Producers distanced the Mexico City student protests from those in New York and sent a message to viewers that it was less significant than protests north of the border.

THIRTEEN DAYS IN OCTOBER 1962

The Cuban Missile Crisis brought the world to the brink of nuclear war and, through televised news reports, provided to a global audience a real and frightening example of the dark side of space technology. In addition, the conflict brought relations between Mexico, Cuba, the United States, and Soviet Union to their most precarious moment in the twentieth century. Moreover, the crisis became a turning point in the country's official stance on Cuba and the Castro regime. As *Noticiero novedades-aceptaciones* reported on October 22, López Mateos remarked while in the Philippines that Mexico would change its attitude toward Cuba if the Antillean country armed itself with offensive missiles.⁵⁵ It should not come as a surprise that non–nuclear-proliferating countries employed the discourse of peace in reference to achievements in space. They did not have much choice.

Noticiero novedades-aceptaciones, which aired on Channel 4, covered the "crisis en el Caribe" (crisis in the Caribbean) extensively on television, as it did another important story, Adolfo López Mateos's trip to Asia. The president embarked on the longest trip of his administration and in the country's history; a tour of India, Indonesia, the Philippines, and Japan between October 3 and 24, 1962.⁵⁶ Because López Mateos was out of the country, he literally distanced himself from the conflict between Cuba, the United States, and the Soviet Union. His coincidental absence from Mexico, which warrants further study, had three results. First, it reduced the possibility of putting the president in a position of having to take a political stand with respect to the crisis as it was unfolding. In short, this allowed him to hold at bay criticism from leftists. Second, his absence reduced the risk of straining his country's relations with the United States, as well as held intact relations with Cuba and the Soviet Union. Third, López Mateos's presence in Asia reduced the United States' obligation to negotiate in the public sphere, such as on television, with another Latin American nation in the midst of the crisis.

President John F. Kennedy imposed a naval blockade against all ships bound for Cuba on October 22, 1962. That night, he appeared on national television alerting citizens of his decision and the reasons for the blockade. The same night, while López Mateos dined with Philippine President Diosdado Macapagal, citizens in Mexico also heard about the blockade.⁵⁷ In television terms *Noticiero novedades-aceptaciones* reports on the subject were quite extensive (two-and-a-half pages devoted to Kennedy's decision to impose the blockade), which provides evidence of the gravity that producers placed on the situation. That the newscast led with reports on the naval blockage before turning to President Adolfo

López Mateos's trip to Asia served to underscore the significance. Channel 4's Pedro Ferriz told viewers:

> This afternoon President Kennedy imposed a naval blockade against Cuba, in view of the Soviet Union's having provided to a military base on the Caribbean island long-range missiles and other arms capable of destroying the very heart of the United States. With the goal of preventing Cuba from continuing to arm itself, President Kennedy ordered the implementation of a seven-point plan, which includes a strict quarantine (notice that President Kennedy eluded using the word blockade), against all military ships with a destination to Cuba, which could be carrying weapons that could be used for an attack. In addition, Kennedy said that he had taken other "initial" steps. Those that are known: continued and heightened vigilance over Cuba and an increase in [U.S.] military forces, with orders that the armed forces "prepare for all eventualities"; a U.S. political declaration that it will consider any nuclear bomb launched from Cuba against any nation in the Western Hemisphere as "an attack by the Soviet Union on the United States, and it will be met with true reprisals against the Soviet Union"; [and] an increase in military forces at the U.S. naval base at Guantánamo and the evacuation of the relatives of military personnel there. Also, the United States has ordered the Strategic Air Command and other military forces to be on heightened alert throughout the world, the state of alert of nuclear bombers and missiles of strategic command, including those in Berlin and West Germany. It is a precautionary measure in the case that the Russians take a countermeasure. At this point, there has not been any known direct response from the Soviet Union or from Cuba related to President Kennedy's forceful speech.[58]

The first two sentences of the report set the tone for the story. Writers portray the Soviet Union as aggressors, because they provided long-range missiles to a Cuban military base. The United

States, as this story implied, was merely taking logical defensive steps. Writers may not have supported President Kennedy actions wholeheartedly, as the second line of the report indicates. The parenthetical phrase on line two was part of the original script. The line suggested a subtle critique of President Kennedy's actions, or least of his failure to respond directly to questions regarding the blockade.

The stories regarding López Mateos's trip in the Philippines shed light on Mexico's reaction to Kennedy's imposition of the blockade:

> Today at a press conference in Manila, the capital of the Philippines, the president of Mexico, Licenciado Adolfo López Mateos, declared before leaving by plane to return to our nation, that Mexico will change its attitude toward Cuba, as the Antillean country arms itself with offensive missiles. The Mexican leader, who ends his goodwill trip to four Asian countries, said that Mexico had been informed that President Kennedy asked that UN Security Council and the OAS council discuss the "new aspects" of the Cuban situation. Within a moment I will return with more news; in the meantime we invite you to listen to this message from our sponsor, the company General de Aceptaciones, Sociedad Anónima.[59]

As noted in the first sentence of the report, López Mateos made it clear that the country's stance toward Cuba, which had either been relatively neutral or supportive since Fidel Castro's takeover of the island nation in January of 1959, was about to shift. With Cuba accepting nuclear weapons from the Soviets, the ante had been raised.

Manuel Tello, secretary of foreign relations, traveled with the president on his lengthy trip through Asia. In his memoirs, Tello describes the night that the U.S. ambassador in the Philippines (whom he does not mention by name) urged Tello to wake up President López Mateos so that he could deliver an important message from President Kennedy. According to Tello, he had no way of contacting the president in the middle of the night, so the news of the Cuban Missile Crisis had to wait until the following morning. The U.S. ambassador would not tell Tello what the message was about, only that it was of utmost importance. Although he was not sure of the contents, when Tello went to bed that night, he had a pretty good idea that the urgent matter had to do with so-called rumors of a Soviet buildup of a nuclear arsenal in Cuba.[60]

López Mateos returned to Mexico on October 24 from his Asian extravaganza, as some of the most critical moments of the crisis were about to unfold. Yet he had already missed the first eight days of the "thirteen days." The Russians had yet to begin withdrawing their missiles from Cuba and a U.S. reconnaissance plane would be shot down three days later.[61] As he had throughout his administration, López Mateos attempted to portray his country as a champion of peace. In his final speech in Manila before returning home, López Mateos distinguished his country from other parts of the world, by stating that Mexicans were conscious of the nuclear age and that "we are fighting for peaceful coexistence among nations, in which human rights will be protected."[62] Despite his remarks in favor of a peaceful resolution to the conflict, López Mateos's physical absence enabled him to keep a political distance from the serious events that transpired. He was literally out of the picture. The result: Mexico did not have to take an immediate stand on the issue in the midst of negotiations between the United States and the Soviet Union, and the United States avoided having to deal with another Latin American nation during the crisis. Although he remained out of the country during most of the thirteen-day crisis, López Mateos managed to receive criticism. In his memoirs, Tello mentions that the country's "leftist press," as much as the U.S. press, criticized López Mateos's actions, a reminder of the political tightrope that the country's leaders walked during the Cuban Missile Crisis and the Cold War.[63]

EL ALUNIZAJE, JULY 1969

While the Cuban Missile Crisis served as an example of one of the most polarizing events of the twentieth century, the lunar landing provided an opportunity for the world to unite. Perhaps, like no other event in history, the *alunizaje* (lunar landing) on July 20, 1969, represented a chance for the world to participate in something greater than itself. A director and editor for Telesistema Mexicano, Gabino Carrandi Ortiz, wrote about the significance of the landing in a letter to his two-year-old son, Mauricio, from the gate of the spacecraft center in Houston: "These lines carry with them all of my hope. My hope for you is a good world, a better world. If my life has been good and full of happiness, may yours also have everything. Today, in my time, a man has landed on the moon. Today, in your time, what is the level of your amazement? God bless you, your father."[64]

The year 1969 represented a landmark year in the history of television news.[65] This was the first time television transmitted simultaneously around the world images of a man on the moon, as Miguel Alemán Velasco put it, "live" and "direct."[66] Beyond that, in July, Telesistema Mexicano created a separate news division within the company, headed by Alemán Velasco, son of former president Miguel Alemán Valdés. The *Apollo 11* mission gave the company a chance to test its new organizational apparatus.

Aléman Velasco recalled that at the urging of President Gustavo Díaz Ordaz, Emilio Azcárraga Milmo decided to create a corporate news division. He asserted that television news coverage of the massacre of at least three hundred students at the Plaza de las Tres Culturas on October 2, 1968, prompted the president to crack down on the news media, including television.[67] According to Aléman Velasco, newspapers influenced greatly the content of television news in 1968, but that would soon change. The creation of the news division brought all news production under two individuals, Alemán Velasco and Azcárraga Milmo. Almost forty years later, Alemán

Velasco would remark that in establishing the news division, its creators sought to eliminate news coverage that favored one political party over another and that was more "fair and balanced than in the past."[68] The network itself also stood to gain a great deal by severing ties with the capital dailies. As the head of the news division, Alemán Velasco had the authority to decide who covered what, and as such he designated himself and Zabludovsky as special correspondents to cover the lunar landing (see figure 5).

In Latin America, press coverage of the lunar landing tended to portray the event as a conquest. In Rio de Janeiro's *Jornal do Brasil*, the newspaper reported, "the privilege of witnessing man's most audacious adventure . . . is enough to justify the efforts of a whole generation. . . . Man's first moon landing is a conquest by all mankind."[69]

Television news coverage resembled newspaper coverage in two ways. First, reports often portrayed the mission to the moon as a human conquest of uncharted territory. Thirty-five years after the event, Alemán Velasco referred to the event as if he were "watching Christopher Columbus arriving on another continent."[70] Second, televised reports, like newspaper coverage, of the Space Race, attempted to portray the U.S.-controlled missions in universal terms.

Su diario Nescafé extensively covered the *Apollo 11* mission. Although the corporate news division had already been created, during this time, Zabludovsky still anchored *Su diario Nescafé*. The transition to *24 horas*, the news division's first program, occurred in September 1970. In his July 9, 1969, newscast Zabludovsky mentioned that he would be leaving for Cape Kennedy along with Alemán Velasco. The next day, *Noticiero Nescafé* aired a report on *Apollo 13*, the successor to *Apollo 11*. *Noticiero Nescafé* reported that the Space Race would not end with the first man on the moon.[71] Writers acknowledged that the alunizaje represented an important benchmark in the race, but by no means signaled the end of the technological competition between the United States and Soviet Union.

5. Miguel Alemán Velasco in front of a rocket at Cape Canaveral, Florida, 1969. Courtesy of Miguel Alemán Velasco, personal collection.

Three days before the lunar landing, *Noticiero Nescafé* aired a report on the *Apollo 11* mission. The following includes a portion of the lead story, which took up two-and-a-half pages of the newscast script:

> Keeping these stations supplied requires an enormous effort. The North American air force uses its airplanes, personnel, and materials, and [has also] contracted private companies for the project. There are thousands of men working on this operation and one of the most important functions is maintaining the supply chain so that they function in accordance with the program outlined. Part of the perimeter's work is to maintain itself at high efficiency, and the staff is constantly simulating emergencies to ensure that the machines are in perfect condition. This is the laboratory where optical equipment is tested with great technical precision to track rockets and vehicles in space orbit, which is so important in the space conquest.[72]

The report demonstrated television news producers' preoccupation with new technology. The story describes with detail, probably not comprehensible to the average viewer, the different aspects of the project. The language used employed highly technological terms likely unfamiliar to most citizens. This would be consistent with the level of understanding of viewers in the United States when *Sputnik* was launched. Television, along with other media, helped to educate the public about new space technology, although it perhaps did not always excel in this area. Simply describing the technology, without giving explanations in lay terms, must often have left viewers more confused than informed.

The following excerpt from the same story provides additional evidence of producers' propensity to focus on technology. In this excerpt of the story, the report describes a piece of equipment, whose name is not given, which measures roundness: "How round is round? At a simple glance a ball appears as round as any other. This space apparatus for measuring roundness shows that it [roundness] has many variations. Every year the laboratory performs fifteen thousand tests of this kind. Optical equipment and electromechanical devices measure the surface of something that looks smooth. The machine finds that there are huge dips. It can register up to five millionths of an inch on a level surface." The same report went on to explain how meteorological tools helped in rocket launches and concluded by stating rather simplistically, "that is how a man is placed on the moon."[73]

Neil Armstrong and Edwin (Buzz) Aldrin landed on the moon on July 20, 1969. As one of the commentators who described the landing live for the nation's viewers, Alemán Velasco remembers the day well because, "We all saw it at the same time, in all parts of the world, which was very exciting to me."[74] The day after the landing, viewers woke up to the report, "Man Has Arrived on the Moon," which led *Noticiero Nescafé*'s newscast:

> The astronauts Neil Armstrong and Edwin Aldrin worked for two hours and twelve minutes on our satellite. Telesistema Mexicano carried a complete image of this feat. Licenciados Miguel Alemán Velasco and Jacobo Zabludovsky were on hand with their commentaries. The emotion and the culminating moments were reflected in their transmission. After staking down the North American flag on the ground of the moon, they were able to communicate with their president, Richard M. Nixon. Neil's first words were, "here's one small step for man, and one giant leap for mankind." Armstrong set foot on the moon at 20:56 hours and twenty minutes later Aldrin did, and his first words were, "Beautiful, beautiful, beautiful! A magnificent desolation." The words of Nixon with the astronauts were, "This must be the most historic telephone call of all time." "I can't express how proud I am. Thanks to what you have done, the heavens are now part of the world of man. Talking with you from the sea of tranquility inspires us to redouble our efforts to bring peace and tranquility to man." After completing with utmost success

6. Mission Control after *Apollo 11* splashdown on Earth, July 24, 1969. Courtesy of NASA.

7. Buzz Aldrin's boot on the surface of the moon, July 20, 1969. Courtesy of NASA.

man's first exploration of the moon's surface, astronauts Neil Armstrong and Edwin Aldrin are resting in the lunar module *Eagle*, waiting for the moment when they will go back into orbit on the spacecraft and initiate Mission *Apollo 11*'s difficult trip of returning to Earth.[75]

The report framed the lunar landing as yet another example of U.S. technological prowess. Other elements of the story reflected the news writer's choice to emphasize Mexico's and Telesistema Mexicano's contributions to bringing the event to viewers. In addition, mentioning Alemán Velasco and Zabludovsky by name strengthened their credibility with viewers. The writer's decision to include President Nixon's quote about the use of technology for peace resembled other space-related stories in print and broadcast of the time, which emphasize the peaceful ends for space advances. Finally, similar to reports on Mexico's involvement with Project Mercury, this lunar landing report highlighted a North American event, at the same time as it emphasized Mexico's participation in it.

LEAPS FORWARD AND STEPS BACK

Reports about the lunar landing underscored a disconnection between human potential and daily realities. Citizens may have watched Armstrong take a giant leap for humankind, but many of those viewers could still not afford an automobile. While the astronauts dined on freeze-dried products manufactured by Nestlé, a large group of citizens continued to be malnourished. All the technology in the world could not seem to conquer the social ills that remained. Watching men walk on the moon must have caused at least some viewers at home and abroad to question the justification for such a mission, when so many of people around the world still suffered from malnourishment and preventable diseases.[76]

By 1969 an estimated 4.5 million television sets throughout the country were capable of tuning into the lunar landing. About half of those viewers lived in Mexico City. Space technology influenced television and daily lives. Between the *Sputnik* launch and the lunar landing, citizens began to adopt and adapt to space terminology and concepts. In 1957 many viewers may not have ever heard the term "satellite," but soon after, shop owners began to name their stores after the new technology, such as a Mexico City's, Tienda Satélite and Satélite Suburb.[77] Over time, viewers interpreted a combination of reports on international and domestic events in a variety of ways. Continued coverage of the Space Race allowed individuals to see the world in a much more global way.

Television reports about the Cold War, Space Race, and nuclear arms race provided evidence to viewers of the country's precarious position. On the one hand, reports showed them the importance of maintaining good diplomatic relations with the United States, and on the other they reaffirmed the country's own revolutionary rhetoric. Coverage of the U.S.-backed Bay of Pigs invasion exposed viewers to heightened tensions between Mexico and the United States, as a growing number of students marched in the streets protesting the invasion. Their messages clearly contrasted with those on the airwaves. By the time the Cuban Missile Crisis unfolded, viewers watched their president's stance toward Cuba's revolution and its revolutionary leader become more critical.

As the Cold War and Space Race ensued on the airwaves, television news writers attempted to appeal to diverse audiences. Stories on the Bay of Pigs invasion demonstrated that news executives could not ignore student protests, but writers chose to emphasize protests abroad rather than those that transpired in Mexico City. Nevertheless, students managed to get their messages across in the streets, and the seeds that would inspire the creation of even more critical messages (hybrid frames) to emerge in 1968 had been sown. The editorial decisions resulted in placating local and international business and political interests without completely alienating a growing number of young viewers.

Between 1957 and 1969 television news often focused on international and mainly U.S. technological advances and events, but news coverage of those events was often portrayed through a national lens. Reports on Project Mercury and a tracking station in Guaymas, Sonora, for example, drew attention to the country's modernity and progress. The reports also set up boundaries regarding U.S. cultural and political influence in the region. Certainly, the United States led the way in terms of technological and economic progress, but Mexico, too, had reached a significant level of modernity by producing its own rockets. The tendency to highlight the country's involvement in U.S.-led Space Race activities such as Project Mercury showed that news producers couched foreign influence in ways that strengthened Mexican nationalism. By portraying international events through a national lens, news producers, as cultural authorities, helped to establish the limits of cultural hegemony.

In addition to covering international events, reporters focused on important domestic events, such as bullfighting and religious pilgrimages. These domestic stories, along with other popular forms of expression, reaffirmed what it meant to be Mexican. In other words, the representation of new technology and traditions shaped self-perceptions, as people began to see themselves as citizens of both the world and the nation. Through informative programming, such as television news, as well through entertainment programming, such as *telenovelas* (soap operas), a sense of nationhood took root.

CHAPTER 6

Olympic Dreams and Tlatelolco Nightmares

ON OCTOBER 12, 1968, Mexico became the first country to broadcast the Olympic Games live and in color. It was an opportunity for government officials and television executives to beam the country's modern and economically successful face into the homes of viewers across the globe. Three years before the games, President Gustavo Díaz Ordaz remarked proudly that "all the eyes of the world would be on Mexico in 1968 and that he hoped Mexicans would respond to their responsibilities in providing a warm and dignified reception for all visitors."[1] But the night before Díaz Ordaz was to register the national Olympic team and ten days before the inaugural ceremony of the games, the government's and television executives' dreams of portraying the country as modern, orderly, and, above all, peaceful, turned nightmarish when the city's riot squad known as *granaderos* and the military moved into the Plaza de las Tres Culturas, also known as the Plaza de Tlatelolco.[2] Gunfire erupted in the plaza around six at night, and several hours later hundreds of students and neighbors had been slain and thousands had been rounded up and detained at Campo Militar Número Uno (Military Camp Number One).[3]

Throughout the summer, Mexico City residents had read about and watched on television the events surrounding student unrest.[4] By September 18 the military had taken over the UNAM, but that seemed only to strengthen the movement and generate support from popular groups outside of the university.[5] Along with Mexico City media, international media converged on the university campus weeks before the Olympics, and on the night of October 2 staff from fourteen news agencies, including twenty foreign correspondents, arrived at the Plaza de las Tres Culturas.[6] Members of domestic and international news media covered the massacre and the Olympics, and the events leading up to both. As this chapter demonstrates, some events received more news coverage than others.

This chapter examines television news coverage of the Tlatelolco massacre and the nineteenth Olympiad aired on Telesistema Mexicano in October 1968.[7] News reports about student movements and the Olympics demonstrate that media executives and government officials pursued a similar goal—to construct positive images of a modern country for viewers at home and abroad.[8] Furthermore, televised news reports reveal that news executives, in their attempt to create positive images of the nation, often sidelined journalistic goals of providing accurate and balanced information. This tendency would resurface again in 1970, when the country hosted the World Cup.

While the country's top-ranking politicians and television executives sought to portray the nation as modern, orderly, and peaceful, citizen viewers often formulated their own distinct interpretations of events. Members of the Consejo Nacional de Huelga (National Strike Committee) and other popular groups, such as intellectuals who supported the students, aired their own countervailing messages—which in this work are referred to as "hybrid frames." While alternative forms of communication, such as street theater and leaflets, could not compete with the power of Telesistema Mexicano, they indicated an unofficial pattern of discourse and showed that the network's writers and producers had a different vision for the country's future than many of their viewers. Hence, viewers, some of whom were young people participating in the student movements of the 1960s and 1970s, generated and disseminated their own ideas about what constituted a just and modern nation.

Television news producers framed events in particular ways, but viewers may have reframed the same events differently, in ways that they deemed just, useful, and meaningful. The concept of hybridity of framing helps explain how news producers may have attempted to downplay student movements, but young people often interpreted the same issues or events in different ways, in ways that in some cases fostered domestic and international solidarity.[9]

TELEVISION AND SOCIETY IN 1968

By 1968 television was on the path to becoming one of the nation's most important forms of mass media. Between 1950 and 1970 the number of television sets throughout the country skyrocketed from a mere hundred receivers to 4.5 million.[10] By the end of the 1960s television stations had been established in twenty-nine of the country's thirty-one states. In the late 1960s news encompassed a large portion of television programming, and by the end of the decade annual news programming produced by commercial and government-owned stations throughout the country totaled approximately 2,847 hours.[11] On a daily basis, regarding events large and small, 1960s television producers generated reports that by and large supported and reinforced the party line. The government's domestic spying program, in full-swing at this time, certainly prevented many journalists from overtly criticizing the PRI and government officials.[12]

Juxtaposing media coverage of students activists and athletes, several audiovisual themes that reflect Cold War politics emerge, including (1) the repression of students as part of a local effort to contain alternative political perspectives, including communism, (2) the United States' effort to contain communism throughout the region, (3) attempts to exclude student voices from the national discourse, (4) the exaltation of athletes, deemed as champions and examples of a successful revolution, and (5) the effort to posit the country as an international peacekeeper, despite the contradiction that its domestic policies promoted the use of violence. One of the stark contradictions and ironies includes the fact that between March 1965 and February 1967 leaders from across Latin America on four occasions convened in the Tlatelolco neighborhood in preparation for the creation of the first nuclear arms free zone in a heavily populated region of the world. The accord became known as the Treaty of Tlatelolco and was signed in Mexico City on April 1, 1968, six months before the massacre in the same neighborhood. Through all this, television news producers played a role in the construction of Cold War meanings and, as a result, functioned as cultural diplomats.[13]

The connection between the 1968 Olympics and the student movement remains an interesting, yet somewhat neglected, area of historical inquiry.[14] By looking at the relationship between student unrest and the Olympics through news coverage, this chapter describes the role of the media at this point of crisis and enriches understanding of Mexican media and society in this period. Mexico's student movements of 1968 were distinct from many other social and political movements throughout the world. Certainly, the historical factors that inspired and led to social unrest were different than movements in the United States, Brazil, France, and Czechoslovakia. However, television and other mass media functioned to connect the movements in no small way.[15]

Finally, this chapter helps to further debate regarding modernity and nationalism by demonstrating how television newscasts both reflected and shaped efforts to construct a modern country. News items that focused on modernity, such as the nation's role as the first country in Latin America to host the Olympic Games, offered evidence of the nation's level of development. Moreover, the country's "economic miracle" enabled television to emerge as one of the most significant forms of mass communication in the twentieth century.[16]

STUDENT MOVEMENTS AND ATHLETES ON THE MOVE

Competing visions for the country's future collided violently in the autumn of 1968. Ten years after his arrest, dissident railway worker Demetrio Vallejo was still in prison. His incarceration inspired thousands of students and workers, who rallied in the streets of Mexico City. Outside of the country, Cuban revolutionary leaders Fidel Castro and Ernesto "Che" Guevara motivated Mexican youth.[17] As students organized, television executives and members of the Mexican Organizing Committee, the national group responsible for the promotion and coordination of the nineteenth Olympiad, worked feverishly to put the country's best face forward, as well as dispel numerous concerns that the country was not ready for an event of such magnitude.

One source of trepidation was Mexico City's altitude (seven thousand feet), which many thought might have deleterious effects on athletes. The concern did not emerge "out of thin air." During the Pan-American Games of 1955 held in the capital city, several athletes collapsed and at least one competitor was rendered unconscious while competing in track and field events.[18] Furthermore, the amount of money the government poured into housing and other Olympic projects drew fire from economically struggling residents in the capital.[19] It is estimated that the government spent US$176 million on the Olympics, which represented another cause for protest among students.[20] Students questioned why so much money was being used to beautify the city, while a large percentage of the country's citizens struggled in extreme poverty and lived in substandard housing. According to one estimate, in 1970 half of the city's residents lived in squatter settlements.[21]

After the military occupied UNAM on September 18, students moved their operations to the neighborhood of Nonoalco-Tlatelolco, and Olympic organizers and television executives worked to make sure the first live worldwide transmission of the games would go off without a hitch. The relocation of student activists to Tlatelolco must have annoyed city planners, who had hoped that the Plaza de las Tres Culturas would function as a prime tourist destination for foreigners attending the games. Indeed, planners called on anthropologists "to furnish authentic background material for the French and Netherlands teams."[22]

On the eve of the games, a generation of young middle-class citizens who had been raised on television waited for the events to begin. Their beliefs, attitudes, and values were partly formed and informed by the programs they watched while sitting in front of television sets showing black and white images. Viewing experiences included everything from telenovelas, bullfights, and newscasts to foreign entertainment programs such as *The Addams Family* (*Los locos Adams*). With respect to news programming, young viewers had come to recognize, though not necessarily trust, Jacobo Zabludovsky as the country's best-known news anchor. Some of these young viewers were the same middle-class students involved in the National Strike Council.

COVERAGE OF THE TLATELOLCO MASSACRE

For the thousands of students who prepared for the late afternoon rally at the Plaza de las Tres Culturas, the threat of violence loomed, but most seemed to be caught off guard by the government's sudden use of force.[23] Intense gunfire erupted, lasting at least an hour and a half.[24] Although they did not appear on television, bodies lay in the esplanade of the square. In Bert Quint's report, hundreds of young residents frantically ran in an effort to seek shelter, as the sound of rapid fire from automatic weapons rang throughout the plaza.[25] The exact number of people killed in the massacre has not yet been determined, but forensic anthropologists who continue to attempt to identify the remains of victims found near the massacre site claim it is "highly probable" that close to five hundred people died in the conflict.[26] Thousands were injured—including Italian journalist Oriana Fallaci—and police detained another two thousand in Campo Militar Número Uno.[27]

The possibility of violence erupting at the Tlatelolco rally that night was no secret to government officials from the United States. The day before the rally, in a confidential memorandum, U.S. Embassy official Covey T. Oliver wrote to the assistant secretary of state for Latin America and noted his concern:

> Though the GOM [Government of Mexico] is acting as if it is confident a compromise is imminent, we remain skeptical. The National Strike Committee is again installed in the University, reiterating its demands and insisting the student strike will continue. The student demands are unmet, tempers continue high, and any violent incident, even if accidental, could easily provoke a new round of disturbances. A mass meeting scheduled for tomorrow, October 2, should provide an opportunity to gauge the amount of support remaining for the students' cause.[28]

Although coverage of the massacre may have gone against the financial interests of Telesistema and the government's political interests, by the time the evening news aired, network executives understood that the events were too significant to ignore. On October 2, 1968, at least three news programs aired on television throughout the city, but only one of the three newscasts on October 2 mentioned the rally or subsequent events at the plaza. News anchors Jacobo Zabludovsky and Pedro Ferríz de Santa Cruz hosted *Su diario Nescafé* from 7:30 to 8:00 in the morning. At 7:15 in the evening, XEW-TV, Channel 2, aired a fifteen-minute news bulletin, which Zabludovsky also hosted. At 11:30 in the evening Guillermo Vela and Jorge Saldaña hosted *Noticiero novedades*, a half-hour program on XHTV, Channel 4. In the late 1960s the length of news broadcasts expanded from fifteen to thirty minutes. This allowed for more breaks to be included within each newscast, increasing the opportunity for more commercials. Similarly, the U.S. model of network news increased from fifteen to thirty minutes in the mid- to late 1960s.

The first newscast of the day, *Su diario Nescafé*, made no mention of the scheduled rally at the Plaza de las Tres Culturas that evening, but a look at the day's rundown, which included reports on several other demonstrations, illustrates the turmoil that engulfed much of the capital. During this period, producers often wrote the estimated time of each story to the right of story titles. Rundowns function as a written backbone of a newscast. They allow all members of a news team to quickly become familiar with the reports of the newscast, such as the order, type, content, and estimated time in seconds. Here is the rundown for the October 2 newscast on *Su diario Nescafé*:

1. Women stage protest at Chamber of Deputies (:15)
2. Jalisco Deputy González resigns from the National Action Party (:15)
3. National University and Polytechnic students rally (:15)
4. Reconstructed pavilions open at tuberculosis hospital (:15)
5. Red Cross hosts cocktail party for Prince Rainier of Monaco (:15)
6. Painter Regina Raúl inaugurates exposition (:15)
7. Artist José Luis Cuevas inaugurates exposition (2:00)
8. Greek artist María Nolohoyu arrives with Olympic Torch
9. Olympic Torch leaving Greece on August 24
10. Noticiero Nescafé to televise "unaltered" scenes of Mexico
11. Díaz Ordaz signs resolutions granting half million hectares to seven thousand peasant families
12. Police capture Guatemalans and German man with arsenal of guns
13. Gun stores closed for the month

14. Headlines of the dailies
15. Olympic Villa, Athletes (1:20, Rosa María)
16. Aspects of Olympic Sports Center (2:18, Alicia "Licha" Piñeda)
17. Baseball World Series in St. Louis to begin
18. Good-bye[29]

Only one report in the morning newscast focused directly on student protests. The lead story reported briefly on a group of mothers who protested at the Chamber of Deputies in support of their children involved in the student movement. The third report centered on students from both the national university and the polytechnic university who staged a "sit-in" in the esplanade of the Ciudad Universitaria (University City) the day before. The text of the story follows: "Students of the [National Autonomous] University and of the Polytechnic gathered for a rally at noon yesterday in the esplanade of the University City. Several speakers reiterated that they would not end their struggle until their entire list of demands is met. They signaled that police and military repression have served only to reaffirm their desire to fight for democratic principles."[30]

The fact that the writer did not mention the meeting at the Plaza de las Tres Culturas scheduled later in the day suggests that television news executives attempted to downplay the student movement, choosing not to publicize their demonstrations. It certainly would be in the best interest of television owners if images that criticized the government remained offscreen. Large-scale demonstrations worked against both the government's and media executives' mutual goal of creating a positive and orderly image of the city. Not including any information about the afternoon meeting at Tlatelolco also gave producers more time to devote to coverage of the Olympic Games. The script alone cannot tell the complete story, but Jorge Saldaña, a news anchor and host for Telesistema Mexicano in the summer and fall of 1968, argued that limiting coverage of the student movements served the financial interests of the television company and that "for television it was important to have no criticism, problems in the country, or the capital so that the natural course of selling goods could continue. It was a business, and businesses are not interested in alternatives or social disturbances."[31]

Certainly, the omission of the scheduled demonstration, as well as a lack of student voices in reports, reflected a tendency of television executives, starting in the 1950s, to downplay social conflicts and limit the voices of popular groups. As covered in chapter 3, during the railway strikes of 1958 and 1959 the labor demands of strikers rarely appeared in news programs.

Returning to the early morning newscast, the scriptwriter made no obvious reference to connections between stories 11, 12, and 13, but looking back at the violence on October 2, an intriguing relationship existed among the reports. First, when examined together, the reports on the reappropriation of land to peasants, the arrest of Guatemalans and a German who allegedly had an arsenal of weapons, and the closing of the city's armories seemed to act as a counterweight to the report on student protests. Second, these three stories related to the upcoming Olympics in an interesting way. They demonstrated the government's *"pan y palo"* (carrot and stick) approach to quelling social unrest, as well as the need to construct a facade of order for foreigners as the games approached.[32]

Consider story 11 about the granting of land to campesinos. Land redistribution provided evidence that the president attempted to help poor peasants. During this time, students criticized the Díaz Ordaz regime for spending money on beautifying Mexico City instead of resolving the country's social ills. Reports that focused on the government's efforts to help the nation's poor may have caused some students to be less critical of the president.

Stories 12 and 13 represented the regime's "stick" approach to social control. Story 12 referred to members of the judicial and secret police, who arrested a group of Guatemalans and one German at the Miguel Alemán government housing complex with a "small arsenal of guns." The arrests coincided with capital police and the military's efforts to maintain order as the Olympics approached, along with authorities' worries about guns falling into the hands of "political dissidents." The producer's decision to mention of the nationalities of the men in story 12 helped to further government officials' contentions that foreign agitators influenced students—a frame that frequently emerged in the scripts regarding student protesters. The same tendency surfaced at other times during the twentieth century. Government officials and media reports made similar accusations about dissident railway workers in 1958 and 1959. Story 13, regarding the closing of armories, served government and network interests by calling attention to the steps that Díaz Ordaz was taking to maintain order in the city leading up to the Olympic Games. The story revealed that in accordance with Federal District ordinances, 128 gun shops closed their doors for business during the month of October.[33]

Although the Olympics did not lead the newscast, the amount of time devoted to the games reflected the importance that news executives assigned to them. Two reports combined made up about three-and-a-half minutes of the newscast. That represented a significant amount of time, especially considering the other four reports mentioned earlier—the student protest, granting of land, arrests at Miguel Alemán housing complex, and closure of gun armories—together contributed approximately one minute to the newscast.[34]

CHANNEL 2'S EARLY EVENING NEWSCAST, OCTOBER 2, 1968

The massacre began at 6:10 in the evening. Channel 2's newscast went on the air one hour and five minutes after gunfire erupted at the Plaza de las Tres Culturas, yet producers chose not to include any reports on the rally or the violence.[35] Hosted by Zabludovsky, the newscast began with international events and contained little national news:

1. Dean Rusk speaks before United Nations about Soviet Union
2. North American Coast Guard in San Diego
3. Vietcong terrorists captured by Saigon police
4. Pope Paulo Sexto supports peace in Vietnam
5. International Communist Conference postponed
6. Olympic "avalanche" at Mexico airport commercial—Domecq
7. Geneva Conference delegates visit Center of Scientific Investigations in Germany
8. West Berlin inaugurates new National Gallery
9. Race car driver Pedro Rodriguez in LeMans Car Race
10. Start of the Baseball World Series
11. Latin American countries criticize industrialized countries
12. Argentine boxer Horacio Agavallo, World Fly Weight champion, resigns
13. Monterrey pre-Olympic basketball game
14. Díaz Ordaz speaks with newspaper directors about tomorrow's Olympic ceremony
15. Soccer teams prepare for the Olympic Games[36]

What remains striking about this early evening newscast is its emphasis on international news and almost complete omission of any national news. Eleven out of the fifteen reports in the news bulletin focused on foreign issues and events.[37] Only one-third of the items in the newscast stressed a national or local event, and all of those reports related to sports.

Analyzing the scripts alone, it remains difficult, if not impossible, to explain why producers of this newscast opted to focus on international events and ignore the events unfolding in the Plaza de las Tres Culturas. From a journalistic perspective, it could be argued that station reporters had not yet gathered enough credible and verifiable information to file a report. This possibility seems unlikely, though, because television news often reported on events that occurred minutes before or during a news broadcast. During the 1958 and 1959 railroad strikes, *Noticiero General Motors* aired a report on a sizable fire that had ignited minutes before airtime (see chapter 3). A lack of images could represent another explanation for the exclusion of the events at the plaza from the newscast. That seems unlikely as well, as anchors frequently voiced stories without images. Regardless of their rationale, the consequence of news producers' exclusion of the Tlatelolco massacre was an emphasis on international affairs, sports, and positive images over social unrest at home.

CHANNEL 4'S 11:30 P.M. NEWSCAST

By 11:30 the evening of the massacre, newscasters began to air reports on the events at the Plaza de las Tres Culturas. Guillermo Vela and Jorge Saldaña anchored *Noticiero novedades*, which, according to its slogan, "wrapped up the most important events of the day and the world."[38] Of the three newscasts aired on October 2, *Novedades*'s 11:30 news was the only television program to include information about the Tlatelolco rally or massacre. Because gunfire initiated at approximately 6:10 that evening reporters, photographers, producers, executive producers, news directors, and all other executives higher in the corporate news ladder had about five hours before this newscast aired to decide how they would or would not cover the violent event.[39]

What follows is the written portion of the report that *Noticiero novedades* aired regarding the events at the Plaza de las Tres Culturas on the evening of October 2. The script ends by indicating that the anchor continued to ad-lib about the events. Anchor Jorge Saldaña delivered the report, which led the newscast:

> Today at 17:30 hours a rally began in the Plaza de las Tres Culturas in Tlatelolco; before 18:00 hours, gunfire started. The facts were confirmed by our team of reporters and photographers. Later, General Marcelino García Barragán, secretary of national defense,

said, "before 18:00 hours in the Plaza de Las Tres Culturas, snipers, who were standing on some Tlatelolco buildings, began to shoot, when soldiers returned fire."[40] General Barragán reported that General José Hernández Toledo was wounded. Also, a corporal from Battalion 44, whose name is unknown, died. General García Barragán added that those detained and wounded are at Military Camp Number One, where they will appear before the appropriate authorities. Beyond that, the secretary of defense made an appeal to the parents of families so that they could prevent their children from attending student activities that could erupt in violence. In addition, he indicated that the Department of the Federal District, by law, is closing armories in the capital. These scenes were filmed by our team of photographers, who are Angel Cabrerq [sic], Tomás Navarrete, and Francisco Ortíz.[41] Our coworkers have fulfilled their duty. We have been working for the past six hours throughout the city. We have confirmed the deaths of five people with the Red Cross. Also, the Central Station of Fire Fighters reported that protestors set fire to five streetcars and three trucks, the majority of them in the Tlatelolco area and the Guerrero neighborhood. There are deaths, but, we repeat, we have not confirmed the total number. A UPI cable reports that the police have found Molotov bombs, M-1–type rifles, and other arms in possession of the demonstrators. Upon entering the Plaza de Las Tres Culturas, the troops said that the neighbors should evacuate the buildings. UPI confirms that there have been seven deaths. Our reporters [ad-libbed portion].[42]

By television standards, this story was much longer than the average story. It took up a page and a half of text, whereas many reports were only three to four sentences. Despite the length of the report, the writer minimized the gravity of the violence that night, especially when considering the reports in the news dailies the following day. What followed after the final sentence was part of an ad-libbed portion of the newscast and Telesistema Mexicano did not initiate the practice of recording news programs until the advent of videotape in the 1970s; therefore it is unlikely that a taped record of this portion of the newscast exists.

This story refers to UPI's confirmation of seven deaths, far less than even the newspapers the following day announced. *El Universal* reported twenty-nine deaths, eighty wounded, and a thousand detained. *El sol de México* reported the deaths of two soldiers and twenty-one civilians as well as one wounded general and eleven wounded soldiers. Even the daily *Novedades*, the sponsor of the late-night news, reported twenty-five deaths and eighty-seven wounded.[43]

An examination of the sources that the news writer chose to include as well as exclude in this report helps elucidate the perspective of news producers and staff. On several occasions, the writer quoted and attributed information to the secretary of national defense, General Marcelino García Barragán. In this report, the general functioned as an expert regarding the events that transpired that night in the plaza. In addition, writers attributed information about General José Hernández Toledo to General Barragán, furthering his role as an "expert" on the events. General Hernández Toledo's four children, who were involved in the student movement, chose not to attend the October 2 meeting at the Plaza de las Tres Culturas.[44]

General Barragán's warning to parents remains telling. That the general made a plea to parents, asking them to watch over their children and keep them from participating in other student activities revealed that by the late 1960s government officials viewed television as an important tool for informing the public, especially in times of crisis. Moreover, the statement provides evidence that television executives as well as those who appeared on it began to recognize that the medium could be manipulated to both build and buckle solidarity.

The other sources in the report included the Red Cross, United Press International, and the company's own reporters and photographers. With respect to Telesistema's staff, only photographers Angel Cabrera, Tomás Navarrete, and Francisco Ortíz were mentioned by name. Curiously, reporters remained anonymous.

Notably missing from this script were names of students or neighborhood bystanders. The absence of student voices in the script suggests a journalistic perspective, especially from the higher echelons of the corporate hierarchy, that students were not credible and not experts on the events, even though there were probably thousands of witnesses. There may have been another possibility for the lack of student and bystander voices in the reports—fear. If neighbors, parents, and students (especially those not involved in the demonstration) felt that they might face reprisals from police, they may have declined requests for interviews. For decades government officials threatened witnesses and families of survivors of the massacre to guarantee silence.[45] Regardless of the reasons, none of the names of the students killed or arrested that night were aired. The anonymity associated with the students who perished or were rounded up and taken to Campo Militar Número Uno resulted in devaluing their voices and lives in relation to their uniformed compatriots.

OCTOBER 3, THE DAY AFTER

The following day, stories surrounding the events at the Plaza de las Tres Culturas and what they meant for the upcoming Olympics filled airtime on Channel 2's half-hour morning program and fifteen-minute nightly news, as well as Channel 4's nightly newscast, which aired at 11:30 p.m.

When viewers turned on their television sets the morning after the massacre, they likely tuned in to see Zabludovsky delivering reports on the events on *Su diario Nescafé*. Producers chose to deviate from the program's usual format of beginning with a news block consisting of national and international news, and instead Zabludovsky began by ad-libbing information about headlines from the nation's dailies, a segment of the newscast that normally aired after the first news block. The first written report regarding the previous night's massacre followed the headlines segment:

> Police have revealed that they have located an organized group of foreigners, professional agitators who are the cause of assaults, crimes, and disturbances. Filmed at nine at night at a press conference, General Marcelino García Barragán, secretary of defense, announced that the military received gunfire from snipers as they approached the Plaza de Las Tres Culturas in Tlatelolco, when they followed the order of the chief of police to support his forces, because the shooting had begun at the meeting that was taking place there. The head of defense added, "We are a free country and we want freedom to continue to prevail, but there's no legal precept that obligates the government to permit disorder."[46]

While rather neutral in tone, the writer framed the script in a way that again pointed to foreign influences and emphasized the voices of government authorities over students. The reference to the alleged participation of foreigners at the beginning of the story, similar to other reports regarding political dissidents, demonstrates the government's continued efforts to place blame on outsiders, giving the impression that the root of the problem originated outside the country's borders. Like many of the reports aired prior to the October 2 crackdown, this one cited only government officials. Officials are named, while students remained nameless. The final sentence of the report offered the defense secretary a pulpit, on which he made it clear to students that their unrest would not be tolerated and that they could expect reprisals if disturbances were to continue. Furthermore, the uncritical tone of the story had the effect of supporting the military's actions.

In all, stories about the violence in the Plaza de las Tres Culturas made up more than three-and-a-half pages of the seven-page early morning newscast script. Five out of a total of thirteen stories in the newscast focused on the violence, and one report mentioned an appeal by federal lawmakers to strike article 145 of the penal code. Known as the law of social dissolution, article 145 gave police authority to arrest and to punish citizens whom government officials identified as threats to the nation.

The amount of time that the newscast writer devoted to the massacre at Tlatelolco demonstrates that producers recognized the importance of the violent events. Rarely did scripts devote that much time to one subject. In 1958, for example, on the second day of the railway strike, *General Motors News* devoted one-and-a-half pages of a six page script to the strike and a fire at a railway station.[47] Three more reports about the events at the Plaza de las Tres Culturas followed the lead story. They included a report on student strikers, a report about vandalism and violence in the square after the shooting, and a report that focused on Red Cross ambulances and emergency workers. When examined together, the perspectives of newscast writers and producers begin to sharpen.

Overall, the reports on the sit-in, disturbances, and the Red Cross discredited the students by framing them in a negative manner. The report titled "sit-in" stuck to the official story—that the military returned fire from a group of unknown snipers: "The gunfire went on for several hours. Snipers standing in windows, on balconies, and roof tops of various adjacent buildings returned the soldiers' fire." In the report about disturbances, news writers employed words such as "terrorist" and "gang members" to describe student activists, which resulted in labeling them as threats to the nation. In the same report, the anchor stated, "The terrorists burned nine street cars and several more buses in more than two hours of terror."[48]

In the report that focused on the Red Cross's response, the anchor stated that, according to the emergency organization, four deaths had occurred and that "in the third district there have been eighteen deaths, fifteen men, and three women," for a death toll of twenty-two people, a much smaller number than international sources and capital news dailies reported. Beyond the low death toll, the report that focused on the Red Cross subtly criticized the students but stopped short of blaming the protestors for the violence by concluding: "And what appeared to be one of the many rallies with people who have the urge to protest turned into a futile slaughter that stained the Plaza de las Tres Culturas with blood, and in which innocent people died, who had nothing to do with what was happening in the city."[49] In short, like other reports regarding student movements, these stories emphasized the official story and silenced popular voices.

The night after the massacre, Saldaña went on the air and eased domestic and international concerns by announcing that the Olympics would go on as scheduled. Avery Brundage, president of the International Olympic Committee, had, Saldaña said, "consulted with Mexican authorities" and nothing would "interfere with the carrying of the Olympic flame to the Olympic cauldron on October 12th."[50] Forty years later, Saldaña remarked that the Olympics served to cover up the massacre, adding that at the time he could not comprehend how the government let the games go on as scheduled.[51] No mention of the disturbances was made, but the inference was understood—those who attempted to stand in the way of the games could expect another violent response.

TO CARRY THE TORCH AND THE BURDEN OF VIOLENCE

On October 12, the opening day of the games, President Díaz Ordaz led a parade of athletes from 112 countries around the Estadio Olympico (Olympic Stadium), and Pope Paul VI delivered these words from the Vatican: "We are profoundly satisfied with you, young athletes who are inaugurating the nineteenth Olympiad in Mexico City, precisely on the day that is remembered as the first encounter between the Old and New World." At the stadium, after the release of forty thousand balloons of all colors and ten thousand doves that "momentarily shadowed the sky," a huge electronic sign illuminated with the phrase, "We offer and wish peace and friendship to people around the earth."[52]

Unlike the student protestors portrayed as threats to the nation, Olympic athletes were described in extremely positive terms. Individual student protestors rarely wound up in the scripts, but television producers did recognize other young people. Twenty-year-old Norma Enriqueta Basilio who hailed from Mexicali, Baja California de Norte, exuded everything the Comité Nacional Organizador (National Organizing Committee) needed to promote the Olympics. Young, shapely and in shape, attractive, and mestiza, she embodied the modern image of Mexico that the organizers wanted foreign visitors to see. On the opening day of the Olympiad, she became the first woman in the history of the modern games to carry the torch and light the Olympic cauldron.

In contrast to her youthful compatriots locked up in the cells of Lecumberri Prison, Basilio, "something of a national heroine," represented the kind of young person television producers sought to include in its news coverage, and government officials wanted in the limelight. Basilio herself remarked that she was chosen because she represented a "new kind of generation."[53] A hurdler for the Mexican Olympic team, she helped to further the goals of television executives to seek viewers and advertisers, as well as the government's objective of portraying the country as modern and progressive. That the organizing committee of the Olympics chose Basilio to carry the torch and light the cauldron was no coincidence.

Twenty-five years after the 1968 Olympics, Basilio appeared on a special program produced by Televisa that commemorated the games. During the program, televised on October 12, 1993, Basilio, as she sat in the studio with a panel of men who also had participated in the event, remembered the Olympics as a proud moment.[54] An archival film clip appeared of her running into the Estadio Olympico, carrying the Olympic torch before a crowd of a hundred thousand. International newspaper reporters described the "golden-olive skinned" athlete, who "laughs easily," as graceful as an antelope, with "sparkling white teeth."[55] Cognizant of the image she would convey on television, Basilio prepared for

8. Norma Enriqueta Basilio carrying the Olympic torch up the ninety-three steps to the cauldron during opening ceremonies in Mexico City, October 12, 1968. AP Photo 681012012.

weeks, which included a careful selection of her attire. Clad in a white sleeveless top, white shorts, and a white headband, the short-haired Basilio ran a lap around the track—an outfit that she had chosen as a "symbol of peace and a peaceful Olympiad." After her lap around the track, she began a ninety-three step trek up a staircase, whose construction sought to evoke a sense of a modern, yet ancient Aztec pyramid. The staircase had been built to coincide with Basilio's stride, although she would remember them as a bit high and wide (see figure 8). She recalled that the experience and responsibility "was unforgettable, and that fortunately she, as a woman, fulfilled."[56]

If the amount of airtime devoted to a particular issue in a newscast serves as a barometer of an event's significance, then opening day of the nineteenth Olympiad was paramount in the eyes of television news producers. The writer of *Noticiero novedades* devoted nearly five pages of a seven-page script to opening day activities. On the whole, Olympic coverage tended to result in the production of three common frames: Mexico as modern, athletes as model youth, and Mexico City as orderly and peaceful. All three of these frames surfaced on the October 12 edition of *Noticiero novedades* in the lead story and the one that followed: "The grand festival of youth was initiated today. In a sporting competition, more than seven thousand athletes will face off and participate in the event. The Olympic flame that was carried from Teotihuacán to Estadio '68 (Stadium '68) brought together in its path more than a million people, who applauded enthusiastically. At the monument of the people there was a brief ceremony. Later, the athletes continued along the torch's route until it was delivered by the Baja Californian athlete Enriqueta Basilio, as she came through the doors of the University City."[57]

The report immediately following the lead story focused on Olympic spectators: "Eighty-thousand spectators arrived, using all means of transportation to '68 Stadium. Transit was well organized. There were no bottle-necks. Mexicans of all ages showed up as early as eight in the morning to take their seats. Security was normal, and no incidents were recorded. Tourists with *charro* hats gave it [the event] an atmosphere of folklore and friendship."[58] The second report's emphasis on transit and security underscored the importance of maintaining order for a successful Olympics. The report highlighted how smoothly traffic flowed, and the "normal" presence of security demonstrated to viewers in Mexico City and around the world that civil disturbances had been brought under control.

When one considers that most of the Olympic Games were held on the UNAM campus, the desire for security becomes all the more relevant. The sit-ins that had occurred throughout the summer and fall, the September 18 military occupation of the campus, and the Olympic events all unfolded in the same vicinity. Meanwhile, the

Consejo Nacional de Huelga had vowed to abstain from protesting during the Olympic Games. Furthermore, the committee asked that young female *edecanes* (hosts), many of whom were students at UNAM, to resist from displaying information related to the movement.[59] Members of the committee understood well that their messages conflicted with those of the government.

The day after the opening ceremony, newscasters called attention to other athletes on the country's Olympic team, such as the soccer team that won its first match of the games against Colombia, one to zero. In addition, distance runner Juan Martinez just missed garnering a bronze medal, finishing fourth in the ten thousand-meter race, after "leading the race for a good while." Images of the youthful athletes worked to further the goals television executives and government officials sought, to demonstrate the country's level of modernity and progress. Furthermore, they aired in stark contrast to the images of the *"pandilleros"* (gangsters) who "terrorized" and torched vehicles on the night of the Tlatelolco massacre.[60]

CONFLICTIVE IMAGES

Despite Telesistema Mexicano's efforts to limit dissident voices during the summer of 1968, students managed to get their messages aired through other means of communication. They formed brigades and took to the streets, where they staged miniplays to inform citizens about their concerns and demands. During demonstrations throughout the city, students collected money from supporters to print information not published in government-supported dailies. For Ana Ignacia "La Nacha" Rodriguez, *las brigadas* formed a vital part of the movement, and the messages they promulgated may have been "the simplest medium, but the most effective. We were like mobile newspapers."[61] The messages delivered through street theater, posters, and flyers served as hybrid frames that countered official voices heard and seen on television.

Students and faculty from the Escuela Nacional de Artes Plásticas (National School of Visual Arts) of the UNAM formed a de facto

Olympic Dreams and Tlatelolco Nightmares 167

9. The nineteenth Olympic logotype juxtaposed against a granadero depicted as a gorilla, 1968. Reprinted by permission from IISUE/AHUNAM/Colección de impresos Esther Montero (foja 507, exp. 13, caja 2).

media production house at the Academia San Carlos, located near the Palacio Nacional. Artists from the school created intense images that overtly criticized the authoritarian regime of President Díaz Ordaz.[62] Their messages targeted everything from the president and the use of granaderos, to the imprisonment of political dissidents, to the Olympics, and at times the news media (see figures 9 and 10). Students pasted their messages on whatever surfaces they could find. As the military increased its presence around the city, small pocket-sized images replaced large posters because they could be carried easily. Thus, "the public got the students' point of view."[63]

As the first generation of citizens raised on television, students understood that the information on broadcast media regarding popular movements in the 1960s represented a limited portrayal of the events. Students were unable to vocalize their disapproval of the mainstream media on Telesistema Mexicano, but they did air their criticisms in student media. Jorge Perezvega became part of the student movements in 1968, when he was an art student at the Escuela Nacional de Artes Plásticas. Perezvega remembered that students viewed the press as a corrupt institution responsible for spewing damaging information. "You had to read between the lines," he said. "You would read a newspaper, and you had to look for the truth within the report, and that happened with television."[64]

10. "Corrupt Press," 1968. Reprinted by permission from IISUE/AHUNAM/Colección de impresos Esther Montero (foja 539, exp. 14, caja 2).

11. Granadero driving with the Olympic symbol as part of the tank, 1968. Reprinted by permission from IISUE/AHUNAM/Colección de impresos Ester Montero (foja 594, exp. 17, caja 2).

While they were not opposed to the games, students criticized the relationship between the Olympics and the increased police presence on the streets of Mexico City. The government created a special force known as the Batallón Olímpia (Olympic Battalion) to maintain order during the games.[65] As many as five thousand plainclothes military troops patrolled the stadium area on the inaugural day of the Olympics.[66] Granaderos provoked ire among students, as members of the Consejo Nacional de Huelga viewed and portrayed them as thoughtless thugs whom the government manipulated as instruments of social control (see figure 11).[67]

Negative portrayals of the government and the president sometimes went beyond posters and other forms of visual media.

Students created chants and songs to make their voices heard, as in an altered version of a familiar children's song:

Di por qué, dime Gustavo,
di por qué, eres cobarde,
di por qué no tienes madre,
dime Gustavo por qué?
[Tell me why, tell me Gustavo,
tell me why you are a coward,
tell me why you have no shame,
tell me Gustavo, why?][68]

The arrival of satellite communications in 1968 linked viewers around the planet and aided government officials who wanted to internationally transmit positive images of the nation, but it could also have an undesirable effect for government officials. The new technology improved opportunities for building student solidarity across national boundaries. For example, following the military's takeover and occupation of UNAM on September 18, students in New York, Paris, and Helsinki protested the army's action. The reports on the student demonstrations in support of Mexican activists in all these cities aired on Mexican television.[69] Reports such as these created windows to the world as well as enabled students to see themselves as part of a movement that went beyond national boundaries. For some participants, such as Perezvega, "knowing that other students were behind Mexican students helped energize us."[70] Through television and other means of communication, Ana Ignacia Rodriguez said, she "felt very supported by students from universities inside the country and out."[71]

At the same time, Rodriguez remembers how she felt after watching television coverage the day after the Tlatelolco massacre. She stated that she was "very angry, but above all, powerless. Because you think, how are the people going to learn about what really happened, if the media negates the truth?"[72] Despite the limited coverage of the massacre at Tlatelolco, over the past forty years,

Olympic Dreams and Tlatelolco Nightmares

activists such as Rodriguez have worked to ensure that their stories are not forgotten. Forty years later, national as well as international mainstream media outlets, such as Televisa, TV Azteca, and the Discovery Channel, allowed former participants in the student movements to play a dominant role in news coverage. In contrast, on the fortieth anniversary of el '68, government officials by and large remained off the air—a sign that the country and its media had changed over the past four decades.

THE GOVERNMENT AND ZABLUDOVSKY RESPOND

The year 1968 represented both the beginning and culmination of an era for the country and the television industry. By the end of the year, the relationship between the state and media executives shifted dramatically and signaled the end of the government's laissez faire attitude toward the media. For network owners, this meant an increase in the state's involvement in the industry. Díaz Ordaz and his successor, Luís Echeverría, laid part of the blame of increasing political dissent on television programming, and in an attempt to reel in the industry, the government placed financial constraints on media owners.[73] Late in the year, Echeverría, then the interior minister, proposed a 25 percent tax on the industry. A strong television lobby fought the proposal and the two sides finally settled on a law that mandated network executives allow the government to use 12.5 percent of a station's total airtime.[74]

As mentioned in earlier chapters, several Mexico City dailies, including *Novedades, Excelsior,* and *El Heraldo,* frequently provided editorial content for the major news programs on Channels 2, 4, and 5—hence the name of some newscasts such as *Noticiero novedades*. For this reason, television news executives tended to argue that newspaper editors were to blame for problems regarding coverage of the massacre.[75] After the massacre at Tlatelolco, newspaper "contracts" with Telesistema Mexicano would expire, through the urging of President Díaz Ordaz.[76] Telesistema Mexicano would create its own news division, which resulted in an increase in corporate censorship rather than direct government censorship.[77]

Following the events at the Plaza de las Tres Culturas, station owners realized they wanted more editorial control over news, giving them another reason to create a corporate news division. Emilio Azcárraga Milmo chose the son of former president Miguel Alemán Valdés (1946–52), Miguel Alemán Velasco, to head up the new Telesistema Mexicano division. Alemán Velasco also served as Televisa's president during the 1980s. A corporate news division allowed executives to centralize and standardize news production, something that they argue had not been possible because of the influence of the various news dailies.[78] Moreover, a centralized news operation further diminished opportunities for alternative voices and perspectives to air on television.[79]

Following the creation of the news division, Jacobo Zabludovsky, who already had eighteen years of experience on television, emerged as the country's most renowned news anchor. Zabludovsky would come to anchor the country's longest-running news program to date, *24 horas*, which aired from September 1970 to January 1998. Long after the bloodstains at the Plaza de las Tres Culturas had been scrubbed clean, though not forgotten, chronicler Elena Poniatowska interviewed Zabludovsky about the student movement of 1968. She asked him whether he thought students in 1968 and 1969 had something to say. Zabludovsky responded with a curt "*sí*." Poniatowska continued, "In 1968 not only did the students think that you weren't with them, they declared you an enemy. Isn't that right?" Zabludovsky quipped, "Before I say or don't say anything, they campaigned against me, and against all journalists, calling all of them 'sold-out.' They didn't make any exceptions."[80]

As the nation's best-known news personality, Zabludovsky has remained silent regarding the issue of state-media relations in 1968. His interviews with journalists have not provided many clues as to what went on in the newsroom in the summer and fall of 1968, though he has admitted that the government applied pressure to

Telesistema Mexicano immediately after the massacre in attempts to limit the amount of information that was broadcast.[81] Because of his influence in newsrooms across the country from the 1950s through the 1990s, Zabludovsky's insights remain critical to understanding the decision-making process during the late 1960s. The details about exactly what happened behind the scenes on the critical days leading up to the massacre and the Olympics have yet to be revealed, and in October 2008 Amnesty International called on the government of Felipe Calderón to initiate another investigation into the events.[82]

Longtime television and radio host Jorge Saldaña represents one of the few news professionals who deviated from the network line, and in retaliation for his actions, he has been fired from Telesistema Mexicano (later Televisa) and Televisión Independiente de México more than a dozen times. Saldaña stated that he was often fired after interviews with news makers who were critical of the government, because, as he put it, he was "responsible not only for what he said on the air but what his guests said."[83]

The moment cameras began to roll at the Estadio Olympico during the inauguration of the games, media moguls and government officials alike could be thankful that the international community saw the images that they wanted transmitted, images that evoked peace, order, and modernity. Airing positive and modern images of the country allowed television executives to achieve their goal of increasing industry profits through commercials and program sponsorship. Owners of foreign companies would be more inclined to invest large sums of money in the industry through television commercials and sponsorship if they knew a growing number of consumers would be available to purchase their products. Indeed, in 1968 national and international advertising agencies directed 40 percent of their publicity to television advertising, totaling more than 973 million pesos.[84] In addition, news about the Olympic Games allowed a certain group of the country's youth to be celebrated — those who possessed the government's and television executives' ideals of desirable national characteristics. Images of athletes aired in contrast to the thousands of students detained in prison after the massacre and provided evidence of deep social fissures between the administration and the nation's "untelegenic" youth.

Both government and media executives worked together to convince national and international audiences that Mexico was indeed a modern country. PRI officials benefited politically from positive images of the country on-screen and broadcast executives such as Emilio Azcárraga Milmo and Rómulo O'Farrill Jr. profited financially. Yet by focusing on the construction of a positive vision of the country, news executives failed to provide the public with a full picture of the nation's political and social ills. Instead, news reports emphasized sports over politics and presented uncritical views of governmental affairs. As a result, reports on the Olympics and the massacre at Tlatelolco, along with the daily news aired throughout the 1960s, helped legitimize the PRI and helped to sustain its power well into the mid-1980s. Despite television news executives' efforts to limit the airing of negative images, the massacre at the Plaza de las Tres Culturas remained too important for them to ignore completely. As a result, through Telesistema Mexicano's scant coverage and through the alternative accounts of students, protestors, and intellectuals, citizen viewers developed an awareness of the events and began to notice the cracks in a facade of modernity and order.

Offering a counterdiscourse to the official story, members of the National Strike Council made their voices heard through the use of alternative forms of media, such as street theater and printed information. While these alternative forms of communication provided dissidents a place in the public arena, their voices could not compete with the enormity and strength of a capitalist enterprise such as Telesistema Mexicano.

Despite their anonymity on-screen, students watched reports about their counterparts protesting for their cause in places such as New York, Paris, and Helsinki. Televised reports and other media helped students build and strengthen transnational solidarity. Watching students across the world protest against the military occupation of UNAM gave young people a sense of belonging to a cause that crossed international boundaries. In short, students framed events in ways that they found just, useful, and meaningful. Their interpretations of the events, though not widely disseminated, did not correspond to those of most television executives or high-ranking government officials.

> Once the new decade was underway, it became clear that if there was one word to characterize the period that just ended, it would be crisis; crisis on all levels, in production, in labor, in education, in rural areas, in the city, in couples, in the individual.
>
> Fátima Fernández Christlieb

CHAPTER 7

Victory for the Brazilians and Echeverría

THE TLATELOLCO massacre and its subsequent political fallout sent two important messages to television news executives. First, they recognized the company lacked total control over the editorial content of its news programs; second, executives began to see the importance of television news, especially in times of national crisis. These two realities, and perhaps with a little coaxing from President Díaz Ordaz himself, prompted executives to rethink the way television news should be gathered, sponsored, and broadcast.[1]

This chapter explains how two major forces attempted to limit the growth and power of Telesistema Mexicano. It describes how the network responded to these forces in ways that established boundaries for the state and the network's competition, allowing Telesistema Mexicano and later Televisa to become one of the world's most profitable media conglomerates. The chapter then turns to the book's final case study, an analysis of news coverage of the presidential elections of 1970 and the World Cup, hosted by Mexico, to illustrate how tele-traditions established during the first five years of television, such as incorporating sports as news and covering national holidays, remained firmly in place two decades later. Finally, the chapter explains that although competition and consolidation—both internally (with the formation of the news division) and externally (merging with Televisión Independiente de México)—initiated a new phase for Telesistema Mexicano, many of the tele-traditions that had been formed in the 1950s would continue into the twenty-first century. The formation of tele-traditions early on in the industry should cause students and researchers of journalism, media, and history to reassess the significance of the early phase of television news production and content, as well as the way that viewers interpreted early news programming.

Similar to the four other case studies, analysis of the news coverage of presidential elections and the World Cup enables investigation of the central question of the study: what are the limits of cultural hegemony? News reports about the elections showed that Telesistema Mexicano towed the PRI line on the air. At the same time, off-the-air tensions brewed between the state and media executives. Like the Space Race and the Olympics, the World Cup represented an international event, but news producers situated it through a nationalistic lens. Similar to reports about the Olympics two years before, the World Cup thrust the country onto the international stage, allowing media executives and government officials to put the nation's modern and orderly face forward. Behind the scenes, the country remained in conflict.

STATE PRESSURE AND TELESISTEMA MEXICANO'S COMPETITORS

Two pressures—one political, the other economic—marked the turning point in the television industry and network news in the late 1960s and early 1970s. The first involved increased tensions with government officials, the second stemmed from pressure from competing television entrepreneurs. As during the 1950s the manner in which Telesistema Mexicano and other network executives responded to these pressures is critical to deepening understanding about the role that television news would play in the country's long and protracted transition to democracy.[2] The media executives' responses to outside influence also remain equally important to this study, because they demonstrate how, through news coverage and negotiations, media owners set the limits of cultural hegemony of the state over the private sector.

Government officials such as Díaz Ordaz and Luis Echeverría attempted to thwart the media's increasing influence in several ways. These efforts, sometimes unsuccessful, marked a dramatic shift in government-media relations from the 1950s to the 1970s. Government pressure included imposing a hefty tax on the industry, the creation of a government TV station, and the threat of nationalization once Echeverría took office on December 1, 1970. Indeed, the first day of his six-year term he created the Subsecretaría de Radiodifusión (Undersecretariat of Broadcasting), a branch of the Secretaría de Comunicaciones y Transporte.[3] One of the responsibilities of the new entity included imposing sanctions on television station owners found in violation of the telecommunications policies. Whether sanctions were actually imposed was another question. Clearly, Ruiz Cortines's attempts to influence the medium in the 1950s through the creation of a government-run station paled in comparison to Echeverría's. By the 1960s it was evident that the state sought to reign in the growing power of electronic media. The company's decision to take control and consolidate news production facilities and personnel were made in part because of government pressure; at the same time, the network would benefit greatly from this arrangement.[4]

Miguel Alemán Velasco, who helped establish Telesistema Mexicano's news division and who later functioned as the president of Televisa, remembers the fallout from Tlatelolco and the growing dissatisfaction among *diazordazistas* (Díaz Ordaz supporters) with big media. Alemán recalled that after the 1968 massacre Díaz Ordaz held a meeting with all television owners. Alemán said that in the meeting the president threatened to send an auditor to monitor the content on each of the company's stations, as well as impose a 30 percent tax on airtime. Exactly what was said in that meeting has not been made public, but when negotiations concluded, the "special supervisor," as Alemán Velasco called it, never appeared and the tax was reduced to 12.5 percent. The "tax" came in the form of free airtime for state-sponsored programming. The meeting resulted in a compromise that allowed Telesistema Mexicano to gain control of news production and content and stopped the government from intervening directly in the stations' operations.[5]

The conflict between Díaz Ordaz and the Mexico City–based network stemmed in part from increasing criticism from various popular groups, such as labor organizations and student activists, whose demands and problems had not been resolved since the strikes of 1958 and 1959. By the time Echeverría took office, representatives from the public sector clashed with television owners. As the secretary general of the Union of Education Workers stated, "enough already with the overreaching [power] of television."[6] The fact that the industry experienced a dramatic increase in production and profits in the 1960s and 1970s rendered broadcasting executives more power and exacerbated tensions between big media and the state.

By July 1970 four television stations in Mexico City produced daily news. Table 2 represents the amount of news produced during the week on an average day as well as company sponsors.[7] Between 1950 and 1970 television news production and personnel skyrocketed.[8] During the early 1950s a few fifteen-minute news bulletins occupied the airwaves, but in the mid-1970s Televisa's annual news production had increased to almost three thousand hours, averaging eight hours of news programming a day. News programming made up 13.3 percent of all programming, or about fifty-five hours a week of news. The number of people employed

TABLE 2. Telesistema Mexicano newscasts and airtimes in 1970

Channel	Time	Program	Sponsors
2	7:30 a.m.	Su diario Nescafé	Nestlé
2	8:00 a.m.	La opinión de hoy	Various
4	3:00 p.m.	Noticiero social de Morelos	State of Morelos
2	3:00 p.m.	Día con día	Various
4	7:15 p.m.	Noticiero General Motors	General Motors
2	7:15 p.m.	Noticiero Domecq	Casa Pedro Domecq
8	7:15 p.m.	Noticiero 15 minutos	Various
8	11:00 p.m.	Tele-periódico notimex	Notimex
2	11:30 p.m.	Noticiero WTV	Various
13	11:30 p.m.	Noticiero trecevisión	Channel 13
2	12:00 a.m.	Agenda de medianoche	Various
4	12:35 a.m.	Noticiero de cierre	Various

Source: González Molina, "Mexican Television News," 103.

TABLE 3. Estimated nationwide viewership from 1950 to 1970

Year	1950	1960	1970
Number of television sets	100	780,000	4.5 million
Number of households	5.8 million	6.9 million	9.9 million
Approximate TV penetration	Less than 1 percent	11 percent	45 percent

Source: Indicadores sociodemográficos de México, 105; Becerra Celis, "Mexico"; Plenn, "Mexico."

by Televisa's news gathering division grew to 250, including 56 national and 33 international correspondents.⁹

The power of television was also evident through the growing number of viewers. Between 1950 and 1970 the number of television sets operating in the country soared from one hundred to more than 4.5 million. Television stations had been established in twenty-nine states around the country. The majority of viewers lived in Mexico City. Table 3 shows that between 1950 and 1970 viewership increased from less than 1 percent of all households to approximately 45 percent. Those who could afford to purchase a television set were part of the upper middle and growing middle classes.

Beyond tensions between the government and Telesistema Mexicano, the network felt pressure from competing media moguls. Through Televisión Independiente de México, the Garza Sada family officially inaugurated XHTIM, Channel 8, on September 1, 1968, with the broadcast of President Díaz Ordaz's fourth informe.¹⁰ Owned and operated by an elite group of entrepreneurs from Monterrey, Nuevo Leon, the station represented the first real challenge to Telesistema Mexicano's monopoly and to Mexico City's media elite in thirteen years.¹¹ Owners of Telesistema Mexicano had enjoyed a monopoly in the news and entertainment market since 1955, when the company consolidated Channel 4 (XHTV), Channel 2 (XEW-TV), and Channel 5 (XHGC) under one roof.

Aside from the Monterrey group, Díaz Ordaz increased Telesistema Mexicano's competition by granting a television concession on July 24, 1967, to radio network owner Francisco Aguirre Jiménez, who started Channel 13 (XHDF).¹² The president's 1968 informe also provided the venue for this station's inaugural broadcast. Yet Díaz Ordaz's address remained momentous among the viewing public for another reason, and to this day it remains in the country's collective popular memory. During his speech, the president reiterated his hard-line position against student activists, and he included a stern warning to young protestors who continued to be a source of consternation for the president, especially as the nation geared up for the Olympic Games. He made his message clear on at least three network stations, when he stated, "We don't wish to make decisions that we don't want to take, but we will if necessary. Whatever our task, we will do it. No matter where we are forced to go, we will."[13] In the same address that was televised on channel 13, the president hailed the country's participation in the nonproliferation of nuclear arms and chided the press for disseminating excessive criticism about the government.

Forced out of the market after four years in operation, Channel 13 went bankrupt and wound up in the hands of the state in 1972. It would remain under government control until 1993, when President Carlos Salinas de Gortari, in a wave of privatization efforts, would sell the station to media magnate Ricardo Salinas Pliego, owner of the electronics company Elektra. The station would become part of the TV Azteca network.[14]

TELESISTEMA MEXICANO'S RESPONSE TO DÍAZ ORDAZ AND THE STATE

Prior to the now infamous 1968 meeting with Díaz Ordaz and station owners, Azcárraga Vidaurreta and Alemán Velasco had begun to contemplate removing newspapers from the editorial picture. The major capital dailies had been contributing editorial content to TV news since 1950. Apparently, some TV producers did not share the same political perspectives as their newspaper counterparts. According to Alemán Velasco, "in 1968 *Excelsior*'s point of view rarely coincided with that of Telesistema Mexicano's."[15] *Excelsior*'s nightly news on Channel 2 was the news program that came closest to criticizing the government in 1968. Julio Scherer García edited the newspaper *Excelsior*, and the paper's critical view of the government's response to student unrest frequently provoked ire among top PRI officials, including Echeverría. The PRI-controlled government officials began to harass Scherer in the late 1960s, and through a government-initiated labor dispute Scherer and other top editors of *Excelsior* were forced to resign from the paper. Scherer described President Echeverría as a leader who "yearned to mandate wherever he was. He wasn't attracted to writers, but to scribes. He didn't want journalists, but publicists instead. He didn't see the nobility in independent men and women, but bowed to his accomplices."[16]

The newscasts prior to 1970 reflected biased and partisan coverage, according to Alemán Velasco.[17] The formation of the news division was part of an attempt to change that. By the end of the 1960s the contracts between the newspapers and Telesistema Mexicano began to expire. The epoch of newspaper influence ended on August 28, 1970, with the last broadcast of *Su diario Nescafé* on XEW-TV, Channel 2.[18]

To gain independence from the capital dailies and to quell criticism from Díaz Ordaz and the state, Azcárraga Vidaurreta devised a two-fold plan that included the creation of a corporate news division and a national news program. He selected Alemán Velasco to lead the corporate news division, referred to as the Dirección General de Información y Noticieros. That Alemán, the son of the former president, was chosen to direct the new division signaled the important role that network executives assigned to the production and content of news.[19]

Azcárraga Vidaurreta told Alemán that he wanted him to work for him on something that is "going to create a lot of problems for us; it's going to give us a lot of headaches; it will have a small audience, and be extremely costly" (see figure 12). Following his boss's orders, Alemán traveled to Europe, Canada, and the United States, taking notes on the various models of news production. He also recruited aspiring journalists from various parts of the country and the world. He searched for the most promising students from the journalism school at the Universidad de Veracruz (Alemán's home state) and recruited them from Mexico City's Universidad Iberoamericana and UNAM. Some of the journalists came from other Latin American countries such as Argentina. Still others came from radio, including BBC radio in London.[20]

12. Miguel Alemán Velasco with Emilio Azcárraga Vidaurreta, when Alemán Velasco was appointed head of the corporate news division, ca. 1970. Courtesy of Miguel Alemán Velasco, personal collection.

The new generation of reporters had to possess several skills before they could begin working. They had to be able to speak at least two languages fluently and needed to have knowledge of modern history. They also had to be skilled communicators and be able to pronounce easily the names of at least ten countries.[21] All of the new and the more veteran journalists now belonged to Telesistema's corporate news division. The effort to incorporate all journalists under the purview of a company news division resulted in a standardized voice of the news, which, as one might expect, became less diverse. The creation of the news division in 1969 consolidated the hierarchy of news production, which worked to generalize both production as well as reporting practices and signaled an increase in the level of professionalization among TV journalists.

The second part of Telesistema Mexicano's response to government pressure was the creation of a national news program titled *24 horas* (24 hours). The first program produced under the guidance of the corporate news division, it served as a model for news production and content for decades to come. Of course, the *24 horas* model was constructed based on what TV producers and executives had learned since 1950. Launched on September 7, 1970, and hosted by Zabludovsky, *24 horas* emerged as one of the most successful programs Televisa would produce for domestic and international audiences. The establishment of a corporate news division had ramifications for advertising revenue as well. When Zabludovsky inaugurated *24 horas*, he could only have imagined the program's and his future success. Having enjoyed one of the longest runs for a news program, it endured for twenty-seven consecutive years. By the time *24 horas* hit the airwaves, studio production of news had become more dynamic. Two cameras, instead of one, focused on the anchors. Having two cameras allowed directors to shoot the anchors from different angles, making the visual experience more interesting for viewers.[22]

At ninety-minutes, the program filled more airtime than any previous newscast. By the late 1960s many news programs increased to a half hour. In 1968 *Su diario Nescafé*, also hosted by Zabludovsky, had already expanded to an hour.[23] The transition from fifteen-minute news bulletins to thirty-minute programs occurred around the same time in the United States, with CBS and NBC expanding to a half hour in 1963 and ABC in 1967.[24] Unlike fifteen-minute news bulletins sponsored by one entity, the half-hour format allowed Telesistema Mexicano to split the program into several shorter blocks and sell numerous commercials during each break. For example, five commercial breaks divided the broadcast of *24 horas* on September 15, 1970. The commercials promoted a variety of products and services, including the Commercial Bank of Mexico and Rico Rum.[25]

News executives standardized the time slots of news programming to coincide with the daily schedules of most viewers. Whereas news bulletins aired at various times of the day, by 1970 they began to air at three specific times: early morning, midday, and late evening. These new time slots aimed to catch as many viewers at one time as possible. From an economic perspective, this allowed the company to sell airtime in a more uniform and organized way.

As one of the longest-running news programs in Televisa history, *24 horas* represented the model that many viewers came to expect, though not necessarily respect. The emphasis on international news influenced viewers to begin to look outward more than they had in the past and to see how they fit into a global village. At the same time, the prominence of international coverage may have also prompted some viewers to reaffirm what it meant to be Mexican. Of course, mexicanidad meant different things to different people. For rural indigenous peasants who had recently moved to the metropolis, news reports focusing on the United States or other foreign countries may have created opportunities for them to see themselves as indigenous and to reaffirm their identities.[26] For the middle class and upwardly mobile capitalinos, television news and images represented either their lifestyle or a lifestyle they sought to achieve. For male elite members of society, the content of television news often included people they knew personally and reaffirmed their rationales for remaining in economic power. For women, the increasing inclusion of females as news makers and as members of on-air talent allowed them to reassess their personal and career goals. For the disenfranchised residents of Mexico City, who by and large remained missing from the scripts, television coverage reemphasized what they already knew: those who controlled the airwaves deemed their voices insignificant.

RESPONSE TO COMPETITION: THE DEATH OF AZCÁRRAGA VIDAURRETA AND BIRTH OF TELEVISA

By the beginning of the new decade, Azcárraga Vidaurreta had been in the broadcast industry for more than fifty years. Over the course of the first twenty years in television, he had watched

Telesistema Mexicano develop into the country's most influential network. By the time Echeverrría moved into Los Pinos, Azcárraga Vidaurreta's health had begun to fail, and Azcárraga Milmo stood by, ready to make critical decisions when the time came.

Azcárraga Vidaurreta died in Houston on September 23, 1972. The following day he was buried in Mexico City, and it was at his funeral that Bernardo Garza Sada, who represented the Monterrey Group, reportedly asked Azcárraga Milmo when they could settle the matter (the matter being the merging of Telesistema Mexicano and Television Independiente de México).[27] With his father no longer able to resist, the son agreed to begin negotiations for a merger. In an effort to end a long-standing regional struggle between *regiomontaños* (residents from Monterrey) and capitalinos, a new company was formed on January 8 of the following year. Azcárraga Milmo was named president, and Alejandro Sada vice president of Televisa.[28] Telesistema Mexicano retained 75 percent of the holdings, while the Monterrey Group received the remaining 25 percent.[29] The 1973 consolidation of Televisión Independiente de México's Channel 8 with Telesistema Mexicano had important implications for news production and content. First, it enhanced the process of standardization and professionalization that was underway. Second, the merger formed a commercial monopoly and strengthened the company's ability to produce programming, including both domestic and foreign news. The name "Televisa," which stands for *"televisión via satélite"* indicated the company's goal to distribute news and entertainment programming to foreign audiences.

Azcárraga Vidaurreta's passing gave Azcárraga Milmo a chance to finally prove that he could walk in the same arena of el León. Prior to assuming the presidency of the company, many of the longtime television executives thought that Azcárraga Junior was incapable of managing.[30] Azcárraga Milmo's astute move toward corporate consolidation further strengthened the television industry, creating a monopoly that would operate without a serious challenge until

1993. More important, the new company made television executives less vulnerable, as the threat of nationalization lingered. Clearly, the successes of Azcárraga Junior, who would become known as el Tigre, and Televisa through the 1970s and 1980s, during which time the company exported programming to more than one hundred countries, proved he had a knack for business after all.

PRESIDENTIAL ELECTIONS AND WORLD CUP COVERAGE

In 1970 the PRI and the government had a serious legitimacy problem. The massacre at Tlatelolco had left a dark cloud hanging over the party and unveiled the shortcomings of the revolution. Díaz Ordaz's choice of Echeverría through the presidential dedazo, created more unrest, given that Echeverría had been the minister of interior in 1968 and had the authority to order the army to open fire on protestors in the Tlatelolco neighborhood on October 2. Although the forty-eight-year-old politician had been indicted by some of the public, he had not been by the party or the courts. A savvy politician, he was no outsider to the PRI, having delivered the nomination speech for candidate Adolfo López Mateos in 1957.[31]

In the eyes of the ruling party, Echeverría's opponent was an outsider. The fact that Efraín González Morfín spoke eight languages did not seem to improve his chance of winning the election, based on the results of the previous nine elections.[32] The forty-one-year-old *panista* (of PAN) from Guadalajara also had a regional mark against him. Given that more citizens lived in the nation's capital than in Guadalajara, Echeverría had an automatic advantage. When election results were announced on July 9, 1970, a week after the vote, Zabludovsky told morning viewers that Echeverría garnered 11,121,714 votes, compared to Morfín's 772,1179. Ballots from seven thousand polling stations remained to be tallied, and official results would be announced the following Sunday.[33] Of course, the outcome of the election was no surprise to most citizens who had grown accustomed to the ruling party's maneuvering of the process through a variety of overt and covert

TABLE 4. Breakdown of election and World Cup coverage in 1970

	Echeverría (PRI candidate)	Morfín (PAN candidate)	World Cup
June 17	3 (11, 12, 13)	1 (16)	9 (1-9)
June 18	3 (14, 15, 16)	1 (20)	7 (2-8)
June 19	1 (8)	0	6 (1-6)
June 20	3 (7, 8, 9)	1 (16)	5 (1-5)
June 22	2 (7, 9)	0	7 (1-6, 13)
June 23	1 (7)	0	4 (9-12)
Total reports	13	3	38

Source: Su Diario nescafé, June 17–23, 1970, FNTEA.

measures. These included everything from stuffing ballot boxes to dominating airtime during the campaign leading up to the election.

Between June 17 and 23, 1970, coverage of the presidential elections and the World Cup filled the news. Before discussion of individual news reports, it is helpful to look at some figures regarding World Cup and presidential campaign coverage that aired on *Su diario Nescafé*. Table 4 lists the number of reports in each category and story placement (in parentheses) on June 17, 18, 19, 20, 22, and 23.[34] On June 17, two weeks before the presidential election, producers devoted four reports to the upcoming vote and nine reports to the World Cup.[35] Reports about the World Cup made up the first nine items in the newscast. Election reports placed eleventh, twelfth, thirteenth, and sixteenth.

The sheer number of reports on a particular subject helps to answer the question: how much importance did news executives assign to each topic? During a six-day period, coverage of the World Cup by far dominated the news, followed by reports on Echeverría, and finally reports on the opposition party candidate, Morfín.

The number of reports on Echeverría more than quadrupled the number of reports on Morfín. Reports on the World Cup were almost three times the number of stories devoted to Echeverría.

The placement of reports in a newscast provided another indicator of the amount of importance news executives assigned to given subjects. World Cup reports led the newscasts four times over the six-day period. Stories on Echeverría and Morfín never led a newscast during this time. In addition, reports on Echeverría always aired before reports on Morfín.

These figures, combined with story placement, demonstrated that the World Cup was by far more important to news producers and other executives than the upcoming election and that the PRI candidate was clearly more important than his PAN opponent. The prevalence of World Cup reports during a presidential campaign elucidated news executives' motives. The number of reports and their placement suggested that economic, rather than political, interests informed the decisions made by news executives, producers, and, as a result, reporters and writers. Increasing viewership for the World Cup would translate to better ratings and hence more profits. Azcárraga Milmo sold his part of the rights to televise the event in the United States to the Spanish International Network for US$500,000.[36] Telesistema Mexicano could increase viewership by promoting the World Cup through its news programs. By 1970 the company had been including sports in news programs for two decades, and news producers and executives drew on this experience again during the World Cup.

The business of sports broadcasting has skyrocketed since 1970. By the beginning of the twenty-first century, the International Soccer Federation Association negotiated a US$425 million cash deal with ABC/ESPN and UNIVISION.[37] In return ABC/ESPN and UNIVISION have the rights to transmit the events on television, the Internet, and mobile telephony. Like the 1968 Olympics, the World Cup created an opportunity for politicians and television executives to put the nation's best face forward.

On June 17, 1970, anchor Zabludovsky led *Su diario Nescafé* with the following lead report:

> Today the semifinalists in the ninth World Cup play. At Aztec Stadium, Germany and Italy will face off, while at Jalisco Stadium, Brazil and Uruguay will go head to head. Yesterday the German team arrived from Guanajuato, León. Immediately they left the airport to Puebla, where they are based. At the Poblano hotel Mesón del Angel, the Teuton coach, Helmuth Shoen, said he feels confident as the game against Italy approaches. Shoen added that it will be difficult to score a goal against the Italians, but he hopes that the strength of his men ends with the defeat of the Italians, and in this way Germany can move on to the finals. Certainly, the German goalie [*el defensa*] Hottges won't be able to play against Italy, because of an injury incurred in the game against England. On the other hand, Grabowski will play against Italy in place of the wing, Libuda. Today, the Germans arrived in Mexico City, and they will have a light practice.[38]

Eight more reports about the World Cup followed the lead story. After a report on the World Bank establishing a line of credit to the country in the amount of 272.5 million pesos, a story on Echeverría's campaign aired:

> Yesterday, Licenciado Luis Echeverría arrived at Tampico Airport to pay a visit to the towns south of Tamaulipas and north of Veracruz. Licenciados Miguel Alemán Velasco and Jacobo Zabludovsky are with the candidate as his guests. At the airport, the state governor, Manuel A. Ravizé, welcomed Licenciado Echeverría. After arriving, he left for northern Veracrúz, where he visited the city of Pánuco. In Pánuco, Licenciado Echeverría spoke. Let's listen to a few points of his speech. . . . Today, the Licenciado will dedicate a monument and pay homage to the journalists who, when working to cover the PRI candidate's campaign, died at Poza Rica. The monument to the fallen companions, Jacobo

says, was erected along Ruiz Cortines Boulevard, 3,400 meters from Meson Hill, where the airplane crashed.³⁹

On January 25, 1970, a twin-engine airplane carrying twenty people, including fourteen Mexico City reporters and photographers and a PRI press officer, had crashed into a rugged hillside, known as Meson Hill in Veracruz.⁴⁰ All but one of those aboard died. The plane had been chartered by the PRI so that journalists could cover the candidate's campaign.

After a story on arts and crafts and a report on the hijacking of a Mexican jet bound for Cuba, the newscast aired a report on PAN candidate Guillermo González Morfín: "Licenciado Guillermo González Morfín, the PAN presidential candidate, is in Santa Rosalia, Baja California. There he conversed with students about national problems. At the same time, Deputy Alfonso Ituarte Servín gave an example of an initiative for the Ley Orgánica de Territorios Federales (Organic Law of Federal Land). Licenciado González Morfín will return from Baja California next week to close his campaign at the end of this month with a rally in front of the Palace of Fine Arts."⁴¹

While reports on the World Cup shed light on the economic interests of news executives, juxtapositioning the reports on Echeverría and González Morfín helps to explain the complex relationship between news producers and politicians. The report on Echeverría emphasized the connections between the PRI candidate and Telesistema Mexicano. The fact that Alemán Velasco and Zabludovsky both traveled with the president provided on-air evidence. To have Alemán Velasco and Zabludovsky (esteemed figures and opinion leaders) both at the candidate's side demonstrated to viewers the significance of the event.

Echeverría's tribute to fallen journalists served the candidate in two ways. First, it allowed him to show compassion for plane crash victims and their families. This served to highlight the human side of the candidate. Second, his dedication of the monument to fallen reporters served to garner support among print and electronic journalists, who would be covering his campaign. The fact that the report aired prior to the report on the opposition candidate sent the message to viewers that Echeverría was symbolically already ahead of his competitor.

The tone of reports about González Morfín, where the reports aired in the newscast, and the lack of coverage about the PAN candidate all revealed political biases in campaign coverage. In the previous report, González Morfín discussed national problems with students.[42] Viewers learned little more than that about the candidate, except that he was scheduled to return to the capital to bring his campaign to a close. Furthermore, in contrast to the reports about Echeverría, no high-ranking correspondents traveled with the candidate. The placement of the report literally put the PAN candidate below the PRI candidate. Finally, the amount of time devoted to the PAN candidate, compared with the PRI candidate, further emphasized Echeverría over González Morfín. Three reports on Echeverría aired that morning, in contrast to one report on González Morfín.

The two election reports on June 17 resembled other stories that aired on *Su diario Nescafé* during the campaign of 1970, which served to bolster Echeverría's position and downplay González Morfín's. Reports always devoted more time to Echeverría and placed reports on the PRI candidate higher than the PAN candidate. It should have come as no surprise to viewers on July 9 that Echeverría won the election by a landslide. According to the "latest calculations," for every vote cast for González Morfín, Echeverría received at least ten.[43]

By June 21 the campaign had drawn to a close, along with the World Cup. Brazil and Italy faced off in the final game of the four-week event. A report on the game's outcome led the morning news the day after the victory:

> Brazil beat Italy, by a score of four to one, the same score as the game between Italy and Mexico. The points made by the

Brazilians gave the Italians a lesson on how to use the ball and how to score a goal. Using his forehead, Pelé nailed the first goal, and it was eighteen minutes into the first half. Italy tied the score at thirty-seven minutes. The referee nullified the second goal by Pelé, because time had run out. The Italians crossed everything, even hands, and got a foul. But they never saw the Brazilians coming. For the Italians, the Brazilians were like ghosts. The Brazilians scored their second goal twenty-one minutes into the second half, by a kick from Gerson. The third goal came at twenty-six minutes, with a penalty kick by Gerson and made by Jair. The fourth goal was a product of Brazilian strength. At this time the Brazilians were in their part of the field. The fourth goal was scored by Carlos Alberto.[44]

The tone of this report sheds light on Brazilian-Mexico relations. The hagiographic portrayal of the Brazilian players in contrast to their Italian counterparts suggested that news writers supported the Latin American over the European team. The demonstrations on the soccer field following the game echoed the favorable sentiment that Mexicans had toward their fellow Latin Americans. A jubilant crowd rushed the field to celebrate with the Brazilian team. Some fans even hoisted team members on their shoulders and placed Mexican hats on the heads of players. The final game, coupled with victory celebrations afterward, must have been too much for some players. A coaching assistant had to help resuscitate player Roberto Rivelino after the fiesta on the field. Or perhaps Mexico City's high altitude did affect players' performances.

The second story the day after Brazil's World Cup victory focused on President Díaz Ordaz's presentation of the Jules Rimet trophy to the team:

> In the midst of an indescribable craziness, President Gustavo Díaz Ordaz presented the Brazilian team captain, Carlos Alberto, with the Jules Rimet cup at the end of the encounter between Brazil and Italy. At the end of the game, the chief executive said

that Italy had played well, but that the Brazilians were better. Right after, Licenciado Díaz Ordaz congratulated the Brazilians. And when asked for his opinion about the event itself, Licenciado Díaz Ordaz said that the spectacle in the stadium had no comparison, except for the stadium at Ciudad Universitaria in 1968. Licenciado Gustavo Díaz Ordaz congratulated the Brazilians and Italians one more time. The president arrived at Aztec Stadium with his daughter and Guillermo Cañedo.[45]

Guillermo Cañedo played a key role in bringing the World Cup to Mexico. He was many things to many people, including vice president of the Federación Mexicano de Fútbol (FMF, Mexican Soccer Federation), part owner of Club América (the soccer team based at Estadio Azteca), vice president of the International Soccer Federation Association, and a personal assistant to and friend of Azcárraga Milmo.[46]

The June 22 report about Brazil's victory served several purposes. First, like the story that aired before it, this report emphasized the Brazilians' athletic prowess over the Italians. Second, by focusing on Díaz Ordaz's presentation of the trophy to team captain Carlos Albert, the report highlighted the president's role in the event. Third, the report provided viewers with evidence of the connections between the government and Telesistema Mexicano. Over time, reports like these served to reinforce the prestige and image of government officials and television executives.

DÍA DE LA INDEPENDENCIA TELE-TRADITIONS CONTINUE

Much like the tele-tradition of selling sports as news, television coverage of Día de la Independencia celebrations continued well into the second half of the twentieth century. In terms of content, coverage of national holidays did not change much, compared with the earliest reports in the 1950s. Part of the reason could be explained by Zabludovsky's continued presence behind the scenes and on the air, which created a certain degree of continuity from his participation as news director of *Noticiero General Motors* on Channel 4 (the first TV news program, established in 1950) to the anchor of *24 horas* on Channel 2. Also, he became vice president of news after Telesistema Mexicano's merger with Televisión Independiente de México. But other factors may have influenced the consistency of tele-traditions, such as viewers' preferences for national holiday coverage, the existence of previously established traditions, technology, and the attitudes and views of television news executives.

The *24 horas* coverage of Día de la Independencia celebrations on September 15, 1970, evoked both new and old concepts. Producers emphasized a new and larger celebration, and at the same time the report reaffirmed a ritual that dated back 160 years. The following report aired after eighteen other international and domestic news items. The third story in the second block of the news program, it began after the program's first commercial break:

> The night of the 15th of September is perhaps the most celebrated in Mexico. The downtown nerve center of a mass of thousands of Mexicans, where the metropolitan plaza's principal arteries begin, there [is] an authentic block party. The public—more together than ever before, without distinction of social class, creates a sense of awareness, excitement, and unbridled happiness, which congregates in the zócalo. It [the zócalo] is invaded. It is impossible to take a step in the midst of this bunch of people, [with their] hats, whistles, masks, and, naturally, indispensable on this occasion, national flags. The shouts occur; the wait is long. . . . Many are accompanied by their children, either holding hands or carried on shoulders, since the early hours of the evening. . . . The tradition requires it that way, to go with the family, listening to the shout from the central balcony of the National Palace. After ringing the same bronze [bell] that in 1810 the father of the nation, Don Miguel Hidalgo, did, the president shouts for our independence, liberty, sovereignty, the

respect of the self-determination of the people, the principal of no intervention of the internal issues of the same, and the lively cries in honor of those who gave us this country.[47]

Although the reporting style did not change much between 1950 and 1970, the importance of the Día de la Independencia celebrations appeared to have diminished, based on where the reports were placed within a newscast. While in 1950 Día de la Independencia celebrations topped the newscast, on *24 horas* they did not appear until after the first commercial break. The difference in placement could be explained by two factors—the overall international focus of *24 horas* and other important nationally significant events. A larger news staff enabled Telesistema Mexicano's news team to increase the number of reports that TV journalists filed and allowed news staff to use stories from different parts of the nation as well as from abroad. Furthermore, while in the 1950s the station had to rely heavily on international news agencies for news from abroad, by 1970 a larger news team, especially one that included multilingual reporters, enhanced the company's own foreign news coverage.

After a report from Graciela Leal at the Palacio Nacional, two other stories followed, focusing on Mexican Día de la Independencia celebrations in Los Angeles, California, and New York City. Reports, such as one filed by *24 horas* correspondent Roberto Cruz from Los Angeles, about Día de la Independencia celebrations abroad demonstrated to viewers the growing importance of the country's diaspora. Consequently, the reports helped to develop a sense of a greater Mexico, a country whose borders did not stop at the Río Bravo/Grande.[48] Stories about Día de la Independencia celebrations abroad provided evidence of both a growing population of Mexicans living *en el extranjero* (abroad) as well as reaffirmed the importance of the country's independence. Like reports about López Mateos's visit to the United States in 1959, they offered proof for citizens that the national imaginary extended beyond the country's borders.

TECHNOLOGICAL ADVANCES AND TELESISTEMA MEXICANO

Aside from consolidation and the establishment of a corporate news division, technological advances helped catapult Telesistema Mexicano (1955–73) and, later, Televisa to a new level of programming and profit. One of the most important developments included the transition from film to videotape. Although videotape had been used since the 1960s, it did not become common in newsrooms until the 1970s. The transition from film to videotape both increased the speed of news production and decreased at least one element of production costs, film stock. In the 1950s work orders for photographers listed a specific amount of film that they should shoot, measured in feet, hence the term "footage." For example, photographer Angel Cabrera was authorized to shoot up to thirty feet of film at a bullfight on March 15, 1953.[49]

In addition, film images had to be processed, that is, developed in a lab, whereas videotaped reports could be aired immediately after they were recorded. Although, videotaped images usually were edited before they were broadcast, in rare cases raw footage could be aired. Another advantage of videotape was that it could be recorded over. In contrast, once exposed, film (which cost more) could not be reused. Since videotape was cheaper than film stock, photographers did not have to be so discriminating with how much they shot.

Not all photographers celebrated the transition to videotape. After two decades of news production, they had grown accustomed to shooting with film, and many resisted the change. Granted, early video cameras were bulky and quite heavy, and photographers would have to learn a new form of editing images. The transition to videotape was met with such resistance that executives had to keep the old sixteen-millimeter cameras "under lock and key" so that photographers would use the new equipment.[50]

The advent of satellite communications dramatically increased the speed at which international as well as national news could be transmitted. Before satellite communications, news items may have been included in the script of a newscast, but it took up to a day or many days for the images to arrive by airplane in Mexico City before they could be broadcast. News footage from major U.S. networks, CBS and NBC, arrived by plane daily.[51] With satellite communications, networks could receive the images as soon they were put up on a satellite feed. Theoretically, this could have positive implications for content. Satellite communications could result in offering a greater diversity of perspectives on the air, both nationally and from abroad. Of course, this did not always happen.

WOMEN HIT THE AIR

The inclusion of women reporters in television news signaled another significant transition in the 1970s. On September 15, Yolanda Sanchez, a Washington correspondent, filed a report for *24 horas*, while Patricia Berumen reported from the Columna of Independencia. Graciela Leal reported on the "usual reception at the National Palace," and Rosa María Campos filed a report on home gardening. In 1950 not one female reporter had generated news content. In contrast, of the nine reporters who filed reports on September 15, 1970, at least four were women.[52]

In 1971 Lolita Ayala began to coanchor *Noticiero teleperiódico Notimex* on Channel 8 with Jorge Kellog and Arturo Ibáñez.[53] Two years later she began to work with Zabludovsky at Televisa. With a trademark rose on her anchor desk, Ayala has become one of the country's most beloved newscasters. Trained by Zabludovsky, she has been on the air for more than four decades. In fact, Ayala stated that Zabludovsky has been a "principal figure" in her professional development as well as that of all TV journalists.[54] She worked with Zabludovsky for fourteen years, between 1974 and 1987.

The increasing presence of women on and in newscasts coincided with women's movements in Mexico and around the world. As women protested in the streets in 1968, some began to reassess their traditional roles, and some probably wound up on the air.[55]

Feminists in the United States and problems at home inspired print journalists Rosario Castellanos and Marta Acevedo to form Mujeres en Acción Solidaria (Women in Solidarity Action). Like the students of '68 who protested in the streets, women journalists found inspiration at home and abroad.[56]

By the 1970s women began to coanchor news programs, but only in the morning and afternoon. Based on anthropological research, Telesistema created news programming and placed women anchors as cohosts of these programs. The research showed that female anchors represented a "motherly figure" to whom viewers could relate, but the studies also demonstrated that they should not be used as anchors of nightly news programs, because if they had to read a negative story, they would appear as if they were "scolding the audience."[57] By 1987 the country and television executives were finally ready for a sole female anchor. That is when Ayala began to host *El noticiero con Lolita Ayala* (The news with Lolita Ayala) (see figure 13). According to her, it took almost four decades before a woman could host her own newscast because "Not only in Mexico, but in so many other countries around the world there is something that is called machismo, no? Which is to think that we women have less credibility, that we have less knowledge, and perhaps that we are worth less. I remember that before I was given my own newscast, they said that women couldn't head a news program because we had less credibility." That way of thinking changed, Ayala said, when Alemán Velasco became president of Televisa for a brief time during the mid-1980s.[58]

CONCLUSION

Despite continued unrest among popular groups, such as student dissidents and guerrillas in Guerrero, news coverage in 1970 generally showed viewers a more peaceful side of the country. This mirrored Echeverría's administration's actions, which publicly attempted to address students' and workers' demands through the announcement of political inclusion but covertly implemented

13. Lolita Ayala, Televisa news anchor and first woman in Mexico to anchor her own newscast. Courtesy of Lolita Ayala, personal collection.

a government spy program and carried out a dirty war against disgruntled citizens.⁵⁹ Critical members of the press, such as Julio Scherer, continued to pressure the president, especially after the Corpus Christi massacre on June 10, 1971. The massacre named for the Catholic celebration on June 10 happened in Mexico City, as students marched from the Instituto Politécnico Nacional on the streets of the San Cosme neighborhood. Halcones (Falcons) — a youth group trained by Federal District authorities — attacked the demonstrators with clubs and chains. The incident left twenty-five students dead and dozens injured.⁶⁰ With the country's social ills unresolved, certain factions of the opposition grew more radical and violent. Social and popular dissatisfaction with the government and its shortcomings hit television executives personally when in 1973 members of the Liga Comunista de 23 de Septiembre (LC-23, Communist League of September 23) murdered Eugenio Garza Sada during an attempted kidnapping. Garza Sada was a prominent member of the Monterrey Group, which had holdings in Televisa. Garza Sada's death only worked to put additional strain on the already tenuous relationship between Echeverría and the media elite.

News coverage of the elections of 1970 and the World Cup ignored the tensions between the president and media executives. Positive treatment of Echeverría during his campaign and the obvious lack of coverage of the PAN candidate told viewers where the network stood. Instead of voicing their criticisms of the administration on the air, media moguls worked to limit the state's hegemonic policies behind the scenes. On an international level, news executives continued to portray the country as modern and orderly, which helped both the government's and the media industry's goals. Furthermore, while the World Cup was a distinctly international affair, news producers chose to highlight the president's, and therefore the country's, participation in hosting the event. This served to emphasize the nation's importance and its ability to host the cup.

> When your life ends and you rest with your forefathers, I shall set up one of your family, one of your own children, to succeed you, and I shall establish his kingdom.
>
> 2 Samuel 7:12

Conclusion

AT ELEVEN o'clock Sunday evening on October 2, 1970, Mexico City viewers tuned into *24 horas*, Telesistema Mexicano's flagship newscast, which had been on the air for almost a month. Zabludovsky led the newscast with a report on President Díaz Ordaz's appointment of Manuel Bernardo Aguirre as secretary of agriculture. The newscast included other national and international reports, as well as a story about the fifth anniversary of the death of Ramón Beteta, narrated by chronicler Salvador Novo—the same Novo who wrote the 1947 report about how television should be implemented. Beteta was the editor of the *News* and *Novedades* between 1958 and 1964, as well as the director of Miguel Alemán Valdés's presidential campaign from 1945 to 1946.[1]

Excluded from the news on October 2 was any mention of the second anniversary of the massacre at Tlatelolco and the nineteenth Olympiad. Certainly, viewers remembered the massacre at the

Plaza de las Tres Culturas as well as the Olympics two years before. Those events were likely more relevant to most viewers than the anniversary of Beteta's death. The decision to omit the two most important national events of 1968, and arguably of the second half of the twentieth century, remained conspicuous. The news division must have supported the producer's decision, because it provided the newscast with its stamp of approval.² After two decades of television watching, many Telesistema viewers had grown accustomed to the news that was included as well as excluded. As '68 activist Jorge Perezvega stated, "you read between the lines" of print and electronic media.³

In the fall of 1970 Echeverría prepared for his next six years at Los Pinos, as hundreds gathered at the Panteón Español (Spanish Cemetery) to bid goodbye to Don Emilio Azcárraga Vidaurreta. The death of the media czar and the ushering in of the left-leaning administration foreshadowed a new era for television news and the country. Echeverría followed Díaz Ordaz's lead and attempted to strengthen the government's grip on television. Whether nationalization was ever a viable possibility or just a tool for political gain remained debatable. Certainly, nationalized television systems became a reality in several countries in Latin America. A military junta in Peru expropriated private television in 1968, along with radio and newspapers. A coup in 1975 returned television to private hands. Between 1970 and 1982 in Venezuela, reformers sought to implement a mixed system, such as in Mexico, where both the government and private industry contributed to television content. In Argentina private interests lost control of television in 1974 when Juan Perón placed it under the authority of the state, arguing that foreign programming and excessive commercialism threatened national culture.⁴ In Brazil the television industry and news production functioned in a manner similar to Mexico—TV remained in private hands throughout the dictatorship (1964–85), but certainly the government had its hands in what ended up on the air.⁵

Nationalization efforts grew out of larger debates about the so-called New World Information and Communication Order. Through UNESCO fora, countries devised national communications policies as part of development strategies and efforts to reduce the power of foreign programming. Herbert I. Schiller warned that the "cultural homogenization that has been underway for years in the United States now threatens to overtake the globe.... Everywhere local culture is facing submission from the mass-produced outpourings of commercial broadcasting."[6] Obviously, the case of Telesistema Mexicano and Televisa called into question Schiller's comments about cultural imperialism, given that by the 1970s the majority of news and entertainment programming was produced domestically. Furthermore, twenty years after the official inauguration of television, Mexican networks had already begun to infiltrate markets in the United States, and by the 1980s Televisa was exporting its programming throughout the world.[7]

The 1970s discussions about cultural hegemony fostered a communications reform environment throughout the hemisphere. Global discussions prompted Televisa to host the Primer Encuentro de Comunicaciones (First World Conference of Communications) in October 1974. At the Acapulco summit, Alemán Velasco entered a heated exchange with President Echeverría about television. During a luncheon at the conference, the president ranted about the failings of television, at which point Alemán stood up and explained the role and responsibilities of television, then told Echeverría that if he wanted to accept the responsibility he could take over the industry.[8] The president declined, but his desire to influence television programming reflected his pressing need to placate popular groups and improve his (as well as the PRI's) image.[9] The debates over nationalization revealed that media executives and politicians did not always see eye to eye, and the 1974 scenario showed that at times capitalists limited the state's attempts to control the media.

The fundamental goal of this book is to define and explain the limits of cultural hegemony during the height of PRI power and the

Cold War. Five case studies of news coverage were analyzed with the goal of deepening understanding about power and culture on an international and national level. In the international realm the book focuses on foreign hegemony, mainly from the United States, on the state and Mexican national media. In the domestic realm the study hones in on the state's influence on national media and on the national media's role in shaping viewers' attitudes.

HEGEMONY ON AN INTERNATIONAL LEVEL

Newscasts between 1950 and 1970 provided powerful public displays of the country's contingent and precarious position during the height of the Cold War. Through coverage of the Cuban Revolution of 1959 and the railway strikes of 1958 and 1959, writers sent two distinct messages to viewers—Cuban rebels were to be hailed, while domestic dissidents were to be assailed. The inconsistent coverage brought to the fore local as well as international tensions, as news reports functioned as audiovisual expressions of the Cold War.

Embracing the new medium, high-ranking government officials at home and abroad sought airtime in efforts to push their distinct diplomatic and Cold War agendas. Coverage about presidents López Mateos and Cárdenas as well as U.S. president Eisenhower, Soviet deputy premier Mikoyan, and Cuban premier Castro illuminated the tenuous quadripartite relations between Mexico, the United States, the Soviet Union, and Cuba. The tensions between the four countries reached an apogee during the Bay of Pigs invasion and the Cuban Missile Crisis, demonstrating that news executives and politicians walked a fine line between keeping the ideas of the revolution alive and maintaining friendly relations with the United States. News coverage of the Space Race suggested that news executives sometimes sided with the United States rather than their country's own politicians. At the same time, news writers often posited international space projects in nationalistic terms, in ways that promoted the country's level of modernity. In this way, television news resembled the coverage of print journalists in other parts of Latin America and established boundaries about how international events would be framed.

From 1950 to 1970 television clearly joined radio, becoming a valuable tool for those interested in winning the hearts and minds of citizens. Television executives, producers, and reporters played a role in that battle. Directed by executives, television producers functioned as political and cultural diplomats. Often using content generated by the big four international news agencies, the reports producers included in newscasts demonstrated the country's alignment with the United States and its less than favorable attitude toward the Soviet Union. At times, producers did include content from the Soviet information agency, TASS, but those instances paled in comparison with the use of the AP and UPI.

News coverage also illuminated the country's contradictions with respect to its international and domestic policies. On the international stage, government officials attempted to be arbiters of peace in discussions regarding the Space Race and nuclear arms race, but at home they waged war against citizens who did not ascribe to the ideas of the authoritarian regime. On television, the nineteenth Olympiad was hailed as the "Olympics of Peace," but witnesses who saw their friends and neighbors shot dead in the Plaza de Las Tres Culturas saw a very distinct side of the country.

HEGEMONY ON A NATIONAL LEVEL

Tensions between media moguls and the government had existed since the inception of television. Alemán's decision to grant the first concession to O'Farrill instead of Azcárraga Vidaurreta certainly did not work to foster the relationship between Azcárraga Senior and the government. The relationship would have to be cultivated over time, so that by the 1970s and 1980s Azcárraga Milmo would call himself a "soldier of the PRI." In the 1950s President Ruiz Cortines, along with Mexico City mayor Ernesto Uruchurtu, attempted to reign in television owners by imposing censorship and banning the broadcasts of *lucha libre* (Mexican wrestling). In 1959, in an effort to improve the quality of television, Ruiz Cortines established XEIPN, Channel 11, a government-owned television station at the Instituto Politécnico Nacional. The station never competed with commercial stations, but its creation provided an example of conflicting corporate and state interests.

Although television newscasts between 1950 and 1970 by and large reiterated and reaffirmed official stories, content included in the newscasts demonstrated that profits more often than politics drove the decisions at Telesistema Mexicano, and later at Televisa. Media executives and politicians did not walk in lockstep, but the goals of creating a modern and orderly nation worked in favor of both the state and the private sector. The Azcárragas and O'Farrills needed a modern and orderly country to lure investors and advertisers, while presidents from Alemán to Echeverría required a level of tranquility and prosperity across the nation to maintain legitimacy and power.

The death of Emilio Azcárraga Vidaurreta put Telesistema Mexicano in the hands of Azcárraga Junior, the "idiot prince." Many of the longtime television executives thought that Azcárraga Junior was incapable of managing. But his ability to complete the construction of Estadio Azteca in 1966 provided his critics with some evidence that he might be able to take over Telesistema Mexicano when the time was right. The elder Azcárraga's death also created an opening for the merging of Televisión Independiente de México and Telesistema Mexicano. At Don Emilio's funeral, Bernardo Garza Sada, a chief executive of Televisión Independiente de México, reportedly asked Azcárraga's son to negotiate a consolidation between to the two companies.[10] The deal was finalized a year later, leaving the Azcárragas with a 75 percent share of Televisa and the Garza Sadas with 25 percent. In an effort to end a longstanding regional struggle between capitalists from Mexico City and from Monterrey, an agreement was signed to create Televisa, with Azcárraga Junior as company president and Alejandro Sada as vice president.[11] As in 1955 corporate consolidation further strengthened the television industry and made it less vulnerable in the face of hostile government officials and potential nationalization efforts. Clearly, the success of Azcárraga Junior through the 1970s and 1980s, during which time he became one of the richest men in the country, proved that he was a media king, and no idiot.

Prior to the consolidation of Televisión Independiente de México and Telesistema Mexicano, television producers established numerous tele-traditions. The invention of tele-traditions reinforced existing traditions and laid the groundwork for standardized news programs. Coverage of national holidays such as El Día de la Independencia helped construct mexicanidad, but it excluded many popular groups from the festivities. Official and elite voices often drowned out those of poor and disenfranchised capitalinos, as well as those from the urban and rural provinces. Television, as the new public square, would ignore a large portion of the population. The consequences of emphasizing elite and official members of society only increased tensions between the nation's rich and poor, and urban and rural populations. Hence, mexicanidad on television tended to reflect an elite and male-dominated version of national identity.

The practice of covering sports as news represents another tele-tradition. The promotion and coverage of sporting events derived from older print and radio traditions and catered to the interests of sports fans as well as the financial interests of television station owners. International sporting events such as the Olympic Games of 1968 and the World Cup of 1970 served both politicians and business owners, in that they created opportunities to promote the nation as modern, orderly, and progressive. The selection of Enriqueta Basilio as the first woman to light the Olympic cauldron was just one example of how politicians and media moguls worked together toward similar ends.

Newscasts often emphasized sports over politics. The amount of coverage devoted to the World Cup compared to the presidential campaign sent a message to viewers that soccer was more important than the electoral process. Consequently, for media executives the strategy of privileging sports over news diminished the possibilities of news producers having to answer to government officials about sensitive and political news coverage. By emphasizing sports over politics, newscasts helped the government carry out the long-standing tactic of what ancient Roman satirist Juvenal called *"panen et circenses"* (bread and circuses).[12] Between 1950 and 1970 television became the vehicle through which modern-day Olympics (circuses) could be beamed to the masses, while government programs such as the food subsidy agency CEISMA, and later the Compañía Nacional de Subsistencias Populares (CONASUPO), distributed the "bread" or, in this case, tortillas.

Student activists protested the shortcomings of government programs and policies and took their frustrations to the streets, but TV producers chose to downplay their concerns and instead highlight the Olympics. Nevertheless, activists managed to disseminate their alternative and hybrid messages through grassroots methods such as street theater, cheap newsprint, graffiti, and counterculture music. The young artists who produced counter-hegemonic images, such as a gorilla dressed in a military uniform, did not have the technological might of Telesistema Mexicano, but the images they produced could sometimes be just as powerful as those transmitted through the airwaves.[13] Student messages and images also proved that there were limits to cultural hegemony imposed by Telesistema Mexicano.

During the first twenty years of television, TV producers aired reports that helped shape and reflect national identity. Newscasts broadcast mexicanidad and demonstrated what made Mexican TV news Mexican. Characteristics of the nation's television news included favorable coverage of the PRI and the president, a preoccupation with modernity and development, and a proclivity for placing economic concerns above educational or informative endeavors. Through corporate and self-censorship, news executives applied the oft-stated "code of honor" that rendered untouchable three pillars of society: the *bandera* (flag, read president), *el ejército* (military), and the Virgen de Guadalupe.[14] Though unwritten, news professionals followed the code if they wanted to remain on the air.[15] Yet this study has shown that the relationship between the state and private media interests was far more complicated and nuanced than simply paying attention to the code of honor and has explained how news coverage and news producers on a daily basis contributed to the longevity of the PRI through a carefully crafted set of guidelines for covering international and national news.

Finally, the treatment of women both on- and offscreen sharpens the picture of Mexican television news and mexicanidad at the middle of the twentieth century. Women reporters did not begin to contribute to news production until the mid-1960s. The first women reporters did not often cover political and hard news events. It took almost three decades before news executives were comfortable enough to have a woman anchor a newscast by herself without a male counterpart. Only politically or economically elite women were covered in the news, which often focused on the activities of presidents' wives who engaged in socially acceptable behavior, such as handing out gifts to poor children on the Día de los Reyes. Rarely did producers grant women opportunities to express their political views. Similarly, the voices of lower-class and indigenous women remained off camera.

News executives' decisions to air coverage within certain political, social, and cultural frames — frames that excluded large portions of the population and alternative viewpoints — came at a price. By the end of the twentieth century, and after three generations of television audiences, Televisa recognized it had a serious credibility problem and that lack of credibility ran the risk of losing viewers. Studies showed that the third generation of viewers had a general distrust of the media, especially with respect to television news.[16]

Despite its inability to include a diverse representation of news and its lack of credibility, *24 horas* must have been popular with enough viewers, having endured for almost three decades. The last edition of the program aired on January 19, 1998, twenty-seven years, four months, and fourteen days after its first broadcast. A day before the final broadcast, the Mexico City daily *Reforma* published an audience survey about the program's influence, in which 40 percent of those surveyed said they watched the program every day. The survey asked two questions: How much influence do you think *24 horas* has had on the life in this country? And, do you think Zabludovsky should continue or retire from anchoring the news? The majority of those surveyed thought that *24 horas* had some or much influence on society. Three-fifths of those interviewed thought that Zabludovsky should continue on the air.[17]

By the turn of the twenty-first century it would be difficult to find a person who had grown up in the capital between the 1950s and 1990s who could not identify Zabludovsky.[18] Despite his familiarity among viewers, the public knows little about the extent to which Zabludovsky controlled the production of daily television news. Through interviews with journalists he has offered some information about the government's influence over news programming. His comments have for the most part been vague, and important details have been omitted. For example, exactly what did government officials tell television and news executives on the night of the Tlatelolco massacre? News executives and government officials continue to contend that the government did not directly influence television coverage regarding the student massacre. Nevertheless, Zabludovsky did admit that Televisa had images of the shooting in the plaza, although it never aired the footage.[19] Zabludovsky's influence among broadcast reporters is unprecedented. Having worked in television news since its inception in 1950 until 1998, he directly or indirectly influenced all Mexican television journalists. Zabludovsky's style of reporting and delivery set the tone and provided a model for those who worked with him and those who came after.[20]

Despite the threat of dwindling audiences, by the first decade of the twenty-first century the television news panorama had been altered. Women such as Lolita Ayala and Adela Micha anchored their own daily news programs. In July 2006, as the country geared up for a presidential election, news personality Victor Trujillo introduced a regular news segment on his morning program on Televisa's Channel 4. The pretaped segment, "If I Were President," included comments from "average" viewers who announced what they would do if they were president. In one sound bite, a mestiza-looking woman declared that she would "improve the conditions of the nation's poor as well as improve the communications media."[21]

By 1998 after the death of Azcárraga "El Tigre" Milmo in 1997, it became apparent that the aging news model and its anchor should retire. Though Zabludovsky left the small screen, he continued to work in broadcasting, hosting a two-hour radio program in Mexico City, Monday through Friday, well into the twenty-first century. Aside from Zabludovsky's departure, several other high-level company executives left Televisa between 1997 and 2000, including Miguel Sabido, vice president of research; Pablo García Sáinz, vice president of special projects; and Alemán, executive vice president. Televisa's incoming president, Emilio Azcárraga Jean, who replaced his father, argued that because the political system was opening, the news system should become more open as well: "We are not rooting for the Institutional Revolutionary Party (PRI), nor any other party, we are rooting for Mexico."[22] In the twenty-first century "rooting for Mexico," from the perspective of big media such as Televisa, continues to be driven by economic interests from "above," following a tele-tradition established during the first decades of television.

Notes

FOREWORD
1. "Foreign Trade."

INTRODUCTION
Becerra Celis, "Mexico."
1. "TV in Mexico," *Newsweek*, December 17, 1951, 50.
2. Today, one of Televisa's news archives is located in the bowels of the stadium in tunnel 27.
3. Leticia Castillo, "História," *Esmas*, 2006, http://www.esmas.com/estadioazteca/quienes/300711.html; *El Noticiero*, May 29, 1966, Filmoteca de Noticieros de Televisa, Estadio Azteca (hereafter cited as FNTEA).
4. *El Noticiero*, May 29, 1966, FNTEA.
5. "Inauguración de Estadio Azteca," XEW-TV, Channel 2, May 29, 1966, Videoteca de Noticieros de Televisa, Chapultepec.
6. *El Noticiero*, May 29, 1966, FNTEA.
7. Fernández Christlieb, *Medios de difusión masiva*; Trejo Delabre, *Redes de Televisa*; Darling and Miller, "Emilio Azcárraga"; Orozco Gómez, "Televisión en México."
8. Noriega and Leach, *Broadcasting in Mexico*, 52, 56, 54.
9. Fernández Christlieb, *Medios de difusión masiva*.
10. Saragoza, *Media and the State*, ch. 5.
11. Fernández and Paxman, *Tigre*, 325.
12. Adolfo Ruiz Cortines, Fondo presidencial, folio 31291, exp. 433/153, caja 452, Archivo General de la Nación.

13. Miguel Alemán Velasco, former vice president and executive president of Televisa and founding director of Telesistema Mexicano's news division, interview by author, Mexico City, August 6, 2009, and March 14, 2006.
14. Fernández and Paxman, *Tigre*, 418; Alemán Velasco, interview.
15. Alemán Velasco, interview.
16. Julia Preston, "News (and State) Anchor Weighs His," *New York Times*, January 20, 1998, A4.
17. Alemán Velasco, interview; Fernández and Paxman, *Tigre*, 144, 161.
18. Zelizer, *Covering the Body*.
19. Martín-Barbero, *Communication, Culture, and Hegemony*.
20. Lears, "Concept of Cultural Hegemony."
21. Hernández Lomeli called attention to these two paradigms in *Racionalidad*.
22. Fernández Christlieb, *Medios de difusión masiva*, 2.
23. Castellot de Ballin, *Historia de la televisión*.
24. Wells and Joseph, *Summer of Discontent*, 4.
25. Hobsbawm, "Introduction," 1.
26. Martín-Barbero, *Communication, Culture, and Hegemony*, 151 and intro.
27. González de Bustamante, "Tele-visiones."
28. Grandin, *Last Colonial Massacre*; Joseph and Spenser, *In from the Cold*; White, *Creating a Third World*; Witherspoon, *Eyes of the World*.
29. Geertz, *Interpretation of Cultures*; Storey, *Introductory Guide*; Schlesinger, introduction to *Communication, Culture, and Hegemony*, by Martín-Barbero, xi.
30. Geertz, *Interpretation of Cultures*; Storey, *Introductory Guide*.
31. González de Bustamante, "First Television Newscasts."
32. Cardoso, "Associated-Dependent Development," 149; Cardoso and Faletto, *Dependency and Development*.
33. Niblo, "British Propaganda"; Arredondo Ramírez and Zermeno Torres, "Política informativa."
34. Zolov, *Refried Elvis*, 13.
35. García Canclini, *Culturas híbridas*; Martín-Barbero, *Communication, Culture, and Hegemony*, 151.
36. Reese, Gandy, and Grant, *Framing Public Life*; Gamson and Modigliani, "Media Discourse."

37. Jorge Perezvega, '68 activist and member of El Comité '68, interview by author, Mexico City, August 6, 2009; Ana Ignacia Rodriguez,'68 activist and member of El Comité '68, interview by author, Mexico City, August 5, 2009.

38. Miguel Sabido, interview by author, Mexico City, March 14, 2006.

39. Two important exceptions are González Molina, "Mexican Television News," and Hughes and Lawson, "Propaganda and Crony Capitalism"; however, their works focus on a later period.

40. Sánchez de Armas, prologue to *Apuntes*, 9, 16; Sánchez Ruiz, *Tendencias*.

41. O'Connor, *Image as Artifact*, 27.

42. Grandin's *Last Colonial Massacre*; Joseph and Spenser, *In from the Cold*; White, *Creating a Third World*; Witherspoon, *Eyes of the World*.

43. Joseph and Spenser, *In from the Cold*, 18.

44. Fein, "Producing the Cold War."

45. Schwoch, *American Radio Industry*, 106.

46. Carrandi Ortíz, *Testimonio*, 81.

47. *Tele* is the Spanish abbreviation for the word "television."

48. Beezley and Lorey, *Viva México*, xi; Anderson, *Imagined Communities*.

49. Sánchez de Armas, *Apuntes*, 535.

50. Paul Kennedy, "Mexico Prepares for 1968 Olympics: Finance Committee Meets on Housing Problems," *New York Times*, July 3, 1965, 13.

1. THE RISE OF TELEVISION IN MEXICO

Guillermo González Camarena, "La televisión: Investigación del Instituto Nacional de Bellas Artes," 39, Miguel Alemán Valdés, Fondo presidencial, exp. 523/14, caja 472, Archivo General de la Nación.

1. "La televisión, el más nuevo adelanto, ya funciona en México," *Novedades*, September 1, 1950, 1–3.

2. Saragoza, *State and the Media*, ch. 5.

3. Fernández Christlieb, *Medios de difusión masiva*, 95–96.

4. Saragoza, *State and the Media*, ch. 5.

5. Hernández Lomeli, "Obstáculos."

6. Mejía Barquera, "Cronología general," 526.

7. Castellot de Ballin, *Historia de la televisión*, 20.

8. Martínez Medellín, *Televisa*, 35.

9. Dorfman and Mattelart, *Donald Duck*.

10. *Novedades*, September 1, 1950, front page.
11. In 1939 Franklin Delano Roosevelt officially inaugurated television at the World's Fair in New York City. Brazil's inaugural transmission occurred seventeen days after Mexico's, with a variety show in Rio de Janiero on TV Tupi.
12. Castellot de Ballin, *Historia de la televisión*, 21.
13. Noriega and Leach, *Broadcasting in Mexico*, 20. The race between Mexico, Brazil, and Cuba offers evidence of the important connection between technology, modernity, and nationalism. While there is a dearth of literature on Brazilian television from a historical perspective, as well as in English, Mattos, *A televisão no Brasil*, has made an important contribution. For a detailed analysis of the early stages of radio and television in Cuba, see Salwen, *Radio and Television*.
14. Mejía Barquera, "Del canal 4," 27.
15. "TV in Mexico," *Newsweek*, December 17, 1951, 50.
16. Alisky, "Early Mexican Broadcasting."
17. Mejía Barquera, "Del canal 4," 29.
18. Mejía Barquera, "Del canal 4," 21.
19. *El Nacional*, May 17, 1935, 1, 2.
20. Fernández Christlieb, *Medios de difusión masiva*, 91.
21. Mejía Barquera, "Del canal 4," 25.
22. Novo and González Camarena, "Televisión," 7.
23. Alisky, "Early Mexican Broadcasting"; Hayes, *Radio Nation*, 34.
24. Fernández Christlieb, *Medios de difusión masiva*, 87–100.
25. Hayes, *Radio Nation*, 34.
26. Noriega and Leach, *Broadcasting in Mexico*, 22.
27. Fernández Christlieb, *Medios de difusión masiva*.
28. Mexico by no means was unique in this regard. Commercial sponsorship and later direct advertising paid for programming in Brazil and the United States since the medium began. In Brazil, for example, Esso (Standard Oil) sponsored the first newscast of record on TV Tupi.
29. Alisky, "Early Mexican Broadcasting."
30. Lewis, *Five Families*, 82.
31. Lewis, *Five Families*, 147.
32. Lewis, *Five Families*, 83.
33. Castellot de Ballin, *Historia de la televisión*, 37.
34. Hernández Lomeli, "Obstáculos," 166.

35. Mejía Barquera, "Cronología general," 529.
36. Hernández Lomeli, "Obstáculos."
37. Hernández Lomeli, "Obstáculos."
38. *Excelsior*, October 28, 1954, 10.
39. Adolfo Ruiz Cortines, Fondo presidencial, exp. 704/208, caja 1282, Archivo General de la Nación.
40. Agustín, *Vida en México*.
41. Rubenstein, *Bad Language*; Kram Villarreal, "Gladiolas."
42. Hernández Lomeli, "Obstáculos."
43. Noriega and Leach, *Broadcasting in Mexico*, 22.
44. Noriega and Leach, *Broadcasting in Mexico*, 30–31.
45. Noriega and Leach, *Broadcasting in Mexico*, 32.
46. Fernández Christlieb, *Medios de difusión masiva*, 158.
47. Baer, "Television and Political Control," 79.
48. Becerra Celis, "Mexico."
49. Mejía Barquera, "Cronología," 517.
50. Mejía Barquera, "Cronología general," 523.
51. The Tokyo Olympics were the first to be transmitted through satellite technology, but images were black and white. Mejía Barquera, "Cronología general," 535.
52. Adriana Labardini, daughter of Jorge Labardini, interview by author, Mexico City, June 2005; see also Mejía Barquera, "Cronología general," 517.
53. Mejía Barquera, "Cronología," 518, 537.
54. Aceves González, "Hermosa provincia mexicana," 263; Sánchez Ruiz, "Medios de difusión."
55. Aceves González, "Hermosa provincia Mexicana," 266.
56. Saragoza, *Monterrey Elite*.
57. Mejía Barquera, "Cronología general," 536.
58. Aceves González, "Hermosa provincia mexicana," 273.
59. Gutierrez Lara, "Industria de la TV," 1:494.
60. Alisky, "Mexico's Rural Radio."
61. Niblo, *Mexico in the 1940s*. Cosío Villegas called the "Revolution exhausted." "Crisis de México," 244.
62. Sherman, "Mexican 'Miracle,'" 576; MacLachlan and Beezley, *Gran pueblo*, 382–420.
63. Sherman, "Mexican 'Miracle,'" 576.

64. The economy had already begun to grow during the Cárdenas administration (1936–42), but it grew at an unprecedented rate after 1946.
65. Kennedy, *Middle Beat*, 77.
66. Sherman, "Mexican 'Miracle,'" 582.
67. Kennedy, *Middle Beat*, 36.
68. Alba and Potter, "Population and Development."
69. For more on the politics of social policy during the twentieth century, focusing on the government's food subsidy program, see Ochoa, *Feeding Mexico*.
70. Ochoa, *Feeding Mexico*, 9.
71. Sherman, "Mexican 'Miracle,'" 588.
72. Blough, "Political Attitudes."
73. Morton, *Woman Suffrage in Mexico*, 94.
74. González de Bustamante, "*Club de señoritas*."
75. Sherman, "Mexican 'Miracle,'" 593.
76. Anderson, *Imagined Communities*; MacLachlan and Beezley, *Gran pueblo*.
77. Arrendondo Ramírez and Zermeno Torres, "Política informativa."
78. Carey, *Plaza of Sacrifices*. Although an extensive literature exists in Spanish, Carey's monograph is one of the first works in English to analyze the Tlatelolco massacre.
79. In 1990 Peruvian writer and intellectual Mario Vargas Llosa called PRI rule the "perfect dictatorship."
80. For more on forms of authoritarianism in Latin America, see O'Donnell, *Bureaucratic Authoritarianism*.
81. Fuentes, *Historia de las comunicaciones*, 150.
82. Mejía Barquera, "Cronología general," 537.
83. Carey, *Plaza of Sacrifices*, 163–66.
84. Fernández Christlieb, *Medios de difusión masiva*, 120–21.
85. Miguel Sabido, former Televisa vice president for research, interview by author, Mexico City, March 14, 2006.
86. Story, "Policy Cycles."

2. THE INVENTION OF TELE-TRADITIONS

1. *Noticiero General Motors*, January 6, 1954, FNTEA. In Mexico children traditionally receive presents on January 6. Over time, December 25 has increased in popularity as the day to distribute gifts to children, in

part because of U.S. cultural influence through the media and migration patterns to and from the United States.

2. Carrandi Ortíz, *Testimonio*, 12, 13.
3. Alemán Velasco, interview by author, Mexico City, March 14, 2006.
4. Fernández and Paxman, *Tigre*, 25.
5. Waisbord, "Latin America." Similarly, the Brazilian television model, dominated by the Marinho family, and early Cuban television (prior to the 1959 revolution) also have been influential throughout Latin America.
6. Hernández Lomeli, "Obstáculos."
7. For an early and significant work on agenda setting and the gatekeeping role of journalists, see Shaw and McCombs, *American Political Issues*. For a cogent and useful discussion of the various levels of agenda setting and framing, see Chyi and McCombs, "Media Salience," 22–35.
8. Beezley and Lorey, *Viva México*.
9. Hughes, *Newsrooms in Conflict*, 91.
10. Castellot, *Televisión en México*, 41.
11. Alemán Velasco, interview.
12. Moreno, *Yankee Don't Go Home!*, 170.
13. Castellot, *Televisión en México*, 41.
14. *Noticiero General Motors*, January 17, 1954, FNTEA. Licenciado is the title given to someone who has received a bachelor's degree.
15. *Noticiero General Motors*, April 7, 1954, FNTEA.
16. González de Bustamante, "Dependency and Development."
17. *Noticiero PEMEX sol novedades*, February 21, 1955, FNTEA.
18. *Noticiero PEMEX sol novedades*, February 28, 1955, FNTEA; *Noticiero General Motors*, December 24, 1954, FNTEA.
19. González de Bustamante, "Dependency and Development."
20. Castellot, *Televisión en México*, 23.
21. Huesca Rebolledo, "Notícia por televisión," 99–102.
22. *Noticiero General Motors*, January 11, 1954, FNTEA.
23. Arrendondo Ramírez and Zermeno Torres, "Política informativa." The creation of the Dirección General de Información y Noticieros is discussed in further detail in chapter 7.
24. Huesca Rebolledo, "Noticia por televisión," 2:71.
25. An interview with Jacobo Zabludovsky was requested, but he declined to sign the researcher's human subjects consent form.
26. Lolita Ayala, interview by author, Mexico City, July 31, 2008.
27. Fernández and Paxman, *Tigre*, 325.

28. Poniatowska, *Todo México*, 173.
29. Huesca Rebolledo, "Noticia por televisión," 102, 71.
30. Poniatowska, *Todo México*, 173.
31. Poniatowska, *Todo México*, 184, 185.
32. Alemán Valdés, *Mejor México*, 633–35.
33. Fromson, "Mexico's Struggle."
34. Camp, *Intellectuals and the State*, 203.
35. Aurélio Pérez, vice president of special affairs, Grupo Televisa, *Dando la noticia*.
36. Smith, "Mexico since 1946," 345–46.
37. Cline, *Mexico*, 160, argues that the PRI rather than Alemán chose Ruiz Cortines as the party candidate.
38. Chorba, *Mexico*.
39. Anderson, *Imagined Communities*; Scott, *Seeing Like a State*; Pérez-Rayon, "Capital Commemorates Independence," 143.
40. Hobsbawm, "Introduction."
41. Castellot, *Televisión en México*, 35.
42. Only scripts and images from 1954 and 1955 are examined in this section because of the limitations of the Televisa news archive. The earliest scripts housed at the archive begin in 1954. The scripts between the years 1950 and 1953 have been lost. All translations are the author's, unless otherwise noted. The source for the following four stories is *Noticiero General Motors*, September 16, 1954, FNTEA.
43. *Noticiero PEMEX-novedades*, September 16, 1954, FNTEA.
44. The newsreel for this story did not include footage of the zócalo, as the script indicated. Because news clips from both newscasts were archived on the same reel, it is possible that at times film was exchanged between producers of both *PEMEX-novedades* and *Noticiero General Motors*.
45. *Noticiero PEMEX-novedades*, September 16, 1954, FNTEA.
46. *Noticiero General Motors*, September 15, 1955; *Noticiero PEMEX-novedades*, September 15, 1955; *Noticiero General Motors*, September 16, 1955; *Noticiero PEMEX-novedades*, September 16, 1955, all in FNTEA.
47. In 1943 women received the right to vote in municipal elections, and in 1953 the National Congress voted to amend the constitution, allowing them to vote in federal elections.
48. Huesca Rebolledo, "Noticia por televisión," 99–104.
49. *Noticiero diario de la tarde aceptaciones*, September 16, 1963, FNTEA.

50. Vizeu Pereira, Porcello, Ladeira Mota, *Telejornalismo*.
51. Hobsbawm, "Introduction," 1.

3. REBELS AND REVOLUTIONARIES

1. *Noticiero General Motors*, January 1, 1959, FNTEA.
2. Castañeda, *Utopia Unarmed*, 67.
3. White, *Creating a Third World*, 44; Zolov, "Lázaro Cárdenas."
4. White, *Creating a Third World*, 21–48.
5. Fidel Castro, "A Cárdenas debo la libertad: A México la inspiración, dice Fidel a la Revista Siempre!," *Siempre!*, August 12, 1959, 32.
6. White, *Creating a Third World*, 55, 54.
7. *Noticiero General Motors*, August 3, 1958, FNTEA.
8. Castañeda, prologue to *México*.
9. *Noticiero General Motors*, January 7, 1959, FNTEA.
10. The favorable coverage of Castro would decrease overtime, especially by the 1963 Cuban Missile Crisis.
11. Alegre, "Contesting the 'Mexican Miracle,'" 222.
12. I thank Robert Alegre for sharing his insights and expertise on the railway workers movements with me.
13. Alegre, "Rieleras."
14. Alegre, "Contesting the 'Mexican Miracle.'"
15. As chapter 6 demonstrates, government leaders used similar anticommunist rhetoric to undermine student dissidents in 1968.
16. González Molina, "Mexican Television News"; Hughes, *Newsrooms in Conflict*, 43.
17. *Noticiero General Motors*, June 27, 1958, FNTEA.
18. Alegre, "Contesting the 'Mexican Miracle.'"
19. The tendency to portray dissidents as rebels continued into the late 1960s (see chapter 6).
20. *Noticiero General Motors*, June 27, 1958, FNTEA.
21. González Molina, "Mexican Television News," has found that in the mid-1980s television news favored some working-class movements over others. For example, while airline and communications strikes occupied a strong position in the news landscape, railway strikes received scant attention.
22. *Noticiero General Motors*, June 28, 1958, FNTEA.
23. Alegre, "Contesting the 'Mexican Miracle.'"

24. *Noticiero General Motors*, June 29, 1958, FNTEA.

25. Alegre, "Contesting the 'Mexican Miracle,'" ch. 5.

26. *Noticiero General Motors*, August 3, 1958, FNTEA.

27. *Noticiero General Motors*, August 3, 1958, FNTEA.

28. Alegre, "Contesting the 'Mexican Miracle,'" 200, 222. For more on the contributions of women during the railway movement, see Alegre, "Rieleras."

29. "El líder Vallejo dio Contraórden," *El Universal*, February 22, 1959.

30. Alegre, "Contesting the 'Mexican Miracle,'" 222.

31. Mallin, *Covering Castro*, 300.

32. Schieffer, *Face the Nation*, 46–49.

33. Ball, *Cold War*, 98.

34. *Noticiero General Motors*, January 1, 1959, FNTEA.

35. *Noticiero General Motors*, January 1, 1959, FNTEA.

36. *Noticiero General Motors*, January 1, 1959, FNTEA. Although the corresponding images for this report were unavailable at Televisa's archive, the script referred to Cubans in Mexico City, which the author assumes referred to images of Cuban exiles at the Cuban embassy, but images did not always logically correspond with the script.

37. For the entire script, see González de Bustamante, "*Tele-visiones*," 117–19.

38. Boyd-Barrett, *International News Agencies*, 14, 91, 92.

39. Tunstall, *Media Were American*; Salwen and Garrison, *Latin American Journalism*, 84–101.

40. *Noticiero General Motors*, January 7, 1959, FNTEA.

41. Jacobo Zabludovsky, "Fidel en Matanzas," *El Universal*, January 14, 2008, http://www.eluniversal.com.mx/columnas/vi_69353.html.

42. White House Memorandum, October 9, 1967, Electronic Briefing Book, no. 5, National Security Archive.

43. Alegre, "Contesting the 'Mexican Miracle,'" 222–23.

44. *Noticiero General Motors*, January 7, 1959, FNTEA.

45. In 1946 the Mexican Revolution was officially institutionalized with the renaming of the ruling party from the Mexican Revolutionary Party (PRM) to the Institutional Revolutionary Party (PRI).

46. Alegre, "Contesting the 'Mexican Miracle,'" ch. 5.

47. Kennedy, *Middle Beat*, 98–99.

48. Moreno, *Yankee Don't Go Home!*

49. Kennedy, *Middle Beat*, 99.
50. Kennedy, *Middle Beat*, 99.
51. Becerra Celis, "Mexico."
52. Lewis, *Five Families*, 82.

4. THE FIRST TELEVISION DIPLOMATS

1. "National Affairs," *Time*, May 12, 1947, 8. In anticipation of his visit, Alemán's image donned the cover of *Time* on April 28, 1947.
2. Virginia Lee Warren, "Alemán Is Greeted by Vast Throngs on Capital Arrival," *New York Times*, April 30, 1947, 1.
3. John O'Donnell, "Capitol Stuff," *New York Daily News*, May 1, 1947.
4. President Adolfo Ruiz Cortines never made an official visit to the United States.
5. Ball, *Cold War*, 98. For a useful theoretical discussion on television and mass media diplomacy, see Gilboa, "Mass Communication."
6. Caprotti, "Information Management"; Fein, "Producing the Cold War."
7. Eric Zolov argues that the period following the Cuban Revolution should be considered a "critical juncture whose outcome was far more contingent than previously assumed." "Lázaro Cárdenas," 9. See also Hamilton, "Whither Cuban Socialism?"
8. Ball, *Cold War*, 101; Doyle, *Double Dealing*; Zolov, "Lázaro Cárdenas."
9. Gilboa, "CNN Effect."
10. Lolita Ayala, Televisa news anchor, interview by author, Mexico City, July 31, 2008.
11. González Molina, "Mexican Television News," 172.
12. Low salaries continue to be a problem for journalists not only in Mexico but throughout Latin America. See Arroyave, Gill, and Blanco, "Latin American Journalists' Perceptions."
13. Aceves González, "Hermosa provincia mexicana," 274.
14. Mejía Barquera, "Televisión y política," 27.
15. *Noticiero General Motors*, December 5, 1959, FNTEA.
16. Becerra Celis, "Mexico."
17. De la Cova, *Moncada Attack*.
18. Loyal supporters referred to him as Tata (Papa) Cárdenas.
19. Hayes, *Radio Nation*, 83.
20. Zolov, "Lázaro Cárdenas," 9. I thank Eric Zolov for sharing his insights about this period with me.

21. Zolov, "Lázaro Cárdenas," 14.
22. *Noticiero General Motors*, July 24–29, 1959, FNTEA.
23. Founded in the nineteenth century, the town of Cárdenas received its named long before Lázaro Cárdenas's 1959 visit. Cárdenas is also home to Elian González, the six-year-old boy who became the subject of global television news in April 2006, when U.S. immigration officials took him from his Miami, Florida, home and sent him to live with his father in Cuba. Television again emerged as the vehicle through which the public learned about the incident. Reports revealed the still-present tensions between the United States and Cuba, after the Cold War.
24. *Noticiero General Motors*, July 24, 1959, FNTEA.
25. *Noticiero General Motors*, July 25, 1959, FNTEA.
26. *Noticiero General Motors*, July 26, 1959, FNTEA. To read the scripts for these three reports, see González de Bustamante, *"Tele-visiones,"* 146–48.
27. Krauze, *Mexico*, 625–64.
28. Pellicer de Brody, *México y la Revolución Cubana*, 92.
29. *Noticiero General Motors*, October 6, 1959, FNTEA.
30. Smith, "Latin American Press."
31. *Noticiero General Motors*, October 14, 1959, FNTEA.
32. Paul Kennedy, "Cardenas Backs Jailed Leftists: Ex-President's Vow to Seek Release of Strike Leaders Causes Stir in Mexico," *New York Times*, October 4, 1959, 40.
33. *Noticiero General Motors*, October 14, 1959, FNTEA.
34. López Mateos, *Pensamiento en acción*, 1:123, 1:124–25.
35. Paul Kennedy, "Cardenas Jolts Mexican Politics: Ex-President Speaks Out on Labor Issues — Stirs Ire by Praising Red China," *New York Times*, October 18, 1959.
36. Kennedy, "Cardenas Jolts Mexican Politics."
37. *Noticiero General Motors*, October 18, 1959, FNTEA.
38. *Noticiero General Motors*, October 19, 1959, FNTEA. This number is close to the estimation of three hundred thousand to five hundred thousand people given by Paul Kennedy, "Mexicans Cheer Lopez on Return," *New York Times*, October 20, 1959, 19.
39. Kennedy, "Mexicans Cheer Lopez."
40. López Mateos, *Pensamiento en acción*, 1:30.
41. *Noticiero General Motors*, February 18, 1959, FNTEA.
42. *Noticiero General Motors*, February 18, 1959, FNTEA. The titles

given to each story are the author's. In some cases, show rundowns (outlines) are included in the script archives, but often they are not, as in this case.

43. On December 31, 1958, members of the Guatemalan Air Force opened fire on Mexican fishing boats. On January 23, 1959, President Adolfo López Mateos ruptured diplomatic relations with Guatemala. A speech he delivered on the subject is in López Mateos, *Pensamiento en acción*, 1:19.

44. González de Bustamante, "Dependency and Development."

45. For an examination of the origins of the tourism industry, see Berger, *Mexico's Tourism Industry*.

46. López Mateos, *Pensamiento en acción*, 1:31.

47. *Noticiero General Motors*, February 20, 1959, FNTEA.

48. *Noticiero General Motors*, February 20, 1959, FNTEA.

49. *Noticiero General Motors*, February 20, 1959, FNTEA.

50. *Noticiero General Motors*, February 20, 1959, FNTEA.

51. Although the script refers to Donato Miranda as foreign relations secretary, Miranda served as secretary of the presidencia, while Manuel Tello served as secretary of foreign relations during the López Mateos administration.

52. *Noticiero General Motors*, November 18, 1959, FNTEA.

53. Archivo Histórico Diplomático Mexicano, num. 4, *Relaciones Mexicano-Soviéticas*, 98.

54. *Noticiero General Motors*, November 18, 1959, FNTEA.

55. *Noticiero General Motors*, November 19, 1959, FNTEA.

56. *Noticiero General Motors*, November 19, 1959, FNTEA. Raúl Salinas is the father of Carlos Salinas de Gortari, president of Mexico between 1988 and 1994.

57. "Mikoyan Leaves for Home: His Trip Is Generally Held a Success Though Press Comment Was Hostile," *New York Times*, November 29, 1959, 27.

58. Jacobo Zabludovsky, "Fidel en Matanzas," *El Universal*, January 14, 2008, http://www.eluniversal.com.mx/columnas/vi_69353.html; Zabludovsky, "26 de julio: Seguí a Fidel que llamó a la puerta cerca de la medianoche," *Zócalo*, http://www.zocalo.com.mx/seccion/opinion-articulo/26-de-julio/.

59. In July 1961 López Mateos announced that he stood on the extreme left side of the Mexican Revolution.

60. García, *Operation Wetback*.
61. "The Americas: Guests of Venezuela," *Time Magazine*, May 26, 1958.
62. Boyd-Barrett, *International News Agencies*.

5. HOT ROCKETS AND COLD WAR

1. Baer, "Television and Political Control," 79. According to Baer three hundred thousand television sets were operating throughout the country in 1957, the majority of them in the nation's capital. It is therefore reasonable to estimate that the potential number of viewers in the capital could have been six hundred thousand.
2. On January 31, 1958, the United States sent into orbit its first satellite, *Explorer I*.
3. Weeks, e-mail message, *Space Monitoring Information*.
4. *Noticiero General Motors*, October 4, 1957, FNTEA.
5. Alemán Velasco, interview by author, Mexico City, March 14, 2006.
6. Deuze, "What Is Journalism?"
7. McLuhan, *Understanding Media*.
8. Doyle, *Double Dealing*.
9. *Noticiero General Motors*, November 17, 1959, FNTEA.
10. Alemán Velasco, interview.
11. Adriana Labardini, interview by author, Mexico City, June 2005.
12. Alemán Velasco, *Secretos*.
13. Alemán Velasco, interview.
14. *Noticiero General Motors*, October 4, 1957, FNTEA.
15. Michael, "Space Age," 574.
16. *Noticiero General Motors*, October 7, 1957, FNTEA.
17. *Noticiero General Motors*, October 4, 1957, FNTEA.
18. Alemán Velasco, interview; Boyd-Barrett, *International News Agencies*.
19. Long, "News for Whom?," in Boyd-Barrett, *International News Agencies*, 22.
20. Smith, "The Latin American Press."
21. Pansters, "Social Movement and Discourse."
22. *Noticiero General Motors*, October 5, 1957, FNTEA.
23. "Satellite Belittled: Admiral Says Almost Anybody Could Launch 'Hunk of Iron,'" *New York Times*, October 5, 1957.
24. *Noticiero General Motors*, October 5, 1957, FNTEA.

25. Fernández and Paxman, *Tigre*.
26. *Noticiero General Motors*, October 5, 1957, FNTEA.
27. *Noticiero General Motors*, October 7, 1957, FNTEA.
28. *Noticiero General Motors*, October 7, 1957, FNTEA.
29. Smith, "Latin American Press," 551.
30. Frutkin and Griffin, "Space Activity."
31. Camp, *Mexican Political Biographies*, 92–93.
32. The Secretaría de Comunicaciones y Obras Públicas and the Secretaría de Comunicaciones y Transporte are essentially the same; the ministry changed names during President López Mateos's administration.
33. *Noticiero General Motors*, November 17, 1959, FNTEA.
34. It is curious that the report on the rocket launching did not occur until three weeks after the launch, but the news report does not offer any explanations for the delay. Also intriguing is the fact that this story aired one day before Anastas Mikoyan's arrival to Mexico.
35. *Noticiero General Motors*, November 17, 1959, FNTEA.
36. Becker, *Virgin on Fire*; Scott, *Seeing Like a State*.
37. This type of criticism surfaced in 1968, as the country spent millions to beautify Mexico City in preparation for the Olympic Games.
38. *Noticiero General Motors*, November 18, 1960, FNTEA. Paul P. Kennedy reported that sixteen stations would be set up around the world. "Mexicans Oppose U.S. Installation," *New York Times*, May 22, 1960.
39. Writers and producers employed the same logic in their portrayal of the 1968 Olympic Games.
40. Kennedy, "Mexicans Oppose U.S. Installation," 33.
41. "Tracking Station Set: 2.5 Million Unit in Mercury Project Planned in Mexico," *New York Times*, April 14, 1960.
42. *Noticiero aeronaves*, June 21, 1961, FNTEA.
43. Martínez, *Troublesome Border*, 1–7.
44. Rankin, "¡México, la pátria!"
45. For more on the propensity to present international events through a national lens, see the following three chapters on Mexican and U.S. English-language and Spanish-language news media coverage of immigration: Chávez and Hoewe, "National Perspectives"; Guerrero and Campo, "Between Heroes and Victims"; and Vigón, Martínez Bustos and González de Bustamante, "Not Business as Usual."
46. *Noticiero aeronaves*, June, 26, 1961, FNTEA.

47. *Noticiero aeronaves*, June 27, 1961, FNTEA.

48. The mass deportation of as many as one million Mexicans during the official U.S program Operation Wetback did not help to improve relations; see García, *Operation Wetback*.

49. *Noticiero aeronaves*, June 27, 1961, FNTEA.

50. Zolov, "*¡Cuba sí, yanquis no!*"

51. Carey, *Plaza of Sacrifices*, 11–16.

52. *Noticiero aeronaves*, April 19, 1961, FNTEA.

53. *Noticiero aeronaves*, April 19, 1961, FNTEA. A protest in the zócalo occurred the day before on April 18, in which tens of thousands of people marched on the plaza; see Zolov, "*¡Cuba sí, yanquís no!*"

54. Some protests against the U.S.-backed invasion erupted in violence. Students in Morelia sacked and destroyed property at the Instituto Cultural Mexico-Norteamericano (Mexican–North American Cultural Institute); see Zolov, "*¡Cuba sí, yanquis no!*"

55. *Noticiero novedades-aceptaciones*, October 22, 1962, FNTEA.

56. *Noticiero novedades-aceptaciones*, October 7, 1962, FNTEA.

57. López Mateos, *Pensamiento en acción*, 1:225.

58. *Noticiero novedades-aceptaciones*, October 22, 1962, FNTEA. News writers did use the words naval blockade (*bloqueo naval*) in the first and second sentences of the report.

59. *Noticiero novedades-aceptaciones*, October 22, 1962, FNTEA.

60. Tello, *México*, 155–57.

61. Hershberg, "Anatomy of a Controversy."

62. *Noticiero novedades-aceptaciones*, October 22, 1962, FNTEA.

63. Tello, *México*, 147.

64. Carrandi Ortíz, *Testimonio*, 113–14.

65. Carrandi Ortíz, *Testimonio*, 85.

66. Alemán Velasco, interview.

67. Coverage of the October 2, 1968, massacre is analyzed in the following chapter.

68. Alemán Velasco, interview by author, Mexico City, March 14, 2006, and August 5, 2009. The former Televisa executive's comment about being "fair and balanced" must be taken in the proper context. Being fair and balanced from 1950 to 1970 under an authoritarian regime was not the same as being fair and balanced in the twenty-first century. Self-censorship, as well as overt censorship by government officials, was part

of the daily news routine. Serious limitations existed about what would be reported on and what would not. In other words, journalism ethics during the first twenty years of television were much different than in 2009, when Alemán Velasco made his statements about the creation of the network news division.

69. Kohler and Harvey, "International Significance," 5.
70. Alemán Velasco, interview by author, March 14, 2006.
71. *Noticiero Nescafé*, July 10, 1969, FNTEA.
72. *Noticiero Nescafé*, July 17, 1969, FNTEA.
73. *Noticiero Nescafé*, July 17, 1969, FNTEA.
74. Alemán Velasco, interview.
75. *Noticiero Nescafé*, July 21, 1969, FNTEA. Apparently Armstrong had meant to say "Here's one small step for [a] man, and one giant leap for mankind." His omission of the indefinite article "a" altered the meaning of one of the most quoted statements in history. The audio tape of the transmission is inconclusive. Newscast scripts for July 12, 13, 14, and 20 are missing from the FNTEA.
76. Kohler and Harvey, "International Significance," 7.
77. Smith, "Latin American Press," 550.

6. OLYMPIC DREAMS AND TLATELOLCO NIGHTMARES
1. Paul Kennedy, "Mexico Prepares for 1968 Olympics: Finance Committee Meets on Housing Problems," *New York Times*, July 3, 1965, 13.
2. The nineteenth Olympiad was dubbed the Olympics of Peace. The three cultures represented in the plaza are the Spanish, indigenous, and modern mestizo.
3. Over the past forty years scores of scholars have generated a sizable body of literature in Spanish focusing on the student movements of 1968 and the massacre at the Plaza de la Tres Culturas from a variety of perspectives. Some of the most prominent works include Aguayo, *1968*; Alvarez Garín, *Estela de Tlatelolco*; Poniatowska, *La noche de Tlatelolco*; Revueltas, *México 68*); and Scherer García and Monsiváis, *Parte de guerra*. Aside from Elena Poniatowska's *Massacre in Mexico* (the translated version of *La noche*), few works in English have emerged. Carey's *Plaza of Sacrifices* is the only scholarly book in English that analyzes the student movements and subsequent massacre at Tlateloloco from a gendered perspective. Focused on the Olympics of 1968, Witherspoon, *Eyes of the World*, analyzes the

myriad controversies surrounding the nineteenth Olympiad, including the government crackdown on students. In *Turbulent Decade Remembered*, Diana Sorensen examines the work of literary figures such as Octavio Paz and their relationship to politics, modernity, and postmodernity.

4. Cano Andaluz, *1968*.

5. Carey, *Plaza of Sacrifices*, 128–30.

6. Aguayo, *1968*, 221.

7. Generally speaking, U.S. viewers who watched the 1968 Olympics remember the games differently than their Mexican counterparts. U.S. viewers recall the raised black-gloved fists of two African American students from San José State University. Tommie Smith and John Carlos protested against discrimination onstage after winning the two hundred–meter Olympic finals. Mexican viewers remember the bloodshed just days prior to the opening of the games.

8. In this way, this chapter furthers the research of Zolov, "Land of Tomorrow," and Witherspoon, *Eyes of the World*.

9. Jorge Perezvega, interview by author, Mexico City, August 6, 2009; Ana Ignacia Rodríguez, interview by author, Mexico City, August 5, 2009.

10. Becerra Celis, "Mexico"; Plenn, "Mexico."

11. Noriega and Leach, *Broadcasting in Mexico*, 58.

12. Aguayo, *1968*.

13. Robinson, "Treaty of Tlatelolco"; González de Bustamante, "'Terroristas' and Torch Carriers."

14. Witherspoon, *Eyes of the World*, is one of the few who has looked at the intersection between these two events.

15. Kurlansky, *1968*, 119. For an intriguing look at student protests around the world and government responses to them, see Kurlansky, *1968*.

16. Sánchez Ruiz, "Medios de difusión."

17. For a cogent discussion of the internal and external factors that inspired the students of 1968, see Carey, *Plaza of Sacrifices*, 29–35.

18. Witherspoon, *Eyes of the World*, 50. Telesistema televised the Pan-Am Games, which served as significant training for personnel who prepared for broadcasts of the nineteenth Olympiad, as did the "Little Olympics" held in Mexico City in 1965.

19. Numerous other international controversies surfaced during the nineteenth Olympiad, including the civil rights protest of Tommie Smith and John Carlos and the threat of boycott by some teams because South

Africa was allowed to participate in the games; see Witherspoon, *Eyes of the World*, 37–47.

20. Zolov, "Land of Tomorrow."

21. Alba and Potter, "Population and Development."

22. Paul Kennedy, "Mexico Redoubles Efforts to Double Tourism," February 7, 1965, *New York Times*, XX21. Tlatelolco was the site of one of the preeminent pre-Hispanic marketplaces in the Valley of Mexico; see C. Gibson, *Aztecs under Spanish Rule*, 352.

23. Krauze, *Presidencia imperial*, 379; Sorensen, "Tlatelolco 1968," 304; Rodríguez, interview.

24. Poniatowska, *Noche de Tlatelolco*, 167.

25. CBS news reporter Bert Quint's account of the massacre provides one of the best audiovisual sources available to the public. See *CBS News*, October 3, 1968, Vanderbilt Television News Archive.

26. Fournier and Martinez, "México 1968," 67–102.

27. MacLachlan and Beezley, *Gran pueblo*, 407.

28. Covey T. Oliver to Acting Secretary, U.S. Department of State, "Mexican Situation-Information Memorandum," October 1, 1968, in Doyle, *Tlatelolco Massacre*.

29. *Su diario Nescafé*, October 2, 1968, FNTEA. While titles tended to be one to three words, in the *Su diario Nescafé* rundown for October 2, 1968, I have expanded the titles to more clearly reflect the topic of each report. Some titles include names of the reporters and times. These were most likely preproduced reports.

30. *Su diario Nescafé*, October 2, 1968, FNTEA. According to the script, images accompanied this report, but I was not granted permission to view them. Directors of Televisa's archive allowed me to view two sets of images related to student movements: a compilation of film images titled "Student Movement" for 1968 and 1971. They did not allow me to dub any of these images. The images did not represent Televisa's entire collection related to the subject. The two tapes that directors allowed me to view are reportedly the same tapes that Televisa's news producers and reporters are permitted to use in their reports.

31. Jorge Saldaña, previous news anchor and host for Telesistema Mexicano, telephone interview by author, Tuscon AZ, August 5, 2008.

32. Historian Enrique Krauze called Díaz Ordaz the "lawyer of order," in *Presidencia imperial*, 8.

33. *Su diario Nescafé*, October 2, 1968, FNTEA.
34. *Su diario Nescafé*, October 2, 1968, FNTEA.
35. Poniatowska, "1968."
36. *Noticiero canal 2*, October 2, 1968, FNTEA. In this rundown, producers did not write estimated times to the right of the story titles.
37. Although Pedro Rodriguez was a Mexican participant in the race, the report focuses on an international event; therefore, this report fits into the international category.
38. *Noticiero novedades*, October 2, 1968, FNTEA.
39. The exact time of gunfire, although listed in the October 2 script at just before 6:00 p.m., was changed to shortly after six on the following day; see *Noticiero novedades*, October 3, 1968, FNTEA, and Poniatowska, "1968."
40. Official documents and testimony have revealed that government officials dressed in plain clothes fired the shots from the top of the Secretaría de Relaciones Exteriores building, which overlooks the Plaza de las Tres Culturas; see Scherer García and Monsiváis, *Los rostros del 68*, 69–70; and Scherer García and Monsiváis, *Tlatelolco, 1968*, 179.
41. Other news scripts refer to a photographer by the name of Angel Cabrera instead of Angel Cabrerq.
42. *Noticerio novedades*, October 2, 1968, FNTEA. When asked about his role as anchor on October 2, 1968, Saldaña stated that he had no recollection of delivering the news on that night. Interview, August 5, 2008.
43. Poniatowska, "1968."
44. Aguayo, *1968*, 221.
45. Fournier and Martinez, "Violencia y memória histórica," 182.
46. *Su diario Nescafé*, October 3, 1968, FNTEA.
47. *Noticiero General Motors*, June 27, 1958, FNTEA.
48. *Su diario Nescafé*, October 3, 1968, FNTEA.
49. *Su diario Nescafé*, October 3, 1968, FNTEA.
50. *Noticiero novedades*, October 3, 1968, FNTEA.
51. Saldaña, interview.
52. *Noticiero novedades*, October 12, 1968, FNTEA. In Mexico and most of Latin America, October 12 is commemorated as the Día de la Raza (Day of the Race/People). It is the day Christopher Columbus arrived in the Americas.

53. "Girl Who Carries Torch for Mexico Also Loves Sports," *New York Times*, October 13, 1968, S3.

54. *México '68*.

55. "Girl Who Carries Torch," S3.

56. *México '68*.

57. *Noticiero novedades*, October 12, 1968, FNTEA. Film accompanied these two reports, but the images were not accessible at Televisa's news archive. "Estadio '68" is known as the Estadio Olympico.

58. *Noticiero novedades*, October 12, 1968, FNTEA.

59. *Noticiero novedades*, October 12, 1968, FNTEA.

60. *Noticiero novedades*, October 3, 1968, FNTEA.

61. Rodríguez was imprisoned three times between 1968 and 1970. She spent almost two years incarcerated in a women's prison from January 3, 1969, to December 31, 1970. Government officials gave Rodríguez the name "La Nacha," a somewhat derogatory term that is a nickname for Ignacia but also means "rear end." Interview, August 5, 2009.

62. Many of the student- and faculty-produced images were published by former students of the Escuela Nacional de Artes Plásticas. Aquino and Perezvega, *Imágenes y símbolos*.

63. Perezvega, interview.

64. Perezvega, interview.

65. Aguayo, *1968*, 222–23; Witherspoon, *Eyes of the World*, 105.

66. Steve Cady, "Mexicans Mix Tears of Pride and Joy as Friendliness Overflows at Olympics," *New York Times*, October 13, 1968, S3.

67. Perezvega, interview.

68. Krauze, *Presidencia imperial*, 359. Gustavo was in reference to President Gustavo Díaz Ordaz.

69. *Noticiero novedades*, September 23, 28, 30, 1968, FNTEA.

70. Perezvega, interview.

71. Rodriguez, interview.

72. Rodriguez, interview.

73. Miguel Alemán Velasco, interview by author, Mexico City, August 6, 2009.

74. Baer, "Television and Political Control," 118.

75. Alemán Velasco, interview, August 6, 2009.

76. Alemán Velasco, interview, March 14, 2006. For television executives this was a convenient argument to make forty years later. Placing

importance on the newspaper "contracts" in describing the events of '68 effectively downplayed the decision-making power that TV executives wielded in the summer and fall of that year.

77. Baer, "Television and Political Control," 123.

78. Alemán Velasco, interview, August 6, 2009.

79. The importance of centralization among mass media, especially with respect to television, is difficult to overstate; see Sánchez Ruiz, "Medios de difusión."

80. Poniatowska, *Todo México*, 172.

81. Fernández and Paxman, *Tigre*, 144.; Julia Preston, "News and (State) Anchor Weighs His," *New York Times*, January 20, 1998.

82. Liliana Alcántara, "AI demanda reabrir indagación sobre el 68," *El Universal*, October 2, 2008, http://www.eluniversal.com.mx/nacion/162735.html.

83. Saldaña, interview.

84. Sánchez Ruiz, "Medios de difusión."

7. VICTORY FOR THE BRAZILIANS AND ECHEVERRÍA

Fernández Christlieb, *Medios de difusión masiva*, 199.

1. Fernández and Paxman, *Tigre*, 143.

2. Martín del Campo and López Levya, "México"; Lawson, *Building the Fourth Estate*, xiii.

3. Fernández Christlieb, *Medios de difusión masiva*, 105, 119. In 1973 the branch's name changed to Secretaría de Radiodifusión.

4. Martínez Medellín, *Televisa*, 55.

5. Miguel Alemán Velasco, interview by author, Mexico City, March 14, 2006.

6. Fernández Christlieb, *Medios de difusión masiva*, 121.

7. The typical or average day in news production runs counter to the logic of news, which is to report the atypical and out of the ordinary. Despite this, the concept of an average day in terms of news production refers to the amount of news generated on a day during which no catastrophic or events of great magnitude occurred.

8. Alemán Velasco said that between 1950 and 1970 as many as 270 different companies sponsored news programs. Only the scripts for the longest-running programs, such as *Noticiero General Motors* and *Su diario Nescafe*, are housed at the FNTEA. Interview, March 14, 2006.

9. Noriega and Leach, *Broadcasting in Mexico*, 58.
10. Mejía Barquera, "Cronología general," 535.
11. Saragoza, *Monterrey Elite*.
12. Mejía Barquera, "Cronología general," 535.
13. Alvarez Garín, *Estela de Tlatelolco*, 67.
14. Mejía Barquera, "Cronología general," 547.
15. González Molina, "Mexican Television News," 106.
16. Scherer García and Monsiváis, *Tiempo de Saber*, 46.
17. Alemán Velasco, interview.
18. González Molina, "Mexican Television News," 108, 109.
19. Martínez Medellín, *Televisa*, 55.
20. Alemán Velasco, interview.
21. Alemán Velasco, interview.
22. *24 horas*, October 2, 1970, FNTEA.
23. Huesca Rebolledo, "Noticia por televisión," 71.
24. W. Gibson, "Network News."
25. *24 horas*, September 15, 1970, FNTEA.
26. Greene, "Cablevision."
27. Fernández and Paxman, *Tigre*, 180–82.
28. Mejía Barquera, "Del canal 4," 50.
29. Mejía Barquera, "Cronología general," 538.
30. Fernández and Paxman, *Tigre*, 89.
31. Camp, *Mexican Political Biographies*, 222. For an analysis of the Echeverría presidency, see Schmidt, *Deterioration*.
32. Camp, *Mexican Political Biographies*, 309.
33. *Su diario Nescafé*, July 9, 1970, FNTEA.
34. June 21, 1970, was missing from the FNTEA.
35. On June 17 Germany and Italy faced off in the semifinals.
36. Fernández and Paxman, *Tigre*, 169.
37. "ABC/ESPN and UNIVISION Awarded US TV Rights for All FIFA Events from 2007 to 2014," *Media Information*, November 2, 2005, http://www.fifa.com/en/media/index/0,1369,110918,00.html.
38. *Su diario Nescafé*, June 17, 1970, FNTEA.
39. *Su diario Nescafé*, June 17, 1970, FNTEA.
40. United Press International, "Newsmen's Plane Crashes in Mexico: 19 of 20 Are Killed," *New York Times*, January 26, 1970, 1.
41. *Su diario Nescafé*, June 17, 1970, FNTEA.

42. *Su diario Nescafé,* June 17, 1970, FNTEA.
43. *Su diario Nescafé,* July 9, 1970, FNTEA.
44. *Su diario Nescafé,* June 21, 1970, FNTEA.
45. *Su diario Nescafé,* June 22, 1970, FNTEA.
46. Fernández and Paxman, *Tigre,* 100.
47. *24 horas,* September 15, 1970, FNTEA.
48. *24 horas,* September 15, 1970, FNTEA.
49. XHTV, *Carpeta,* March 4–April 8, 1953, FNTEA.
50. Alemán Velasco, interview.
51. González Molina, "Mexican Television News," 100.
52. *24 horas,* September 15, 1970, FNTEA.
53. Huesca Rebolledo, "Cronología de noticiarios televisivos" 105.
54. Lolita Ayala, interview by author, Mexico City, July 31, 2008.
55. Carey, *Plaza of Sacrifices,* 177.
56. Egan, "Feminine Perspectives."
57. Alemán Velasco, interview by author, March 14, 2006, and August 6, 2009.
58. Ayala, interview.
59. Aguayo, *1968;* Carey, *Plaza of Sacrifices,* 170; Doyle, *Mexico's Dirty War.*
60. Doyle, *Corpus Christi Massacre.*

CONCLUSION

2 Samuel 7:12 (Revised English Bible with the Apocrypha).
1. Camp, *Mexican Political Biographies,* 77–78.
2. *24 horas,* October 2, 1970, FNTEA.
3. Jorge Perezvega, interview by author, Mexico City, August 6, 2009.
4. Waisbord, "Latin America," 256; Skidmore, *Transition to Democracy.*
5. Becker and González de Bustamante, "Brazilian Television News."
6. Schiller, "National Development."
7. Gutierrez and Reina Schement, "Spanish International Network."
8. Alemán Velasco, former head of Telesistema Mexicano news division, former Televisa executive vice president, interview by author, Mexico City, March 14, 2006.
9. To this day, Echeverría denies he ordered government troops to fire on protesters in Tlatelolco. "Mexico Ex-leader Genocide Charge: Special Prosecutors in Mexico Have Filed Genocide and Kidnapping Charges

against a Former Mexican President," BBC News, September 20, 2005, http://news.bbc.co.uk/1/hi/world/americas/4263472.stm.

10. Fernández and Paxman, *Tigre*, 89, 181.
11. Mejía Barquera, "Del canal 4," 50.
12. Jones, *Juvenal*.
13. Perezvega, interview.
14. Alemán Velasco, interview; Lawson, *Building the Fourth Estate*, 50.
15. Lolita Ayala, Televisa news anchor, interview by author, Mexico City, July 31, 2008; Jorge Saldaña, former Televisa news anchor, telephone interview by author, Tuscon AZ, August 5, 2008.
16. Guerrero and Corduneaunu, "Trust, Credibility and Relevance."
17. Huesca Rebolledo, "Noticia por televisión," 2:78, 2:79.
18. Carrandi Ortíz, *Testimonio*, 115.
19. Fernández and Paxman, *Tigre*, 144.
20. Alemán Velasco, interview.
21. "Si yo fuera presidente," segment on Victor Trujillo, *El cristal con que se mira*, XHTV, Channel 4, Televisa, March 15, 2006, FNTEA.
22. Andrés Oppenheimer, "New Televisa CEO Promises Sweeping Changes: Networks Will Shun Political Biases of the Past, He Says," *Miami Herald*, November 9, 1997.

Bibliography

ARCHIVES AND LIBRARIES
Archivo General de la Nación (AGN), Mexico City
  Ramo de Presidentes
  Miguel Alemán Valdés (1946–52)
  Adolfo Ruiz Cortines (1952–58)
  Adolfo López Mateos (1958–64)
  Gustavo Díaz Ordaz (1964–70)
Archivo Histórico de la Universidad Nacional Autónoma de México–Centro de Estudios Sobre la Universidad (AHUNAM-CESU), Mexico City
Archivo Miguel Alemán Valdés (AMAV), Mexico City
Biblioteca Mexicana de la Fundación Miguel Alemán (BMFMA), Mexico City
Biblioteca Nacional, Mexico City
Filmoteca de Noticieros de Televisa, Estadio Azteca (FNTEA), Mexico City
Hemeroteca Nacional, Mexico City
National Security Archive, Washington DC
Television News Programs (1954–70)
  El Noticiero
  General Motors
  Noticiero Aeronaves
  Noticiero Canal 2
  Noticiero Superior
  Novedades-Aceptaciones
  PEMEX-Sol
  Su Diario Nescafé

Vanderbilt Television News Archive, Nashville TN
Videoteca de Noticieros de Televisa, Chapultepec (VNTC), Mexico City

PUBLISHED WORKS

Aceves González, Francisco de Jesús. "Hermosa provincia mexicana: Televisión monopolize." In *Las redes de Televisa*, edited by Raúl Trejo Delabre, 263–84. Mexico City: Claves Latinoamericanas, 1988.

Aguayo, Sérgio. *1968: Los archivos de la violencia*. Mexico City: Grijalbo / Reforma, 1998.

Agustín, José. *La vida en México, 1940–1970*. Vol. 1 of *Tragicomedia Mexicana*. Mexico City: Planeta, 1990.

Alba, Francisco, and Joseph E. Potter. "Population and Development in Mexico since 1940: An Interpretation." *Population and Development Review* 12, no. 1 (1986): 47–75.

Alegre, Robert F. "Contesting the 'Mexican Miracle': Railway Men and Women Struggle for Democracy, 1943–1959." PhD diss., Rutgers University, 2007.

———. "Las rieleras: Gender, Politics, and Power in the Mexican Railway Movement, 1958–1959." *Journal of Women's History* 23, no. 2 (2011): 162–86.

Alemán Velasco, Miguel. *Los secretos y las leyes del espacio*. Mexico City: Helio-México, 1962.

Alemán Valdés, Miguel. *Un mejor México: Pensamientos, discursos, e información*. Mexico City: Diana, 1988.

Alisky, Marvin. "Early Mexican Broadcasting." *Hispanic American Historical Review* 34, no. 4 (1954): 513–26.

———. "Mexico's Rural Radio." *Quarterly of Film, Radio and Television* 8, no. 4 (1954): 405–17.

Alvarez Garín, Raúl. *La estela de Tlatelolco: Una reconstrucción histórica movimiento estudiantíl del 68*. Mexico City: Grijalbo, 1998.

Alvarez Garín, Raúl, Gilberto Guevara Niebla, Hermann Bellinghausen, and Hugo Hiria, eds. *Pensar en 68*. Mexico City: Cal y Arena, 1988.

Alwood, Edward. "Watching the Watchdogs: FBI Spying on Journalists in the 1940s." *Journalism and Mass Communication Quarterly* 84, no. 1 (2007): 139–50.

Andaluz Cano, Aurora. *1968: Antología periodística*. Mexico City: Instituto de Investigaciones Bibliográficas, Universidad Nacional Autónoma de México, 1993.

Anderson, Benedict. *Imagined Communities: Reflections on the Origins and Spread of Nationalism.* London: Verso / NLB, 1983.

Aquino, Arnulfo, and Jorge Perezvega. *Imágenes y símbolos del 68: Fotografía y gráfica del movimiento estudiantil.* Mexico City: Universidad Nacional Autónoma de México, 2004.

Arredondo Ramírez, Pablo, and María de Lourdes Zermeno Torres. "La política informativa de Televisa en los Estados Unidos: El caso de '24 horas.'" *Mexican Studies / Estudios Mexicanos* 2, no. 1 (1986): 83–105.

Arroyave, Jesús, Juliet Gill, and Iscar Blanco. "Latin American Journalists' Perceptions of the Profession: Between Exhaustion and Fascination." *Florida Communication Journal* 36, no. 2 (2007): 67–76.

Baer, Miriam Delal. "Television and Political Control in Mexico." PhD diss., University of Michigan, 1991.

Ball, S. J. *The Cold War: An International History, 1947–1991.* London: Arnold, 1998.

Becerra Celis, Luis. "Mexico." In *International Television Almanac: Who, What, Where in Television,* edited by Charles S. Aaronson, 733. New York: Quigley, 1961.

Becker, Beatriz, and Celeste González de Bustamante. "The Past and the Future of Brazilian Television News." *Journalism: Theory, Practice and Criticism* 10, no. 1 (2009): 44–68.

Becker, Marjorie. *Setting the Virgin on Fire.* Berkeley: University of California Press, 1995.

Beezley, William H., and David E. Lorey, eds. *¡Viva México! ¡Viva la Independencia!* Wilmington DE: Scholarly Resources, 2001.

Benjamin, Thomas. *La Revolución: Mexico's Great Revolution as Memory, Myth and History.* Austin: University of Texas Press, 2000.

Berger, Dina. *The Development of Mexico's Tourism Industry: Pyramids by Day, Martinis by Night.* New York: Palgrave Macmillan, 2006.

Blough, William J. "Political Attitudes of Mexican Women: Support for the Political System among a Newly Enfranchised Group." *Journal of Inter-American Studies and World Affairs* 14, no. 2 (1972): 201–24.

Boyd-Barrett, Oliver. *The International News Agencies.* London: Constable, 1980.

Camp, Roderic Ai. *Intellectuals and the State in Twentieth-Century Mexico.* Austin: University of Texas Press, 1985.

———. *Mexican Political Biographies, 1935–1993*. Austin: University of Texas Press, 1995.

Cano Andaluz, Aurora. *1968: Antología periodística*. Mexico City: UNAM, Instituto de Investigaciones Bibliográficas, 1993.

Caprotti, Federico. "Information Management and Fascist Identity: Newsreels in Fascist Italy." *Media History* 2, no. 3 (2005): 177–92.

Cardoso, Fernando Henrique. "Associated-Dependent Development: Theoretical and Practical Implications." In *Authoritarian Brazil: Origins, Policies, and Future*, edited by Alfred Stephan, 142–78. New Haven CT: Yale University Press, 1973.

Cardoso, Fernando Henrique, and Enzo Faletto. *Dependency and Development in Latin America*. Translated by Marjory Mattingly Urquidi. Berkeley: University of California Press, 1971.

Carey, Elaine. *Plaza of Sacrifices: Gender, Power, and Terror in 1968 Mexico*. Albuquerque: University of New Mexico Press, 2005.

Carrandi Ortíz, Gabino. *Testimonio de la televisión mexicana*. Mexico City: Diana, 1986.

Castañeda, Jorge. Prologue to *México y la revolución cubana*. By Olga Pellicer de Brody. Mexico City: El Colegio de México, 1972.

———. *Utopia Unarmed: The Latin American Left after the Cold War*. New York: Vintage Books, 1994.

Castellot, Gonzalo. *La televisión en México: 1950–2000*. Mexico City: Edamex, 1999.

Castellot de Ballin, Laura. *Historia de la televisión en México: Narrada por sus protagonistas*. Mexico City: Alpe, 1993.

Chavez, Manuel, and Jennifer Hoewe. "National Perspectives on State Turmoil: Characteristics of Elite U.S. Newspaper Coverage of Arizona SB 1070." In *Arizona Firestorm: Global Immigration Realities, National Media, and Provincial Politics*, edited by Otto Santa Ana and Celeste González de Bustamante. New York: Rowman and Littlefield, 2012.

Chorba, Carrie. *Mexico, from Mestizo to Multicultural: National Identity and Recent Representations of the Conquest*. Nashville TN: Vanderbilt University Press, 2003.

Chyi, Hsiang Iris, and Maxwell McCombs. "Media Salience and the Process of Framing: Coverage of the Columbine School Shootings." *Journalism and Mass Communication Quarterly* 81, no. 1 (2004): 22–35.

Cline, Howard F. *Mexico: Revolution to Evolution, 1940–1960*. New York: Oxford University Press, 1983.

Cole, Richard, ed. *Communication in Latin America*. Wilmington DE: Scholarly Resources, 1996.

———. "Mass Media in Mexico: Ownership and Control." PhD diss., University of Minnesota, 1972.

Cosío Villegas, Daniel. "La crisis de México," 1947. In Niblo, *Mexico in the 1940s*, 244.

Dando la noticia: Historia de la TV Mexicana 3. Directed by Hank Heifetz. Mexico City: Clio, 2001. Videocassette (VHS), 43:10 min.

Darling, Juanita, and Marjorie Miller. "Emilio Azcárraga and the Televisa Empire." In *A Culture of Collusion: An Inside Look at the Mexican Press*, edited by William A. Orme Jr., 59–70. Miami: North-South Center Press, 1997.

De la Cova, Antonio Rafael. *The Moncada Attack: Birth of the Cuban Revolution*. Columbia: University of South Carolina, 2007.

Deuze, Mark. "What Is Journalism? Professional Identity and Ideology of Journalists Reconsidered." *Journalism* 6, no. 4 (2005): 442–64.

Dorfman, Ariel, and Armand Mattelart. *How to Read Donald Duck: Imperialist Ideology in the Disney Comic*. New York: International General, 1975.

Doyle, Kate. *The Corpus Christi Massacre: Mexico's Attack on Its Student Movement*. Electronic briefing book. Washington DC: National Security Archive, 2003, http://www.gwu.edu/~narchiv/NSAEBB/NSAEBB91/.

———. *The Dawn of Mexico's Dirty War: Lucio Cabañas and the Party of the Poor*. Electronic briefing book. Washington DC: National Security Archive, December 5, 2003. http://www.gwu.edu/~nsarchiv/NSAEBB/NSAEBB105/index.htm.

———. *Double Dealing: Mexico's Foreign Policy toward Cuba*. Electronic briefing book. Washington DC: National Security Archive, 2003. http://www.gwu.edu/~nsarchiv/NSAEBB/NSAEBB83/index.htm.

———. *The Tlatelolco Massacre: U.S. Documents on Mexico and the Events of 1968*. Document no. 36. Electronic briefing book. Washington DC: National Security Archive, 2003. http://www.gwu.edu/~nsarchiv/NSAEBB/NSAEBB99/index.htm.

Egan, Linda. "Feminine Perspectives on Journalism: Conversations with Eight Mexican Women." *Studies in Latin American Popular Culture* 12 (1993): 175–88.

Fein, Seth. "Producing the Cold War in Mexico: The Public Limits of Covert Communications." In Joseph and Spenser, *In from the Cold*, 171–213.
Fernández, Claudia, and Andrew Paxman. *El Tigre: Emilio Azcárraga y su imperio Televisa*. Mexico City: Grijalbo, 2000.
Fernández Christlieb, Fátima. *Los medios de difusión masiva en México*. Mexico City: Pablos, 1982.
Ferreira, Leonardo. *Centuries of Silence: The Story of Latin American Journalism*. Westport CT: Praeger, 2006.
"Foreign Trade." U.S. Census Bureau, 2011. http://www.census.gov/foreign-trade/top/dst/current/balance.html.
Fournier, Patricia, and Jorge Martinez. "México 1968: Entre las fanfarrias olímpicas, la represión gubernamental y el genocidio." In *Arqueología de la represión y resistencia en América Latina: 1960–1980*, edited by Pedro Paulo A. Funari and Andrés Zarankin, 67–102. Córdoba, Argentina: Encuentro Grupo Editor, 2006.

———. "Violencia y memória histórica: Tlatelolco 1968." In *Antropología y Simbolismo*, edited by Patrica Fournier, Saúl Millán, and María Eugenia Olavarría. Mexico City: Instituto Nacional de Antropología e Historia, 2007.
Fox, Elizabeth, and Silvio Waisbord, eds. *Latin Politics: Global media*. Austin: University of Texas Press, 2002.
Fromson, Murray. "Mexico's Struggle for a Free Press," in Cole, *Communication in Latin America*, 115–38.
Frutkin, Arnold W., and Richard B. Griffin Jr. "Space Activity in Latin America." *Journal of Inter-American Studies* 10, no. 2 (1968): 185–93.
Fuentes, Gloria. *Historia de las comunicaciones y los transportes en México*. Mexico City: Secretaría de Comunicaciones y Transportes, 1987.
Gamson, William, and André Modigliani. "Media Discourse and Public Opinion on Nuclear Power: A Constructionist Approach." *American Journal of Sociology* 95, no. 1 (1989): 1–37.
García, Juan Ramón. *Operation Wetback: The Mass Deportation of Mexican Undocumented Workers in 1954*. Westport CT: Greenwood, 1980.
García Canclini, Néstor. *Culturas híbridas: Estratégias para entrar y salir de la modernidad*. Buenos Aires: Paidós, 2001.
Geertz, Clifford. *The Interpretation of Cultures: Selected Essays*. London: Hutchinson, 1975.

Gibson, Charles. *Aztecs under Spanish Rule: A History of the Indians of the Valley of Mexico (1519–1810)*. Palo Alto CA: Stanford University Press, 1964.
Gibson, William. "Network News: Elements of a Theory." *Social Text* 3 (1980): 88–111.
Gilboa, Eytan. "The CNN Effect: The Search for a Communication Theory of International Relations." *Political Communication* 22 (2005): 27–44.
———. "Mass Communication and Diplomacy: A Theoretical Framework." *Communication Theory* 10, no. 3 (2000): 275–309.
González de Bustamante, Celestine. "*Club de señoritas*: Productions of Mexican Femininity in the 1950s." *Studies in Latin American Popular Culture* 28 (2010): 132–40.
———. "Dependency and Development: The Importance of TV News in the History of Mexican Television." *Revista Galáxia* (São Paulo), December 18, 2009, 254–70.
———. "The First Television Newscasts: The Importance of News in Mexican Television History." *Revista Galáxia* 18 (December 2009): 254–70.
———. "*Tele-visiones* (tele-visiones): The Making of Mexican Television News, 1950–1970." PhD diss., University of Arizona, 2006.
———. "'*Terroristas*' and Torch Carriers: Televising the Cold War in Mexico, 1968." Paper presented at the American Historical Association Conference on Latin American History, San Diego CA, January 7–10, 2010.
González Molina, Gabriel. "The Production of Mexican Television News: The Supremacy of Corporate Rationale." PhD diss., University of Leicester, 1990.
Grandin, Greg. *The Last Colonial Massacre: Latin America in the Cold War*. Chicago: University of Chicago Press, 2004.
Greene, Alison. "Cablevision (Nation) in Rural Yucatán: Performing Modernity and Mexicanidad in the Early 1990s." In *Fragments of a Golden Age: The Politics of Culture in Mexico since 1940*, edited by Gilbert M. Joseph, Anne Rubenstein, and Eric Zolov, 415–51. Durham NC: Duke University Press, 2001.
Guerrero, Manuel Alejandro. *The Emergence of Political Pluralism in Mexican Broadcasting*. Saarbrücken, Germany: VDM Verlag, 2009.
Guerrero, Manuel Alejandro, and Maria Eugenia Campo. "Between Heroes and Victims." In *Arizona Firestorm: Global Immigration Realities, National*

Media, and Provincial Politics, edited by Otto Santa Ana and Celeste González de Bustamante. New York: Rowman and Littlefield, 2012.

Guerrero, Manuel Alejandro, and Victoria Isabela Corduneanu. "Trust, Credibility and Relevance in the Consumption of Information among Mexican Youth; Third Generation TV Audiences." In *Empowering Citizenship through Journalism, Information, and Entertainment in Iberoamerica*, edited by Manuel Alejandro Guerrero and Manuel Chavez, 157–98. Mexico City: Universidad Iberoamericana, 2009.

Gutierrez, Felix F., and Jorge Reina Schement. "Spanish International Network: The Flow of Spanish-Language Television to the United States." *Communication Research* 11, no. 2 (1984): 241–56.

Gutierrez Lara, Aníbal. "La industria de la TV en el desarrollo económico." In Sánchez de Armas, *Apuntes*, 1:485–509.

Hamilton, Douglas. "Whither Cuban Socialism? The Changing Political Economy of the Cuban Revolution." *Latin American Perspectives* 29, no. 3 (2002): 18–39.

Hayes, Joy Elizabeth. *Radio Nation: Communication, Popular Culture, and Nationalism in Mexico, 1920–1950*. Tucson: University of Arizona Press, 2000.

Hernández, Omar, and Emile McAnany. "Cultural Industries in the Free Trade Age: A Look at Mexican Television." In *Fragments of a Golden Age: The Politics of Culture in Mexico since 1940*, edited by Gilbert M. Joseph, Anne Rubenstein, and Eric Zolov, 389–414. Durham NC: Duke University Press, 2001.

Hernández Lomeli, Francisco. "Obstáculos para el establecimiento de la televisión comercial en México (1950–1955)." *Comunicación y Sociedad* 28 (September–December, 1996): 147–71.

———. "Racionalidad limitada y efectos perversos: Ensayo sobre el origen de la televisión en México." *Consejo Nacional para la Enseñanza y la Investigación de las Ciencias de la Comunicación Universidad de Guadalajara* 9 (2002): 323–46.

Hershberg, Jim. "Anatomy of a Controversy." *Cold War International History Project Bulletin* 5 (Spring 1995). National Security Archive. http://www.gwu.edu/~nsarchiv/nsa/cuba_mis_cri/moment.htm.

Hobsbawm, Eric. "Introduction: Inventing Traditions." In *The Invention of Tradition*, edited by Eric Hobsbawm and Terrence Ranger, 1–14. Cambridge: Cambridge University Press, 1983.

Hobsbawm, Eric, and Terrence Ranger, eds. *The Invention of Tradition.* Cambridge: Cambridge University Press, 1983.

Huesca Rebolledo, Sabás. "Cronología de noticiarios televisivos." In Sánchez de Armas, *Apuntes,* 2:99–107.

———. "La noticia por televisión." In Sánchez de Armas, *Apuntes,* 2:67–112.

Hughes, Sallie. *Newsrooms in Conflict: Journalism and the Democratization of Mexico.* Pittsburgh: University of Pittsburgh Press, 2006.

Hughes, Sallie, and Chappell Lawson. "Propaganda and Crony Capitalism: Partisan Bias in Mexican Television News." *Latin American Research Review* 29, no. 3 (2004): 81–105.

Indicadores sociodemográficos de México, 1930–2000. Aguascalientes, Mexico: Instituto Nacional Estadística, Geografía e Informática, 2001.

Jones, Frederick. *Juvenal and the Satiric Genre.* London: Duckworth, 2007.

Joseph, Gilbert M., and Daniela Spenser, eds. *In from the Cold: Latin America's New Encounter with the Cold War.* Durham NC: Duke University Press, 2008.

Kennedy, Paul. *The Middle Beat: A Correspondent's View of Mexico, Guatemala, and El Salvador.* Edited by Stanley Ross. New York: Teachers College Press, 1971.

Kohler, Foy D., and Dodd L. Harvey. "The International Significance of the Lunar Landing." *Journal of Inter-American Studies and World Affairs* 12, no. 1 (1970): 3–30.

Kram Villarreal, Rachel. "Gladiolas for the Children of Sanchez: Ernesto P. Uruchurtu's Mexico City, 1950–1968." PhD diss., University of Arizona, 2008.

Krauze, Enrique. *Mexico: Biography of Power; A History of Modern Mexico, 1810–1996.* Translated by Hank Heifetz. New York: HarperPerennial, 1998.

———. *La presidencia imperial: Ascenso y caída del sistema político mexicano, 1940–1996.* Mexico City: Tusques, 2002.

Kurlansky, Mark. *1968: The Year That Rocked the World.* New York: Ballantine, 2004.

La France, David G. "Politics, Violence, and the Press in Mexico." *Studies in Latin American Popular Culture* 12 (1993): 215–21.

Lawson, Chapell. *Building the Fourth Estate: Democratization and the Rise of a Free Press in Mexico.* Berkeley: University of California Press, 2002.

Lears, T. J. Jackson. "The Concept of Cultural Hegemony." *American Historical Review* 90, no. 3 (1985): 567–93.
Lewis, Oscar. *Five Families: Mexican Case Studies in the Culture of Poverty.* New York: Basic Books, 1959.
Long, Gerald. "News for Whom?" Seminar. St. Anthony's College, Oxford, 1975. In Boyd-Barrett, *International News Agencies.*
López Mateos, Adolfo. *Pensamiento en acción.* 2 vols. Mexico City: Oficina de Prensa, 1963.
MacLachlan, Colin M., and William H. Beezley. *El gran pueblo: A History of Greater Mexico.* Upper Saddle River NJ: Simon and Schuster, 1999.
Mallin, Jay, Sr. *Covering Castro: Rise and Decline of Cuba's Communist Dictator.* New Brunswick NJ: Transaction; Washington DC: U.S.-Cuba Institute Press, 1994.
Martín-Barbero, Jesús. *Communication, Culture, and Hegemony: From the Media to Mediations.* Translated by Elizabeth Fox and Robert A. White. London: Sage, 1993.
Martín del Campo, Julio Labastida, and Miguel Armando López Levya. "México: Una transición prolongada (1988–96/97)." *Revista Mexicana de Sociología* 66, no. 4 (2004): 749–806.
Martínez, Oscar J. *Troublesome Border.* Tucson: University of Arizona Press, 1995.
Martínez Medellín, Francisco J. *Televisa: Siga la huella.* Mexico City: Claves Latinoamericanas, 1992.
Mattos, Sérgio. *A televisão no Brasil: 50 anos da história, 1950–2000.* Salvador: Inamá, 2000.
McLuhan, Marshall. *Understanding Media: The Extensions of Man.* New York: McGraw-Hill, 1964.
Mejía Barquera, Fernando. *1920–1960.* Vol. 1 of *La industria de la radio y la política del Estado Mexicano.* Mexico City: Fundación Manuel Buendía, 1989.
———. "Cronología: Del desarrollo technológico de la TV." In Sánchez de Armas, *Apuntes*, 1:513–20.
———. "Cronología general de la televisión Mexicana." In Sánchez de Armas, *Apuntes*, 1:521–66.
———. "Del canal 4 a Televisa." In Sánchez de Armas, *Apuntes*, 1:19–98.
———. "Televisión y política." In Sánchez de Armas, *Apuntes*, 2:21–66.

Mello e Souza, Cláudio. *15 anos de história: Jornal Nacional*. Rio de Janeiro: Rede Globo, 1984.

México '68: 25 años después. Mexico City: Televisa, 1993. Videocassette (VHS), 120 min.

Michael, Donald N. "The Beginning of the Space Age and American Public Opinion." *Public Opinion Quarterly* 24, no. 4 (1960): 573–82.

Moreno, Julio E. "J. Walter Thompson, the Good Neighbor Policy, and Lessons in Mexican Business Culture, 1920–1950." *Enterprise and Society* 5, no. 2 (2004): 254–80.

———. *Yankee Don't Go Home! Mexican Nationalism, American Business Culture, and the Shaping of Modern Mexico, 1920–1950*. Chapel Hill: University of North Carolina Press, 2003.

Morley, Morris. "The U.S. Imperial State in Cuba, 1952–1958: Policymaking and Capitalist Interest." *Journal of Latin American Studies* 14, no. 1 (1982): 143–70.

Morris, Steven D. *Gringolandia: Mexican Identity and Perceptions of the United States*. Lanham MD: Rowman and Littlefield, 2005.

Morton, W. M. *Woman Suffrage in Mexico*. Gainesville: University of Florida Press, 1962.

Niblo, Stephen R. "British Propaganda in Mexico during the Second World War: The Development of Cultural Imperialism." *Latin American Perspectives* 10, no. 4 (1983): 114–26.

———. *Mexico in the 1940s: Modernity, Politics, and Corruption*. Wilmington DE: Scholarly Resources, 1999.

Noriega, Luis Antonio de, and Frances Leach. *Broadcasting in Mexico*. London: Routledge and Kegan Paul, 1979.

Novo, Salvador, and Guillermo González Camarena. "La Televisión: Investigación del Instituto Nacional de Bellas Artes." Unpublished manuscript. Mexico, 1948.

Ochoa, Enrique. *Feeding Mexico: The Political Uses of Food since 1910*. Wilmington DE: Scholarly Resources, 2000.

O'Connor, John. *Image as Artifact: The Historical Analysis of Film and Television*. Malabar FL: Krieger, 1990.

O'Donnell, Guillermo. *Bureaucratic Authoritarianism: Argentina, 1966–1973, in Comparative Perspective*. Berkeley: University of California Press, 1988.

Orozco Gómez, Guillermo. "La televisión en México." In *Históricas de la televisión en Ámerica Latina: Argentina, Brasil, Colombia, México,*

Venezuela, edited by Guillermo Orozco Gómez and Nora Maziotti, 59–70. Barcelona: Gedisa, 2002.

Pansters, Wil. "Social Movement and Discourse: The Case of the University Reform Movement in 1961 in Puebla, Mexico." *Bulletin of Latin American Research* 9, no. 1 (1990): 79–101.

Pellicer de Brody, Olga. *México y la Revolución Cubana*. Mexico City: El Colegio de México, 1972.

Pérez-Rayon, Nora. "The Capital Commemorates Independence at the Turn of the Century." In *¡Viva México! ¡Viva la Independencia!*, edited by William H. Beezley and David E. Lorey, 141–66. Wilmington DE: Scholarly Resources, 2001.

Plenn, Virginia. "Mexico." In *International Television Almanac: Who, What, Where in Television*, edited by Charles S. Aaronson, 748. New York: Quigley, 1970.

Poniatowska, Elena. "1968: Año del movimiento estudiantil en México." Paper presented at COMEXUS, Mexico-U.S. Commission for Educational and Cultural Exchange, Mexico City, 2005.

———. *Massacre in Mexico*. Translated by Helen R. Lane. Columbia: University of Missouri Press, 1992.

———. *La noche de Tlatelolco: Testimonios de historia oral*. Mexico City: Era, 1971.

———. *Todo México*. Vol. 5. Mexico City: Diana, 1999.

Rankin, Monica Ann. *¡México, la patria! Propaganda and Production during World War II*. Lincoln: University of Nebraska Press, 2010.

Reese, Steven D., Oscar H. Gandy Jr., and August E. Grant. *Framing Public Life: perspectives on media and our understanding of the social world*. Mahwah NJ: Erlbaum, 2001.

Relaciones Mexicano-Soviéticas, 1917–1980. Mexico City: Secretaría de Relaciones Exteriores / URSS Academia de Ciencias, 1981.

Revueltas, José. *México 68: Juventud y revolución*. Mexico City: Era, 1978.

Robinson, Davis R. "The Treaty of Tlatelolco and the United States: A Latin American Nuclear Free Zone." *American Journal of International Law* 64, no. 2 (1970): 282–309.

Rodriguez-Castañeda, Rafael. *Prensa vendida: Los periodistas y los presidentes; 40 años de relaciones*. Mexico City: Grijalbo, 1993.

Rubenstein, Anne. *Bad Language, Naked Ladies, and Other Threats to the Nation: A Political History of Comic Books in Mexico*. Durham NC: Duke University Press, 1998.

Salwen, Michael B. *Radio and Television in Cuba: The Pre-Castro Era*. Ames: Iowa State University Press, 1994.

Salwen, Michael B., and Bruce Garrison. *Latin American Journalism*. Hillsdale NJ: Erlbaum, 1991.

Sánchez de Armas, Miguel Ángel, ed. *Apuntes para una historia de la Televisión Mexicana*. 2 vols. Mexico City: Revista Mexicana / Televisa, 1998.

Sánchez Ruiz, Enrique. "Los medios de difusión masiva y la centralización en México." *Mexican Studies / Estudios Mexicanos* 4, no. 1 (1988): 25–54.

———. Prologue to *Apuntes*, ed. Sánchez Ruiz, 1:9–16.

———. *Tendencias en la investigación sobre la televisión en México 1950–1990*. Mexico City: Universidad de Guadalajara, 1992.

Saragoza, Alex. *The Media and the State in Mexico: The Origins of Televisa*. Austin: University of Texas Press, forthcoming.

———. *The Monterrey Elite and the Mexican State, 1888–1940*. Austin: University of Texas Press, 1988.

Scherer García, Julio, and Carlos Monsiváis. *Los rostros del 68*. Vol. 2 of *Parte de guerra*. Mexico City: Nuevo Siglo, 2002.

———. *Tiempo de Saber: Prensa y Poder en México*. Mexico City: Nuevo Siglo/Aguilar, 2003.

———. *Tlatelolco, 1968: Documentos del General Marcelino García Barragán; Los hechos y la historia*. Vol. 1 of *Parte de guerra*. Mexico City: Nuevo Siglo / Aguilar, 1999.

Schieffer, Bob. *Face the Nation: My Favorite Stories from the First 50 Years of the Award-Winning News Broadcast*. New York: Simon and Schuster, 2004.

Schiller, Herbert I. "National Development Requires Some Social Distance." *Antioch Review* 29, no. 1 (1967): 63–67.

Schlesinger, Philip. Introduction to *Communication, Culture, and Hegemony: From the Media to Mediations*. By Jesús Martín-Barbero. Translated by Elizabeth Fox and Robert A. White, 1–12. London: Sage, 1993.

Schmidt, Samuel. *The Deterioration of the Mexican Presidency: The Years of Luis Echeverría*. Tucson: University of Arizona, 1991.

Schwoch, James. *The American Radio Industry and Its Latin American Activities, 1900–1939*. Urbana: University of Illinois Press, 1990.

Scott, James C. *Seeing Like a State: How Certain Schemes to Improve the Human Condition Have Failed*. New Haven CT: Yale University Press, 1998.

Shaw, Donald Lewis, and Maxwell E. McCombs. *The Emergence of American Political Issues: The Agenda-Setting Function of the Press*. St. Paul MN: West, 1977.

Sherman, John W. "The Mexican 'Miracle' and Its Collapse." In *The Oxford History of Mexico*, edited by Michael C. Meyer and William H. Beezley, 575–608. Oxford: Oxford University Press, 2000.

Skidmore, Thomas. *Television, Politics, and the Transition to Democracy in Latin America*. Washington DC: Woodrow Wilson Center Press, 1993.

Sinclair, John. "Dependent Development and Broadcasting: 'The Mexican Formula.'" *Media, Culture and Society* 8, no. 1 (1986): 81–101.

———. *Latin American Television: A Global View*. New York: Oxford University Press, 1999.

———. "Neither West nor Third World: The Mexican Television Industry within the NWICO Debate." *Media, Culture and Society* 12, no. 3 (1990): 343–60.

Sinclair, John, Elizabeth Jacka, and Stuart Cunningham, eds. *New Patterns in Global Television: Peripheral Vision*. Oxford: Oxford University Press, 1996.

Smith, Peter H. "The Latin American Press and the Space Race." *Journal of Inter-American Studies* 6, no. 4 (1964): 549–72.

———. "Mexico since 1946: Dynamics of an Authoritarian Regime." In *Mexico since Independence*, edited by Leslie Bethell, 321–98. Cambridge: Cambridge University Press, 1991.

Sorensen, Diana. "Tlatelolco 1968: Paz and Poniatowska on Law and Violence." *Mexican Studies/Estudios Mexicanos* 18, no. 2 (2002): 297–321.

———. *A Turbulent Decade Remembered: Scenes from the Latin American Sixties*. Palo Alto CA: Stanford University Press, 2007.

Storey, John. *An Introductory Guide to Cultural Theory and Popular Culture*. New York: Havester / Wheatsheaf, 1993.

Story, Dale. "Policy Cycles in Mexican Presidential Politics." *Latin American Research Review* 20 (1985): 139–61.

Tello, Manuel. *México: Una posición internacional*. Mexico City: Cuadernos de Joaquín Mortiz, 1972.

Tlatelolco: La claves de la masacre. Directed by Carlos Mendoza Aupetit. Mexico City: La Jornada and Canalseisdejulio, 2005. DVD, 57 min.

Trejo Delabre, Raúl, ed. *Las redes de Televisa*. Mexico City: Claves Latinoamericanas, 1988.

——, ed. *Televisa: El quinto poder*. Mexico City: Claves Latinoamericanas, 1985.

Tunstall, Jeremy. *The Media Were American: U.S. Mass Media in Decline*. Oxford: Oxford University Press, 2008.

Vigón, Mercedes, Lilliam Martínez Bustos, and Celeste González de Bustamante. "Not Business as Usual: Spanish-Language Television Coverage of Arizona's Immigration Law, April–May 2010." In *Arizona Firestorm: Global Immigration Realities, National Media, and Provincial Politics*, edited by Otto Santa Ana and Celeste González de Bustamante. New York: Rowman and Littlefield, 2012.

Vizeu Pereira, Alfredo Eurico, Jr., Flávio Porcello, and C. Ladeira Mota, eds. *Telejornalismo: A nova praça pública* [Television journalism: The new public plaza] (Florianopolis, Brazil: Insular, 2006).

Waisbord, Silvio. "Latin America." In *Television: An International History*, edited by Anthony Smith, 254–63. Oxford: Oxford University Press, 1998.

Weeks, Albert L. E-mail message. *Space Monitoring Information Support News*. September 2, 2003. http://smis.iki.rssi.ru/news_e.htm.

Wells, Allen, and Gilbert M. Joseph. *Summer of Discontent Season of Upheaval*. Palo Alto CA: Stanford University Press, 1996.

White, Christopher M. *Creating a Third World: Mexico, Cuba, and the United States during the Castro Era*. Albuquerque: University of New Mexico Press, 2007.

Witherspoon, Kevin B. *Before the Eyes of the World: Mexico and the 1968 Olympic Games*. DeKalb: Northern Illinois University, 2008.

Zelizer, Barbie. *Covering the Body: The Kennedy Assassination, the Media, and Shaping of Collective Memory*. Chicago: University of Chicago Press, 1992.

Zolov, Eric. "¡Cuba sí, yanquís no! The Sacking of the Instituto Cultural Mexico-Norteamericano in Morelia, Michoacán, 1961." In Joseph and Spenser, *In from the Cold*, 214–52.

——. "Lázaro Cárdenas and the Cuban Revolution: A Political and Cultural Perspective." Paper presented at the Society for Latin American Studies, Leiden, The Netherlands, 2004.

——. *Refried Elvis: The Rise of the Mexican Counterculture*. Berkeley: University of California Press, 1999.

——. "Showcasing the 'Land of Tomorrow': Mexico and the 1968 Olympics." *Americas* 61, no. 2 (2004): 159–88.

Index

Photos and tables are indicated by page numbers in *italics*.

ABC News, 186, 191
Academia San Carlos, 168
Acevedo, Marta, 200
Adenauer, Konrad, 47
advertisers and advertising, 9–10, 12, 15, 19–20, 34–36, 58, 174, 186, 210. *See also* commercials
Agence France-Presse (French Press Agency), 69, 113
Aguirre, Manuel Bernardo, 205
Aguirre Jiménez, Francisco, 182
airtime, taxation of, 28, 179–80
Aldrin, Edwin (Buzz), 139, 141, *141*
Alemán Valdés, Miguel: and Acapulco tourism development, 96; and adoption of commercial television model, 7, 9; broadcast of fourth informe, 1–4; and Día de la Independencia, 44; and establishment of television in Mexico, 1–4, 6–7; and freedom of the press, 42–43; and O'Farrill Sr., xxiii; passing of party leadership, 43–44; political, economic, social, and cultural changes under, 23–26, 29; and railway strikes of 1958–59, 56; as television diplomat, 79–80, 227n1; visit to Washington DC, 79–80, 227n1
Alemán Velasco, Miguel: and corporate news division, 135–36, 173, 183–84, *185*; on "fair and balanced" news coverage, 232–33n68; as head of Dirección General de Información y Noticieros, 40; and nationalization debate, 207; and PRI, xxiv; and Space Race, 110–12, 135–36, 137, 139, 141; and Tlatelolco massacre fallout, 179–80; and 24 horas, xxxvi, 40

el alunizaje. See *Apollo 11*
Amorós, Roberto, 37, 59, 61–63
AP. *See* Associated Press
Apollo 11, 134–42, 137, 140–41, 233n75
Apollo 13, 136
Armstrong, Neil, 139, 141, 233n75
Arredondo Ramírez, Pablo, xxviii
Associated Press (AP), xxvi, xxx, 69, 113–14
attribution of news stories, 112–14
Ayala, Lolita, 83, 200–201, 202, 214–15
Azcárraga, Emilio, 117
Azcárraga, Luis, 8
Azcárraga, Raul, 8
Azcárraga Jean, Emilio, 186, 215
Azcárraga Milmo, Emilio: at Aztec Stadium opening, xxi–xxii; and Cañedo, 196; and corporate news division, 135, 173; and hegemony on national level, 209; and PRI, xxiii, 175, 209; and refusal of Spanish-language monopoly in U.S., xxviii; and technological advances, 22; and tele-traditions, 33; and Telesistema Mexicano, 38, 188–89; and World Cup, 22, 191
Azcárraga Vidaurreta, Emilio: and consolidation into Telesistema Mexicano, 12; and corporate news division, 183–84, 185; death of, 187–88, 206, 209–10; and establishment of television in Mexico, 2–3, 5–6, 8; on his own radio and television prominence, xxi; master plan of, 34; in newscasts, 37–38; and regional markets expansion, 21
Aztec Stadium. *See* Estadio Azteca

Barragán, Marcelino García, 157–59, 161
Basilio, Norma Enriqueta, 164–66, 165
Batallón Olímpia, 170
Batista, Fulgencio, 53, 64, 66–68, 70–72, 80, 83, 86
Bay of Pigs invasion, 105, 110, 128–30, 143, 208, 232n53, 232n54
Becerra Celis, Luis, 17
Becerril, Porfirio, 122
Belmont, Antonio, 117
Bennett, Rawson, 116
Berumen, Patricia, 200
Betancourt, Ernesto, 53, 66
Beteta, Ramón, 205
Bracero Program, 27, 103
Brazilian-Mexican relations, 195–96. *See also* World Cup of 1970
bribes, 42. *See also* corruption
las brigadas, 167
Brundage, Avery, 163
Brunet, Meade, 4
Buchanan, Walter C., 122
bullfighting, 116–17, 144

business and capital enterprises news coverage, 34

cable television, 20
Cablevisión, 20
Cabrera, Angel, 47, 160, 199
Café matutino. See *Su diario Nescafé*
Campo Militar Número Uno, 151, 158, 160
Campos, Rosa María, 200
Cañedo, Guillermo, 196
Cantillo, Eulogio, 66
Cárdenas, Lázaro: and Alemán Valdés, 23; first televised image of, 6; and Ley de Vías Generales de Comunicaciones of 1940, 84; as television diplomat, 81–82, 86–93, 102–3, 105; undermining López Mateos, 91–93, 103; visit to Cuba, xxxiv, 54, 81–82, 86–93, 102–3, 105, 228n23
Carlos, John, 234–35n19, 234n7
Carrandi Ortiz, Gabino, 33, 111, 135
Casas Alemán, Fernando, 43
Castellanos, Rosario, 200
Castellot, Gonzálo, 10–11, 39
Castro Ruz, Emma, 68–69
Castro Ruz, Fidel: and Bay of Pigs invasion, 129–30, 208; as champion of democracy, 55, 225n10; and Cuban Missile Crisis, 130, 133, 208; and Cuban Revolution, 53–55, 64–66, 65, 68–78; and López Mateos, 110; and Mexican student movements, 149, 208; motivating Mexican youth, 149; named prime minister of Cuba, 98; as television diplomat, 80, 86–91, 98, 102
Castro Ruz, Lidia, 68–69, 72
CBS News, 2, 64–65, 186, 200
CEIMSA (Compañía Exportadora e Importadora Mexicana), 25–26, 212
Celanese Mexicana (CelMex), 117–18
censorship, 16, 42–43, 85, 173, 209, 212, 232–33n68
Central American Games of 1954, 34
charrazo, 56
charrismo, 56
charros, 56
Chávez, Carlos, 7
chayotes, 42, 83, 85
A child's paradise, 19
china poblana, 13, *14*
"Cinderella Years," 24
Club América, xxi, 196
Cold War, 107–44; *Apollo 11*, 134–42, *137*, *140–41*; Bay of Pigs invasion, 105, 110, 128–30, 143, 208; citizens political ideologies about, 75; Cuban Missile Crisis, xxxiv, 26, 41, 74–75, 102, 110, 114, 130–34, 143, 208; and Cuban Revolution, 53–55; effects on television news, 142–44; and international news agencies, 69; interruptions in coverage

Index 261

Cold War (cont.)
   of, 116–18; and nationalism,
     45; overview, 107–11; Project
     Mercury, 19, 124–28, 143,
     231n38, 231n39; and railway
     strikes of 1958–59, 57; SCT-1
     rocket, 86, 88–90, 92–94,
     96–102, 121–24, 231n34,
     231n37; Sputnik, xxxiv, 107–
     16, 118–21, 138, 142; and tele-
     traditions, 32; and television
     diplomacy, 80, 82, 90–92, 95,
     97, 99, 102–5; and television
     news, effect on, 142–44
color television, 19
Columna de Independencia
   (Column of Independence), 46,
   48–49, 52, 100–101, 105
Comité Nacional Organizador,
   149, 164
commercials, 20, 35–36, 152,
   174, 186. See also advertisers
   and advertising
communism, 26, 82, 148
Communist League of September
   23 (LC-23), 203
Compañía Exportadora e
   Importadora Mexicana
   (CEIMSA), 25–26, 212
Compañía Nacional de Subsistencias Populares (CONASUPO),
   25–26, 212
CONASUPO (Compañía Nacional
   de Subsistencias Populares),
   25–26, 212
Consejo Nacional de Huelga, 146,
   151, 167, 175

Cooper, Gordon, 19
corporate news division, 135,
   172–73, 183–84, 237–38n76
Corpus Christi massacre, 29, 203
corruption, 2, 17, 23, 168, 169
Cry for Independence, 43
Cuba, Cárdenas visit to, 81–82,
   86–93, 102–3, 105. See also
   Castro Ruz, Fidel
Cuba-Mexico relations, 54. See
   also quadripartite relations
   between Mexico, the United
   States, the Soviet Union, and
   Cuba
Cuban Missile Crisis, xxxiv, 26,
   41, 74–75, 102, 110, 114,
   130–34, 143, 208, 232n58
Cuban Revolution, xxxiii–xxxiv,
   26, 53–55, 64–78, 82, 87–89,
   208, 226n36, 227n7
cultural hegemony: definition
   and value of, xxv; international, 208–9; limits to, xxv–
   xxvi, 33, 55–56, 78, 82, 143,
   178–79, 207, 212; national,
   209–15; and Space Race, 108
cultural hybridity, xxix
cultural imperialism, xxviii–xxix,
   16, 207
CYJ radio, 8
CYL radio, 8

Day of the Revolution. See Día de
   la Revolución
Day of the Three Wise Men, 31,
   222n1

Day of the Virgin of Guadalupe, 117
de Léon, Jesús, 56
Día de la Independencia, 32, 44–52, 108, 196–98, 211, 224n42, 224n44
Día de la Revolución, 32, 99, 102, 104
Día de la Virgen de Guadalupe, 117
Día de los Reyes Magos, 31, 222n1
Díaz Guerra, Alejandro, 20–21
Díaz Ordaz, Gustavo: at Aztec Stadium opening, xxi–xxii; broadcast of fourth informe, 182; choosing Echeverría as successor, 189; and corporate news division, 135, 237–38n76; and government-media relations, 179–80, 183–84; and Olympics of 1968, xxxv, 145, 155, 163; political, economic, social, and cultural changes under, 28; and student protest movements, 168; and technological advances, 21–22; and termination of newspaper contracts, 172; and Tlatelolco massacre, xxiii; and World Cup, 195–96; and Zabludovsky, 42, 58, 83
Dirección General de Información y Noticieros, 34, 40, 184
Dorticós, Osvaldo, 75
Dulles, John Foster, 47, 55

Echeverría Alvarez, Luís: and expansion of television to remote areas, 22; goals in common with television, 210; and government-media relations, 22, 28–29, 172, 179–80, 183–84, 201–3, 206–7; and nationalization debate, xxiii, 207, 240–41n9; and plane crash at Meson Hill, 193–94; and presidential elections of 1970, xxxvi, 189–94, 206; Scherer on, 183–84
Ed Sullivan show, 64–65
Eisenhower, Dwight D., xxxiv, 47, 80–82, 94–98, 101, 103–5, 109, 115, 120, 208
el '68 student protest movement. *See* student protest movements; Tlatelolco massacre
elections of 1970, xxxvi, 189–96, 190, 211–12
El Heraldo, 172
embutes, 42, 83, 85
Erazo, Eleazar, 120
Escuela Nacional de Artes Plásticas, 167–68, 237n62
ESPN, 191
Estadio Azteca, xxi–xxii, xxxi, 22, 192, 196, 210
Excelsior, 5, 29, 172, 183–84
Explorer I, 230n2

Falcons, 203
Fallaci, Oriana, 151
Federal Law of Radio and Television of 1960, 11, 15–16, 85

Index 263

Fernández Christlieb, Fátima, xxvi, 16, 117
Ferríz de Santa Cruz, Pedro, xxii, 36, 41, 87, 132, 151
Ferrocarriles Nacionales de México (FNM), 61
first official television broadcast, xxxii, 1–4
First World Conference of Communications, 207
Fonseca, Amelia, 6
Fonseca, Miguel, 6
framing, xxix–xxx. *See also* hybrid frames
freedom of expression, 16, 85
freedom of the press, 42–43
French Press Agency, 69, 113

gacetillas, 42, 77
Garcia, Rodolfo, 117
García Sáinz, Pablo, 215
Garza Sada, Bernardo, 188, 210
Garza Sada, Eugenio, 203
Gateway to suspense, 18
General Division of Information and News, 40, 184
General Motors News. *See Noticiero General Motors*
Gomez, Rosa, 10
González, Elian, 228n23
González Camarena, Guillermo, 1, 4, 6–7, 12, 15, 19
González Morfín, Efraín, 189–91, 190, 193–94
government-media relationships, xxiii–xxiv, xxvi, 15–17, 28–29, 172–84, 196, 201–3, 206–10, 212–13

granaderos, xxxv, 145, 168, 170, 170
Grito de Dolores, 45, 51
Grito de la Independencia, 43
Guadalajara, 17, 20–21, 77, 84, 129, 189
Guaymas tracking station, 124–28, 143
Guerra Leal, Mario, 93
Guevara, Ernesto "Che," 72–74, 89, 149

Haggerty, James, 116
Halcones, 203
hegemony. *See* cultural hegemony
Henríquez Guzmán, Miguel, 43
Hidalgo de Costilla, Miguel, 43–44
Hill, Robert C., 125
holiday broadcasts: Día de la Independencia, 32, 34, 43–52, 108, 196–98, 211, 224n42, 224n44; Día de la Revolución, 32, 99, 102, 104; Día de los Reyes Magos, 31; ongoing significance of, 178
hybrid frames, 56, 64, 78, 143, 146, 167
hybrid framing, xxix–xxx

Ibáñez, Arturo, 200
independence celebrations. *See* Día de la Independencia
Independence Day. *See* Día de la Independencia
Iñíguez, José Alberto, Institutional Revolutionary Party, 72

Institutional Revolutionary
Party. *See* PRI (Partido Revolucionario Institucional)
INTELSAT (International Organization of Satellite Communications), 19
International Organization of Satellite Communications (INTELSAT), 19
Izaguirre de Ruiz Cortines, María Dolores, 31–32, 45, 48, 52

Jenkins, William, 3–4
journalists, television: professionalization of, 109, 185; wages of, 84, 227n12
Juárez, Alberto, 117

"kaleidoscope" color television, 19
Kellog, Jorge, 200
Kennedy, John F., 19, 129, 131–33
Kennedy, Paul, 24, 76, 92
kinescope, 18

Labardini, Jorge, 20, 111
Law of Public Thoroughfares and Communications of 1940, 15–16, 84
LC-23 (Liga Comunista de 23 de Septiembre), 203
League for Decency, 13
Leal, Graciela, 200
Lears, T. J. Jackson, xxv
Lewis, Oscar, 10
Ley de Vías Generales de Comunicaciones of 1940, xxxv–xxxvi, 15–16, 84
Leyendo Novedades. *See Noticiero novedades*
Ley Federal de Radio y Televisión of 1960, 11, 15–16, 85
Liga Comunista de 23 de Septiembre (LC-23), 203
Liga de la Decencia, 13
López Chávez, Salvador, 20–21
López Mateos, Adolfo: and agrarian reform, 88–89; and Castro, 110; and Cuban Missile Crisis, 130–34; and Cuban Revolution, 53–54, 75–76; and Día de la Independencia, 46, 51; economic and political policies of, 25–27; and Federal Law of Communications, 85; and Guatemala, 96, 229n43; hosting Eisenhower, 80, 94–96, 115; hosting Mikoyan, 100–101; laying first stone of Aztec Stadium, xxii; and Ley Federal de Comunicaciones, 85; and Mexican Revolution, 229n59; and press independence, 41–42; and railway strikes of 1958–59, 56–58; as television diplomat, 80–83, 86–87, 90–96, 100–101, 103, 105; undermined by Cárdenas, 91–93, 103; visit to Asia, 130–34; visit to United States, 80–83, 86–87, 90–94, 93, 103, 228n38
lucha libre, 13, 209
lunar landing. *See Apollo 11*

Index   265

Martinez, Juan, 167
Mascarua Alonso, Alfonso, 45
matadors, 116–17
media-government relationships. *See* government-media relationships
Meson Hill plane crash, 193–94
Mexican Exporting and Importing Company (CEIMSA), 25–26, 212
mexicanidad, xxvi, xxviii, 13, 32, 43, 117, 187, 211–13
Mexican Railway Workers Union, 56
Mexican Revolution, 54, 71, 74, 87–88, 90, 93, 101, 226n45, 229n59
Mexico-Brazil relations, 195–96
Mexico-Cuba relations, 54. *See also* quadripartite relations between Mexico, the United States, the Soviet Union, and Cuba
Mexico-U.S. relations, 26, 45, 87, 102–3, 126. *See also* quadripartite relations between Mexico, the U.S., the Soviet Union, and Cuba
Micha, Adela, 214–15
microwave transmission, 3, 21–22
Mikoyan, Anastas, xxxiv, 80–82, 98–102, 104–5
Military Camp Number One, 146, 151, 158, 160
Ministry of Communications and Public Works, 15, 122, 231n32

Ministry of Communications and Transportation, 122, 231n32
Miranda, Donato, 99, 229n51
Molotov, Viacheslav, 40–41
Monterrey, 21
movie industry, 12
Movimiento de 26 de Julio, 86
Mujeres en Acción Solidaria, 200

National Autonomous University of Mexico. *See* Universidad Nacional Autónoma de México
National Company of Popular Subsistence Foods (CONASUPO), 25–26, 212
national holidays. *See* holiday broadcasts
national identity, 27–28, 32, 34, 44, 48, 211–12
National Microwave Network, 19
National Network of Telecommunications, 19
National Organizing Committee, 149, 164
National Railways of Mexico (FNM), 61
National Revolutionary Party (PNR), 6
National School of Visual Arts, 167–68, 237n62
National Strike Committee, 146, 151, 167, 175
Navarrete, Tomás, 160
NBC News, 2–3, 8, 35, 116, 186, 200
news, television. *See* television news

newspapers: and corruption, 168; influence on television content, 33, 35, 39–42, 58, 108–9, 135; influence on television content, end of, 183–84; and Olympics of 1968, 164; and Space Race, 116, 120–21, 126, 136; and Tlatelolco massacre, 172–73, 237–38n76

The news with Lolita Ayala. *See El noticiero con Lolita Ayala*

New World Information and Communication Order, 207

Nixon, Richard, 104, 139, 141

Noticias del día. See Noticiero novedades

Noticiero aeronaves, 126–27, 129

El noticiero con Lolita Ayala, 201

Noticiero General Motors: and bullfighting, 117; and Cuban Revolution, 66–68, 70; and Día de la Independencia, 44–49; early content of, 40; establishment of, 41; Molotov interview, 39–40; and railway strikes, 58–59, 62–63, 77, 157, 162; and SCT-1 rocket, 86, 88–90, 92–94, 96–102, 122; self-promotion of, 86; and *Sputnik*, 107, 111–12, 115–16, 118–20; and tele-traditions, 31, 36–41, 44–49, 197

Noticiero Nescafé, 40, 136, 138–41. See also *Su diario Nescafé*

Noticiero novedades, 36, 39–40, 151, 157, 166, 172

Noticiero PEMEX, 40, 44, 47–49

Noticiero PEMEX sol novedades, 37–38

Noticiero superior, 39

Noticiero teleperiódico Notimex, 200

Novedades, 1, 4, 35, 39–40, 159, 172, 205

Novo, Salvador, 7, 205

Novo Report, 7, 205

nuclear arms race, 91–92, 109, 130–34, 142, 148, 183, 209

Nuevo Leon, 182

O'Donnell, John, 80

O'Farrill Silva, Rómulo, Jr., 37–38, 98, 175

O'Farrill Silva, Rómulo, Sr.: and adoption of commercial television model, 8; and Alemán Valdés, xxiii; business ties to U.S. companies, 3; and consolidation into Telesistema Mexicano, 12, 15; and Día de la Independencia coverage, 44; at Eisenhower banquet, 98; and establishment of television in Mexico, 1–5; and government-media relations, 209–10; news coverage of, 34, 37–38, 98, 108, 115; and Televisora de Guadalajara, 21

Oliver, Covey T., 151

Olympic Battalion, 170

Olympic Games of 1968: and Basilio, 164–66, 165; as evidence of Mexico's economic development and modernity,

Index   267

Olympic Games of 1968 (*cont.*) 148–49, 167, 172, 174–75; and hegemony on national level, 211–12; as Olympics of Peace, 146, 209, 233n2; opening ceremonies of, 163–66, 236n52; overview, 145–46; public perception of, 146, 209, 234n7; satellite transmission of, 19–20, 221n51; second anniversary of, 205–6; student protests during, xxxv, 145–46, 148–50, 152–55, 160, 166–70, 168–70, 174–75, 234–35n19; training for coverage of, 34
Operation Wetback, 103, 232n48
Organization of American States, 89
Ortíz, Francisco, 160

Palavicini, Félix F., 8
Pan-American Games of 1955, 34, 149, 234n18
Paraíso infantil, 19
Partido Nacional Revolucionario (PNR), 6
Partido Revolucionario Institucional. *See* PRI
payoffs, 42
Pedra, Carlos Manuel, 66
Pelé, xxxvi, 22, 195
Pérez, Aurelio, 43
Perezvega, Jorge, 168, 171, 206
peso, devaluation of, 12, 56
Plan de Rehabilitación Ferroviaria, 56

plane crash at Meson Hill, 193–94
Plaza de las Tres Culturas massacre. *See* Tlatelolco massacre
Plaza de Tlatelolco massacre. *See* Tlatelolco massacre
PNR (National Revolutionary Party), 6
political prisoners, 91, 103
Poniatowska, Elena, 42, 173
Pope Paul VI, 163
population of Mexico, 24–25
poverty in Mexico, 149
presidencialismo, xxx
presidential elections of 1970, xxxvi, 189–96, 190, 211–12
PRI (Partido Revolucionario Institucional): Azcárraga Jean on, 215; and coverage of Olympics and Tlateloco massacre, 175; formation of, 6, 23; harassment of Scherer, 183; naming of, 226n45; and news reports, 32; and plane crash at Meson Hill, 193–94; relationship with Telesistema Mexicano, xxii; Tlatelolco massacre fallout, 189; two factions within, 115
Primer Encuentro de Comunicaciones, 207
print media, 11, 33, 172–73, 237–38n76
Project Mercury, 19, 124–28, 143, 231n38, 231n39
Puerta al suspenso, 18

quadripartite relations between Mexico, the U.S., the Soviet

Union, and Cuba, xxxiii, 53, 98, 104, 208
Quint, Bert, 150, 235n25
quotas on importation of television sets, 12–13

radio: availability of, 9; and Azcárraga Vidaurreta, 2, 5–6; and Cuban Revolution, 68, 70, 72; direct government participation in, 6; influence of, xxxi, 7–9, 22; regulation of, 15–16, 43, 85; and Zabludovsky, 41, 83, 215
Radio Moscow, 107, 112
Railroad Rehabilitation Plan, 56
railway strikes of 1958–59, xxxiii, 55–64, 73–78, 91, 103, 117, 162, 208, 225n15, 225n19, 225n21
Ravizé, Manuel A., 192
Rebel Radio (Cuba), 68, 70
Red Cross, 158–59, 162–63
regional markets for television, 20–21
religious pilgrimages, 116–18, 144
Reuters, 69, 113
Ridgeway, Matthew, 45–46
Rodriguez, Ana Ignacia "La Nacha," 167, 171–72, 237n61
Rodriguez, Pedro, 156, 236nn36–37
Ruiz Cortines, Adolfo: and corruption, 17; and Día de la Independencia, 46–49, 52, 108; establishment of XEIPN Channel 11, 8, 209–10; and government-media relations, 179; and hegemony on national level, 209–10; and labor unrest, 25; moralizing television transmissions, 13; as PRI party leader chosen by Alemán, 43, 224n37; and railway strikes of 1958–59, 57; and women's suffrage, 26; and Zabludovsky, 41
Russian Expo, 99, 102
Russian Revolution, 101

Sabido, Miguel, xxx, 29, 215
Sada, Alejandro, 188, 210–11
Saldaña, Jorge, 151, 153, 157, 163, 174, 235n30, 236n42
Salinas, Raúl, 101, 229n56
Salinas de Gortari, Carlos, 183, 229n56
Salinas Pliego, Ricardo, 183
Sanchez, Yolanda, 200
satellite communications, 19–20, 171, 199–200
Scherer García, Julio, 183–84, 203, 233n3
Schiller, Herbert I., 207
SCT-1 rocket, 86, 88–90, 92–94, 96–102, 121–24, 231n34, 231n37
Secretaría de Comunicaciones y Obras Públicas, 122, 231n32
Secretaría de Comunicaciones y Transporte, 122, 231n32
self-censorship, 43, 85, 212, 232–33n68

Index   269

self-promotion, 38, 86
sharing of news content, xxxvi, 39, 114
Sindicato de Trabajadores Ferrocarrileros de la República Mexicana, 56
Siqueiros, David, 76
Slim, Carlos, 34
Smith, Tommie, 234–35n19, 234n7
Soviet press, 99–100
Soviet Union. See Cold War; Cuban Missile Crisis; quadripartite relations between Mexico, the U.S., the Soviet Union, and Cuba; Sputnik
Space Race: and Alemán Velasco, 110–12, 135–36, 137, 139, 141; coverage slant of, 208; first U.S. satellite *Explorer I*, 230n2; and Telesistema Mexicano, 108, 114–15; and Zabludovsky, 110–11. See also *Apollo 11*; Cold War; SCT-1 rocket; *Sputnik*; tracking station at Guaymas
sports as news, 5, 34, 47, 178, 191, 211. See also Olympic Games of 1968; World Cup of 1970
Sputnik, xxxiv, 107–16, 118–21, 138, 142
Stavoli, Francisco Javier, 6
student protest movements, xxxv, 28–29, 145–63, 167–76, 168–70, 182–83, 203, 212, 214, 225n15. See also Tlatelolco massacre

Subsecretaría de Radiodifusión, 179, 238n3
Su diario Nescafé, 40, 136, 151–52, 160, 184, 186, 190, 192, 194. See also *Noticiero Nescafé*

tariffs on importation of television sets, 12
TASS, 47, 69, 112–13, 209
taxation of airtime, 28, 179–80
Telemundo, 111
Telesistema Mexicano: and *Apollo 11*, 135, 139; attribution of news stories, 111–12; and Bay of Pigs invasion, 129–30; competition between stations, 182–83, 187–89; creation of, 11–15, 182; creation of corporate news division, 172–75, 183–85; creation of Televisa, 15, 187–89; and Cuban Revolution, 74; and cultural imperialism, 207; and election of 1970, 193; foreign news coverage by, 198; and government-media relations, 177–82, 196; and hegemony on national level, 210; merger with Televisión Independiente de México, 15, 187–89; and Olympics of 1968, 146–47; and railway strikes, 62–63; relationship with government and PRI, xxii; response to government pressure, 183–87; and Space Race, 108, 114–15;

270 Index

and sports news coverage, 34; technological advances and expansion, 18–21, 199–200; and tele-traditions, 50, 212; and television diplomacy, 84, 90; and Tlatelolco massacre, 146–47, 151, 153, 158, 160, 167–68; and *24 horas*, 186–87; and World Cup, 191

tele-teatros, 51

tele-traditions, 31–52; business and capital enterprises coverage, 34; Día de la Independencia, 32, 34, 43–52, 108, 196–98, 211, 224n42, 224n44; Día de la Revolución, 32, 99, 102, 104; Día de la Virgen de Guadalupe, 117; Día de los Reyes Magos, 31, 222n1; impact beyond Mexico, 33–34, 223n5; media owners, coverage of, 98, 108, 115; news programs as, 35–43; ongoing significance of, 178, 196–98; overview, xxxii–xxxiii, 31–35; self-promotion, 86; and social divide, 50–52; sports as news, 5, 34, 47, 178, 191, 211

Televimex, 5, 15. *See also* XEW-TV Channel 2

Televisa: and Azcárraga Milmo, 38; and Basilio, 164; credibility of, 213; establishment of, 15, 187–89, 210; expansion of, 22; foreign news sources, end of dependence on, 70; implications of success of, xxviii; news production capacity in mid-1970s, 180–81; and payoffs to reporters, 83–84; popularity of, 213–14; and Primer Encuentro de Comunicaciones, 207; relationship with government and PRI, xxii; and satellite broadcasting, 111; and technological advances, 199; and Tlatelolco massacre anniversary, 172; and women in television news, 200–201

Televisión de México, XHTV. *See* XHTV Channel 4

television diplomats, 79–105; Alemán Valdés, Miguel, 79–80; Cárdenas, Lázaro, xxxiv, 81–82, 86–93, 102–3, 105; Castro Ruz, Fidel, 64–65, 80, 86–91, 98, 102; and Cold War tensions, 80, 82, 90–92, 95, 97, 99, 102–5; Dwight D. Eisenhower, xxxiv, 94–98, 101, 103–5, 109, 115, 208; López Mateos, xxxiv, 86–87, 90–96, 100–101, 103, 105; Mikoyan, Anastas, 80–82, 98–102, 104–5; overview, xxxiv, 79–82; and presidential politics, 82–86

Televisión González Camarena, 4, 15. *See also* XHGC Channel 5

Televisión Independiente de México, 15, 21, 174, 178, 182, 188, 197, 210–11

television in Mexico: in 1960s, 17–22; advertising on, 12; cable, 20; color, 19; commercial

Index 271

television in Mexico (*cont.*)
vs. state-run, 7–9, 220n28; competition among stations, 182–83; consolidation into Telesistema Mexicano, 11–15; early establishment of, 1–7; early legal considerations, 15–17; early social influence of, 9–11; first official public transmission, 1–4, 220n13; first televised images, 6; first televised news program, 31–32, 222n1; government pressure on, 178–82; government role in, 15–17; influence of radio on, 7–9; microwave transmission of, 3, 21–22; and morality, 13; movie industry, competition from, 12; and national identity, 28; nationalization debate, 206–7; and political, economic, social, and cultural changes 1950–70, 23–29, 221n64, 221n79; vs. print media, 11; public availability of, 3, 9–10, 12–13, 17, 51, 77, 86, 107, 147, 230n1; quotas and tariffs on importation of sets, 12–13; regional markets expansion of, 20–21; rise of, xxxii, 1–29; satellite transmission, 19–20, 171, 199–200; selling of viewing time, 9–10; and social divide, 50–52; as social status symbol, 10; and society in 1968, 147–49; technological advances and expansion of, 199–200; videotaping of, 19; violence in, 29

television journalists: professionalization of, 109, 185; wages of, 84, 227n12

television news: attribution of news stories, 112–14; business and capital enterprises coverage, 34; centralization of, 173, 238n79; consolidation into Telesistema Mexicano, 15; corporate news division, 135; effects of Cold War coverage on, 142–44; evolution of, 39–43; first simultaneous world transmission, 135; first television news program of record, 31–32, 222n1; growth from 1950 to 1970, 180–81, 181, 238nn7–8; importance of in times of national crisis, 177; national and international tensions, 54–55, 69–70; newscasts produced in 1959, 85; origins of, 33–38; satellite transmission of, 19–20; sharing of news content, xxxvi, 39, 114; sports coverage, 5, 34, 47, 78, 191, 211; technological advances in producing, 18–19; as tele-tradition, 35–43; television executives coverage, 37–38; women in, 52, 68–69, 187, 200–201; and women's suffrage, 27. See also *Noticiero General Motors*

Televisión Tapatía, 20–21

Tello, Manuel, 125, 133–34, 229n51
Tlatelolco massacre: as beginning of political transformation, 28; coverage during Olympics of 1968, 145–63, 167–76, 233–34n3, 234n7, 235n22, 235n25, 235nn29–30, 236nn39–42; and creation of corporate news division, 135; criticism of television coverage by Díaz Ordaz, xxiii; government influence on coverage of, 214; and Olympics of 1968, xxxv; political fallout from, 177, 179–80, 189; public perception of, 209; second anniversary of, 205–6. *See also* student protest movements
Toledo, José Hernández, 158–59
Torres Bodet, Jaime, 101
tortuguismo movement, 56
tracking station at Guaymas, 124–28, 143, 231n38, 231n39
Treviño, Nacho, 116–17
Trujillo, Victor, 215
Truman, Harry, 79–80
The truth about space, 111
TV Azteca, 172, 183
TV-world, 111
24 horas, xxviii, 40, 84, 136, 173, 186–87, 197–98, 200, 205, 213–14
26th of July Movement, 86

UNAM. *See* Universidad Nacional Autónoma de México

Undersecretariat of Broadcasting, 179, 238n3
Union of Electricians, 62
United Press International (UPI), xxvi, xxx, 69, 112–14
United States: Alemán Valdés visit to, 79–80, 227n1; Bracero Program, 27–28; counterrevolutionary activities in Cuba, 89–90; and Cuba, 26; and Cuban Revolution, 71, 74, 76; and hegemony, xxvi, 82; importation of early equipment from, 7; infiltration of Mexican networks in, 207; López Mateos visit to, 80–83, 86–87, 90–94, 93, 103, 228n38; news stories on, 47; as political barometer for western hemisphere, 71; sharing of news content, 114; U.S.-Mexico relations, 26, 45, 87, 102–3. *See also Apollo 11*; Bay of Pigs invasion; Cold War; Cuban Missile Crisis; quadripartite relations between Mexico, the U.S., the Soviet Union, and Cuba
Universidad Nacional Autónoma de México (UNAM), 118, 146, 150, 166–68, 171, 176, 184
UNIVISION, 191
UPI. *See* United Press International
Urrutia, Manuel, 70, 88, 98
Uruchurtu, Ernesto, 209
U.S.-Mexico accord of 1960, 126

Vallejo, Demetrio, 55, 57–58, 62–64, 73–74, 76, 91, 149
Vela, Guillermo, 41, 151, 155
Velasco de Alemán, Beatríz, 44
La verdad del espacio, 111
videotape, 18, 199
Villegas, Ramón, 117
violence on television, 29

Warren, Virginia Lee, 79
Weeks, Albert L., 107
WBM Channel 3, 107–8
White, Christopher M., 54
Women in Solidarity Action, 200
women in television news, 50, 52, 68–69, 187, 200–201, 213–15
women's suffrage, 26–27, 50, 224n47
World Cup of 1970, xxxv–xxxvi, 22, 34, 146, 178, 189–96, 190, 203, 211–12

XEIPN Channel 11, 8, 209
XEQ radio, 2
XEW radio, 2, 5–6, 8
XEW-TV Channel 2, 5, 11–12, 21, 34, 39, 85, 151, 182, 184
XHDF Channel 13, 28, 182
XHGC Channel 5, 4, 11–12, 85, 182
XHTIM Channel 8, 21, 182
XHTV Channel 4: advertisers and advertising, 35; at Aztec Stadium opening, xxii–xxiii; broadcast of Alemán Valdés's fourth informe, 1; china poblana and charro on camera, *14*; consolidation into Telesistema Mexicano, 11–12, 15, 182; Día de la Independencia broadcasts, 44–47; establishment of, 3; first televised news program, 31; self-promotion of producers, 38; sharing of news content, 39–40; and Tlatelolco massacre, 151

Your Nescafé daily. See *Su diario Nescafé*

Zabludovsky, Jacobo: and *Apollo 11*, 110, 136, 139, 141; and Ayala, 200–201; and Azcárraga Milmo, xxiv; at Aztec Stadium opening, xxii; background of, 40–42; as best-known news personality, xxii, xxxvi, 150, 173; blurring of television role with political life, 58; Cárdenas in Cuba interview, 87–88; Castro interviews, 102; and Cuban Revolution, 64, 70–72, 77; and election of 1970, 189, 192–93; host of *La verdad del espacio*, 111; influence of, 40–41, 214, 223n25; López Mateos in U.S. interview, 90; moon landing coverage, 139–41, *141*; on presidential election of 1970, 189; and radio, 41, 83, 215; retirement of, 215; and Space Race, 110–11; on state-media relations in 1968, 172–74; and tele-traditions, 196; and television diplomacy, 82–84,

87–88, 90, 102; and Tlatelolco massacre, 150–51, 155–57, 160–61; and 24 horas, 186, 205, 214–15; on World Cup of 1970, 192

Zermeno Torres, María de Lourdes, xxviii
zócalo of Mexico City, 45, 51, 61, 63, 78, 130, 197, 224n44, 232n53

IN THE MEXICAN EXPERIENCE SERIES

*Mexicans in Revolution,
1910–1946: An Introduction*
William H. Beezley and
Colin M. MacLachlan

*Celebrating Insurrection: The
Commemoration and Representation
of the Nineteenth-Century
Mexican "Pronunciamiento"*
Edited and with an introduction
by Will Fowler

*Forceful Negotiations: The
Origins of the Pronunciamiento in
Nineteenth-Century Mexico*
Edited and with an introduction
by Will Fowler

*Malcontents, Rebels, and Pronunciados: The Politics of Insurrection
in Nineteenth-Century Mexico*
Edited and with an introduction
by Will Fowler

*"Muy buenas noches": Mexico,
Television, and the Cold War*
Celeste González de Bustamante
Foreword by Richard Cole

*Gender and the Negotiation of Daily
Life in Mexico, 1750–1856*
Sonya Lipsett-Rivera

*Mexico's Crucial Century,
1810–1910: An Introduction*
Colin M. MacLachlan and
William H. Beezley

*¡México, la patria! Propaganda and
Production during World War II*
Monica A. Rankin

*Pistoleros and Popular Movements:
The Politics of State Formation in
Postrevolutionary Oaxaca*
Benjamin T. Smith

To order or obtain more information on these or other University of
Nebraska Press titles, visit www.nebraskapress.unl.edu

www.ingramcontent.com/pod-product-compliance
Lightning Source LLC
Chambersburg PA
CBHW021346300426
44114CB00012B/1098